TOWARDS REALIZATION OF THE HIGHER INTENTS OF ISLAMIC LAW

TOWARDS REALIZATION OF THE HIGHER INTENTS OF ISLAMIC LAW

Maqāṣid al-Sharīʿah
A Functional Approach

GAMAL ELDIN ATTIA

Translated from the Arabic by
NANCY ROBERTS

THE INTERNATIONAL INSTITUTE OF ISLAMIC THOUGHT
LONDON • WASHINGTON

THE INTERNATIONAL INSTITUTE OF ISLAMIC THOUGHT
P.O. BOX 669, HERNDON, VA 20172, USA
www.iiit.org

LONDON OFFICE
P.O. BOX 126, RICHMOND, SURREY TW9 2UD, UK
www.iiituk.com

ISBN 978-1-56564-437-3 PAPERBACK
ISBN 978-1-56564-438-0 HARDBACK

Typesetting and cover design by Sideek Ali
Printed in the United Kingdom by Cromwell Press Ltd

CONTENTS

FOREWORD

Of knowledge, we have none, save what
You have taught us. (The Qur'an 2:32)

The International Institute of Islamic Thought (IIIT) has great pleasure in presenting this scholarly work on the topic of *Towards Realization of the Higher Intents of Islamic Law: Maqāṣid al-Sharīʿah, A Functional Approach*. The author, Dr. Gamal Eldin Attia, is a well-known scholar and specialist in the field, and the Arabic edition of his work entitled, *Naḥwah Tafʿīl Maqāṣid al-Sharīʿah*, was originally published by the Institute in 2001. This is a work of serious scholarship in which the author offers a detailed discussion of how the realization of *maqāṣid* is to take place. We hope that this English edition with its innovative approach, analysis and ideas, will not only make an important contribution to the field of *maqāṣid al-Sharīʿah*, but also attract wider attention and generate greater interest among readers.

Since few works, if any, are available in the English language on this important subject, *al-maqāṣid*, the IIIT decided to fill the vacuum by initiating the translation and publication of a series of books on the subject to introduce this important area of thought to English readers. In addition to this particular volume the series so far includes: *Imam al-Shāṭibī's Theory of the Higher Objectives and Intents of Islamic Law*, by Ahmad al-Raysuni, and *Ibn Ashur Treatise on Maqāṣid al-Sharīʿah* by Muhammad al-Tahir ibn Ashur. Although the topic is a complex and intellectually challenging one, it needs to be emphasized that these books are not for specialists, scholars and intellectuals alone, but works that also provide very interesting and useful reading for the general reader. Knowledge of *al-maqāṣid* is a prerequisite for any attempt to address and resolve contemporary issues challenging Islamic thought. Indeed such knowledge can help in the process of developing a much needed objectives-based fiqh for minorities; and is essential for anyone who is interested in understanding and appreciating the concept of divine wisdom underlying Islamic rulings.

Not only are the ideas presented in this work subtle and challenging but equally challenging has been our effort to render the term *maqāṣid* accurately into English, the Arabic original having a much deeper and more precise level of meaning. The term has largely been translated as "higher objectives/intents" throughout the book, although this does not do justice to its proper meaning.

The IIIT, established in 1981, has served as a major center to facilitate sincere and serious scholarly efforts based on Islamic vision, values and principles. Its programs of research, seminars and conferences during the last twenty six years have resulted in the publication of more than two hundred and fifty titles in English and Arabic, many of which have been translated into several other languages.

We would like to express our thanks and gratitude to the translator, Nancy Roberts, who throughout the various stages of the book's production, cooperated closely with the editorial group at the IIIT's London Office. Ms. Roberts' accuracy, thorough attention to detail as well as continuous attempts to revise and improve the quality of her translation, is a credit to her. She has managed to render with great lucidity and clarity a very complex subject.

We would also like to thank the editorial and production team at the IIIT London Office and those who were directly or indirectly involved in the completion of this book: Dr. Gasser Auda, Shiraz Khan, Dr. Maryam Mahmood, Maida Malik, and Sideek Ali. May God reward them, the author, and the translator for all their efforts.

Ramadan 1428 AH
October 2007 AC

ANAS S. AL-SHAIKH-ALI
IIIT Translation Department
London, UK

PREFACE TO THE ARABIC EDITION

Praise be to God (SWT)[1], and may blessings and peace be upon our master, the Messenger of God (ṢAAS)[2], upon his descendents and Companions, and upon all who have been his allies and friends.

God sent His Messenger with right guidance and the religion of truth in order to manifest it as superior to all other creeds. He caused him to be the seal of the prophets and messengers, revealing the Holy Qur'an as a final covenant for humanity and as a decisive word after which no further revelation would be sent from heaven to earth, and by virtue of which divine legislation would likewise come to an end. In view of the finality of this message, God addresses through it every human being answerable to His commands in all times and places and under all circumstances. Moreover, these distinctive qualities of Islamic law – that is, its finality, its universality, and its capacity to transcend boundaries of time and place – necessitate the flexibility, inclusiveness and balance appropriate to the situations with which the Law concerns itself.

Given this doctrinal view of Islamic law and of the nature of the holy writ in which they place their faith, Muslims have pondered and reflected on God's words and, as a consequence, have come to see that the divine speech is associated with the profoundest of wise purposes and the sublimest of aims. In fact, it was through this realization that Muslims came to perceive God's purpose in bringing the created realm into existence. What God desires of His creation and His aims relating thereto are, in essence, for human beings to worship Him and to populate and civilize the earth. As God Almighty has declared, "I have not created the invisible beings and men to any end other than that they may [know and] worship Me"(51:56), and, "He brought you into being out of the earth, and made you thrive thereon" (11:61).[3] Certain *maqāṣid** relating to the welfare of human beings are observable in every

---

* It was a challenging effort to render the term *maqāṣid* in English. However, throughout the book, it has been translated as: goals, objectives, higher objectives, principles, intents, purposes, and ends, depending on context. In addition, words marked with an asterisk are defined in the Glossary of Terms at the end of the book [translator's note].

obligation laid down by the Law, namely, the preservation of human life, the preservation of the faculty of human reason, the preservation of religion, the preservation of honor, and the preservation of material wealth. This is the order in which they are mentioned by al-Ghazālī in his *al-Mustaṣfā*, where he gives the preservation of religion priority over the preservation of both human life and reason. Following al-Ghazālī's lead, *uṣūl* scholars detailed these five essentials of human welfare in the context of discussions of that which is 'appropriate' (*munāsib*)*; the concept of 'appropriateness'* is subsumed under the quest to identify the occasion or basis (*ʿillah*) of Islamic legal rulings, which itself represents one of the most important pillars of analogical deduction (*qiyās*).* By 'appropriate,' such thinkers are referring to the situation or condition on the basis of which a given legal ruling was issued. Such a situation or condition might, in turn, involve other, interrelated situations or conditions by means of which we can, in the end, arrive at those higher aims (*al-maqāṣid al-ʿulyā*) which were mentioned by al-Ghazālī, and were discussed so exhaustively by al-Shāṭibī in his book, *al-Muwāfaqāt*, and to which all scholars of Islamic jurisprudence throughout the ages have devoted such concern. Indeed, the theme of *maqāṣid* appears most clearly in the writings of those who are renowned for the exhaustiveness of their efforts such as, for instance, Ibn Taymiyyah, al-ʿIzz ibn ʿAbd al-Salām, al-Qarrāfī, Ibn Daqīq al-ʿĪd, and others.

These *maqāṣid* represent the human interest, or welfare, which Islamic law seeks to preserve and protect and which is, in fact, the Law's most vital concern and aim; as such, they have continued to dominate the thought of those who labor in the realm of Islamic jurisprudence and legislation. It is the *maqāṣid* which inform Muslim consciousness and which, indeed, may be viewed as the 'public order' that no one is permitted to challenge or violate and the authoritative point of reference providing the framework for all Muslims' activity and their understanding of Islamic law. Even so, however, the proper formulation, clarification, arrangement and activation of *maqāṣid* call for such a major effort that there have been calls for these endeavors to be treated as an independent discipline in order for them to receive the attention they merit. If such a step were taken, efforts could be made to glean whatever is useful from other disciplines so that such findings could be employed in the service of *maqāṣid*-related research; in this manner, it would become easier to highlight the applications of the *maqāṣid* and to clarify the manner in which they need to be dealt with and put to use for the sake of a more thorough understanding of Islamic law and for the sake of rendering the *maqāṣid* useful and accessible to people in their daily lives.

A number of writings have appeared in this area, including both academic dissertations and book-length works, beginning with the eminent scholar of his age, the commentator and authority Shaykh al-Tahir ibn Ashur,[4] followed by Professor Allal al-Fasi. Such contributions include a discussion of *maqāṣid* in a book by Shaykh Muhammad al-Ghazali, as well as *al-Maqāṣid ᶜInd al-Imām al-Shāṭibī*[5] by Ahmad al-Raysuni and *Naẓariyyah al-Maqāṣid ᶜInd al-Imām Muḥammd al-Ṭāhir ibn ᶜĀshūr* by Ismail al-Hasani, as well as numerous other writings whose titles appear in the bibliography of the present work.

We then come to the author of this book. Dr. Gamal Eldin Attia is founder of the *Al-Muslim Al-Muᶜāṣir* magazine, which for more than a quarter of a century has contributed to the dissemination of committed Islamic thought. He has a Ph.D. in law from Geneva University (1959). Dr. Attia has shown concern for the practical application of Islamic economics through a combination of action and reflection. He held posts as professor of Islamic Law at the University of Qatar for a number of years and as an academic consultant for the International Institute of Islamic Thought, in which capacity he supervised academic theses, research projects, seminars, conferences and cultural fora. As a result of his extensive experience and knowledge, Dr. Attia has become a leading figure in this field, eminently qualified to write on the theme of *maqāṣid*, the means by which they may be identified and verified, which of them are speculative* and which of them may be viewed as definitive, the issue of adding to or subtracting from the number of *maqāṣid*, the order in which the *maqāṣid* are to be arranged, their importance, and their realization, that is to say, their translation into concrete action.

The present work consists of three chapters, each of which contains detailed discussions of issues relating to *maqāṣid*. In Chapter One, "Central Issues," the author discusses the role of reason, innate understanding and experience in the determination and verification of *maqāṣid*, establishing the order of the *maqāṣid* in relation to each other, establishing the order of the means (*wasā'il*) associated with each of the *maqāṣid*, and practical applications of these processes.

In Chapter Two, "A New Conceptualization of *Maqāṣid*" the author discusses the traditional limitation of the *maqāṣid* to the five essentials, namely, the preservation of religion, human life, reason, progeny and material wealth, the types of *maqāṣid* and a proposed alternative of conceiving the *maqāṣid* in terms of the four areas of the individual, the family, the greater Muslim community, and humanity as a whole. In this way, the author expands the spheres in which *maqāṣid* are given consideration and renders them more subject to practical application.

In Chapter Three, "Realization of the *Maqāṣid*," the author offers a detailed discussion of how the activation of *maqāṣid* is to take place. In this context, he deals with the current uses of *maqāṣid*, *maqāṣid*-based independent reasoning, or ijtihad, juristic theorization, the *maqāṣid*-based mindset on the individual and communal levels, the future of *maqāṣid*, and lastly, the question of whether the study of *maqāṣid* is likely to become a self-contained discipline in the future.

The study of *maqāṣid* by means of this innovative approach (an approach which makes use of our understanding of today's world and the experience gained through contact with reality, be it advancing or deteriorating, the preservation of Islamic law and the determination to establish it as our ultimate concern in life, and deliberate application of the notion of *maqāṣid* on a practical level rather than contenting ourselves with hopes or wishes) is the type of discussion which merits our attention. Similarly, it is this type of approach which we ought to adopt with greater frequency not only in relation to Islamic law, but in relation to all those themes with which we engage ourselves (be they in the realm of the fundamentals of jurisprudence, jurisprudence and its applications, or the broader realm of Islamic thought) in the service of Islam and for the sake of delivering Muslims from their intellectual and practical crises.

May God employ this book to great benefit and cause it to weigh in the balance of its author's good deeds. May it be the first step in the author's ongoing productiveness and the beginning of an era of *maqāṣid*-based construction and progression.

ALI JUMAH
Professor of Uṣūl, Al-Azhar University
Current Mufti of the Arab Republic of Egypt

Cairo, 13 February, 2001 AC
19 Dhu al-Qaʿdah, 1421 AH

INTRODUCTION TO THE FIRST EDITION

This book forms part of the *maqāṣid al-sharīʿah* series which has been recently initiated, and to which I hope to make a contribution by helping to bring this topic out of the phase of traditional writings and into the phase of innovation, planning and programs of action. It has not been my intention here to cover all themes relating to *maqāṣid*; rather, I have chosen only what is of relevance to the aim of this study. I have divided the book into three chapters. The first deals with central issues of relevance, the second presents a new conceptualization of *maqāṣid*, and the third concerns itself with the realization of *maqāṣid* in our lives, both in the field of Islamic jurisprudence and on the level of our practical experience. The extensive quotations given from other writers have been included deliberately, my purpose therein being to allow readers to share my thought process. Then, whether or not they agree with my conclusions, I will be content to know that at the very least, they have accompanied me on my journey of reflection. Mention should also be made here of the unparalleled genius with which this theme was treated by our forebears, from al-Juwaynī to al-Shāṭibī, as well as the laudable efforts to resume writing on this topic by Muhammad al-Tahir ibn Ashur, Allal al-Fasi and those of subsequent generations who have followed so ably in their footsteps, including Yusuf al-Alim, Ahmad al-Raysuni, Ismaʿil al-Hasani and others. I salute all these thinkers and hope that I may have added something of use to what they achieved and that the words uttered by al-Juwaynī concerning "those who went before and those who will come after"[1] might be true of me as well. There is always the possibility of error; hence, I ask those who read this book to correct and send me whatever errors they happen to discover so that, even if I should fall short of the reward of the *mujtahid** whose conclusions are flawless, I might, at the very least, enjoy the reward of the *mujtahid* who strove, but missed the mark. *And to God is due all success.*

Cairo, 10 February 2001 AC
16 Dhu al-Qaʿdah 1421 AH

GAMAL ELDIN ATTIA

INTRODUCTION TO THE SECOND EDITION

When copies of the first edition of this book ran out, I was asked by the IIIT to highlight the section dealing with the use of *maqāṣid* in the Islamization of the human, social and physical sciences. I, therefore, undertook to compile what had been scattered throughout the pages of the first edition in connection with this theme. In addition to minor additions, this edition also includes two papers of mine which were not included in the first; I have also devoted the third chapter to this topic.

In the period which lapsed between the first and second editions, other important studies were published on the subject of *maqāṣid*, the most significant of which are listed below:

1. Hasan Muhammad Jabir, *Al-Maqāṣid al-Kulliyyah wa al-Ijtihād al-Muʿāṣir*, (Beirut: Dār al-Ḥiwār, 2001).
2. Abd al-Jabbar al-Rifaʿi, *Al-Mashhad al-Thaqāfī fī Irān* (*Falsafah al-Fiqh wa Maqāṣid al-Sharīʿah*), (Beirut: Dār al-Hādī, 2001).
3. Nur al-Din Mukhtar al-Khadimi, *Al-Maqāṣid fī al-Madhhab al-Mālikī*, (Riyad: Maktabah al-Rushd, 2002).
4. Numan Jughaym, *Ṭuruq al-Kashf ʿan Maqāṣid al-Shāriʿ*, (Jordan: Dār al-Nafā'is, 2002).
5. *Al-Muslim al-Muʿāṣir* Magazine, No. 103 devoted to the theme of *maqāṣid*, 2002.
6. *Ḥuqūq al-Insān, Miḥwar Maqāṣid al-Sharīʿah*, (*Kitāb al-Ummah*), No.87, 2002.
7. Muhammad Mahdi Shams al-Din, et. al., *Maqāṣid al-Sharīʿah*, (Beirut: Dār al-Fikr al-Muʿāṣir and Damascus: Dār al-Fikr, 2002).

I have also perused a number of studies published prior to the first edition, the most important of which are:

1. Bin Zughaybah Izz al-Din, *Al-Maqāṣid al-ʿĀmmah li al-Sharīʿah al-Islamiyyah*, (Cairo: Dār al-Ṣafwah, 1996).
2. Muhammad Saʿd al-Yubi, *Maqāṣid al-Sharīʿah wa ʿAlāqatuhā bi al-'Adillah al-Sharʿiyyah*, (Riyad: Dār al-Hijrah, 1998).
3. Ahmad al-Raysuni, "Al-Jamʿ wa al-Taṣnīf li Maqāṣid al-Sharʿ al-Sharīf," an unpublished paper commissioned by the International Academy of Islamic Jurisprudence, 1998.
4. Mustafa Bin Karamat Allah Makhdum, *Qawāʿid al-Masā'il fī al-Sharīʿah al-Islamiyyah*, (Riyad: Dār Ashbīlyah, 1999).
5. Nur al-Din Buthuri, *Maqāṣid al-Sharīʿah*, (Beirut: Dār al-Ṭalīʿah, 2000).
6. Yusuf Ahmad Muhammad al-Badawi, *Maqāṣid al-Sharīʿah ʿInd ibn Taymiyyah*, Jordan: (Dār al-Nafā'is, 2000).
7. Abd al-Rahman al-Kilani, *Qawāʿid al-Maqāṣid ʿInd al-Imam al-Shāṭibī*, (The International Institute of Islamic Thought and Dar al-Fikr, 2000).
8. Abd al-Latif Muhammad Amir, *Maqāṣid al-Sharīʿah ʿInd al-Imam al-Shāṭibī*, no date.
9. Abd al-Rahman Yusuf al-Qaradawi, "Maqāṣid al-Sharīʿah bayn ibn Taymiyyah wa Jumhūr al-Uṣūliyyīn," unpublished MA thesis, Kulliyyāh Dār al-ʿUlūm, Cairo University, 2002.

And to God is due all success.

GAMAL ELDIN ATTIA
Cairo, 2004 AC

Chapter One

Central Issues

[THEME 1]

The Role of Reason, Innate Understanding and Experience in Identifying and Verifying Maqāṣid[1]

§*First:* The positions taken by *uṣūl* scholars on the question of how we are to identify the *maqāṣid* or, to use Ibn Ashur's phrase, methods of verification.

(a) Whoever investigates the theme of *maqāṣid* will note that what was written on this subject by scholars who came after al-Shāṭibī was limited either to summarizing or rearranging what al-Shāṭibī had already formulated.[2] According to al-Shāṭibī, the means by which the intents (*maqāṣid*) of the Lawgiver may be ascertained are as follows:

1. Explicit texts from the Qur'an or the Sunnah which identify the basis or occasion (*ʿillah*) of Islamic legal rulings.

2. Inductive analysis of the actions of the Lawgiver, which may be divided into two types. The first type is an inductive reading of the legal rulings whose bases (*ʿilal*) have been determined by means of recognized approaches (*masālik al-ʿillah*), yet without an explicit text from the Qur'an or the Sunnah. The second is an inductive reading of the various pieces of textual evidence in support of legal rulings which have a common purpose (*ghāyah*) and basis (*bāʿith*).

3. The Companions' understanding of the rulings found in the Qur'an and the Sunnah.

However, such thinkers failed to take into account what al-Shāṭibī's predecessors had recognized, the role of reason and innate understanding in the determination of what is beneficial and harmful in cases where we lack an explicit text from the Qur'an and the Sunnah.

(b) The following is a passage from Ibn Sīnā's *al-Najāt* as quoted by Ibn Ashur:

> Innate understanding (*fiṭrah*) might be illustrated by imagining someone who has been brought into existence in the world all at once as a rational being, yet without having heard anyone's opinion, embraced a point of view, lived with a community [through whom his thinking may have been influenced] or been acquainted with this or that policy. He has, however, perceived concrete realities and derived knowledge of specific cases. Then something is presented to his mind about which he is doubtful; if doubt is possible for him, his innate understanding will not attest to it. If, on the other hand, doubt is not possible, then his innate understanding must affirm it of necessity. However, not everything affirmed by human beings' innate understanding is true. Rather, what is true is the inborn capacity (*fiṭrah al-quwwah*) known as the mind, or reason. As for the innate tendency to ponder and consider (*fiṭrah al-dhihn*), it is subject to error. Such error manifests itself in connection with realities which are not accessible to the physical senses as such but which are, rather, conceptualizations of concrete realities. The true innate understanding may be seen in widely recognized, praiseworthy premises and points of view which it is our duty to affirm and believe either by virtue of others' unanimous testimony (as in the case of the affirmation that "justice is good"), the testimony of the majority, or the testimony of scholars or the most virtuous among them. However, it is not represented by commonly held notions which people tend to believe by nature [yet which are actually false].[3]

(c) Al-Juwaynī, the Imam of the Two Sacred Shrines, devotes a chapter [of his book, *al-Burhān*] to a discussion of *istidlāl** in which he states,

1. "There has been disagreement among recognized scholars and imams involved in the process of *istidlāl*, namely, [the search for evidence and] meanings which, in the absence of an agreed-upon text [from the Qur'an or the Sunnah], point to a given ruling and are appropriate thereto based on rational thought, and to which also applies the *taʿlīl*[4] which the scholar has in mind."[5]

2. There are three schools of thought on *istidlāl*: Adherents of the first school repudiate the practice of *istidlāl*, restricting themselves solely to those significations which have a textual basis in the Qur'an or the Sunnah. Adherents of the second school hold to the permissibility of adopting the results of *istiṣlāḥ** and the search for what is most correct regardless of whether they reflect precisely the causes on account of which Islamic texts came into being (*mawārid al-naṣṣ*), provided that they do not conflict with any of the three 'roots' (*uṣūl*) [of Islamic law and doctrine], namely, the Qur'an, the Sunnah, and the consensus of the Muslim community. As for the third school, which is associated with the Shafiʿite school of jurisprudence, it holds to the signification [arrived at through *istidlāl*] even if it cannot be traced to a textual basis in the Qur'an or the Sunnah, provided that such a signification is close to the meanings found in the established 'roots'.[6]

3. Al-Imam al-Shāfiʿī supported this latter position by noting that whoever does a thorough investigation of the approach taken by the Companions – bearing in mind that they provided a model for us to emulate in the process of investigation and reflection – will find that not a single one of them adopted some fixed rule upon which he based his legal decisions. Rather, they would proceed directly to an exchange of points of view without reference to fixed rules, even if they were available. Then, if it was determined that their independent interpretation, or ijtihad, accounted for the situation at hand, if it proved impossible to restrict their interpretation to what is stated explicitly in Islamic texts, and if it was confirmed by the fact that the scholars among the Companions did not support an appeal to fixed rules, then such a situation was considered to constitute a justification for resorting to *istidlāl*.[7]

(d) We turn now to the views of al-ʿIzz ibn ʿAbd al-Salām.[8]

1. He states in this regard:

> Most sources of earthly benefit and harm are discernible through human reason; moreover, the truth of this affirmation is recognized by most divinely revealed laws. After all, there is no sensible person who – even before the revelation of the divine Law – would fail to realize that the attainment of pure benefit and the prevention of pure harm, whether for one's own sake or for someone else's, is a praiseworthy, desirable thing, as is favoring that which is of greater benefit over that which is of lesser benefit and favoring the

prevention of that which is of greater harm over the prevention of that which is of lesser harm. There is agreement among the wise and prudent, as well as among the various divinely revealed Laws, on the sacredness of human life, chastity, material wealth and honor...and wherever disagreement has occurred, this has most often been due to differences of priority and degree...Be aware, then, that the tendency to favor what is of greater benefit over what is of lesser benefit and to favor the prevention of what is of greater harm over the prevention of what is of lesser harm is ingrained in human nature as a mercy to us from the Lord of lords....If you give a young child a choice between something which is delicious and something which is more delicious, he is sure to choose the more delicious; if he is given a choice between something which is good and something which is better, he will choose what is better; if he is given a choice between a *fils* and a *dirham*, he will choose the *dirham*; and if he is given a choice between a *dirham* and a *dinar*, he will choose the *dinar*. In short, no one favors that which is good over that which is better unless he happens to be ignorant of the advantage inherent in that which is better, or unless he is the mischievous, contrary type who willfully disregards the disparity between these two degrees.

2. Elsewhere, he states:[9]

Otherworldly sources of benefit and harm and their causes may only be ascertained through the law of Islam; hence, if any of them is concealed from our knowledge, we may seek such knowledge through the evidence provided by the Law, namely the Qur'an, the Sunnah, the consensus of the Muslim community, recognized *qiyās* or analogy, and sound *istidlāl*. As for earthly benefits and sources of harm and their causes, they are recognized on the basis of human needs, experiences, customs, beliefs, and sound, commonly acknowledged suppositions. If any of these sources of benefit or harm or their causes is concealed from us, we may seek knowledge of them through the appropriate types of evidence. Moreover, whoever wishes to recognize the occasions for benefit and harm and to identify those which are more or less probable must consult his own reason if no mention of them is made in the Law, then base his judgments on this. Hardly will one find a legal judgment which departs from this rule with the exception of those having to do with forms of worship which have no rationally discernible basis and which are, therefore, to be adhered to in unquestioning submission. In the case of

> this latter type of ruling, God has not apprised His servants of the benefit to be derived or the harm to be averted through adherence to it such that they might perceive the goodness or evil of this or that action. At the same time, God, Almighty and Majestic is He, is under no obligation to bring benefit out of what is good, nor to prevent the harm that results from what is evil. Indeed, He is under no obligation to create, to provide His creatures with sustenance, to impose obligations upon His servants, or to reward or punish them. Rather, He brings benefit out of what is good and prevents the harm that arises from what is evil out of His forbearance and graciousness toward His servants. Moreover, if He were to reverse everything, this would not be evil, since no one has any claim or authority over Him.

3. In a third passage of relevance,[10] ʿIzz al-Dīn ibn ʿAbd al-Salām affirms that this is the approach embodied in Islamic law, saying,

> Whoever investigates the intents of the Law (*maqāṣid al-sharʿ*), which are to achieve benefit and prevent harm, will arrive at a conviction or recognition that this or that benefit must not be neglected and that this or that source of harm must be avoided. For even if there is no consensus, text or analogy which deals specifically and explicitly with the source of benefit or harm in question, an understanding of the Law itself necessitates such a conclusion. The situation might be likened to one in which someone has lived in close communion with a companion of virtue, wisdom and discernment and gained an understanding of this person's likes and dislikes in all sorts of situations. If this person is then presented with a source of benefit or harm about which he or she has never heard his/her companion express an opinion, he or she will nevertheless – based on his or her accumulated experience of this companion's manner of thinking and habits – know that this companion would incline toward a particular benefit and be averse to a particular source of harm.
>
> Moreover, if we investigate the *maqāṣid* manifested in the Qur'an and the Sunnah, we will realize that God has enjoined all that is good, from the most trifling to the most momentous, and that He has forbidden all that is evil, from the most insignificant to the most heinous. In speaking of 'good,' He is referring to the pursuit of benefit and the prevention of harm, and in speaking of 'evil,' He is referring to the pursuit of harm and the prevention of what is beneficial, as He has declared, may He be Exalted, "And so, he who shall have done an atom's weight of good, shall behold it; and he who shall have done an atom's weight of evil, shall behold it" (99:7-8).

> This may be seen easily in cases of pure goodness and unmitigated evil. The difficulty arises when it is not known which is the greater of two goods or which is the greater of two evils, or when we do not know whether a given benefit is of greater weight than a corresponding source of harm, or whether the source of harm is of greater weight than the corresponding benefit; or, alternatively, when we do not know which things are of benefit and which are harmful. There are some sources of benefit and harm which can only be recognized by those with sound understanding and virtuous character, by means of which they are able to discern the fine gradations of what is beneficial and what is harmful, from the most negligible to the most significant, and which of these should be given greater weight. People differ in their capacity for such discernment depending on the factors I have just mentioned. Hence, an intelligent, 'superior' person might fail to be aware of some things which are clearly discernible to a stupid, 'inferior' person, few though they may be. The Qur'anic verse which is most inclusive in terms of its exhortation to all that is beneficial and its proscription of all that is harmful reads, "And behold, God enjoins justice, and the doing of good, and generosity towards [one's] fellow-men; and He forbids all that is shameful and all that runs counter to reason, as well as envy; [and] He exhorts you [repeatedly] so that you might bear [all this] in mind" (16:90).

4. Similarly, he states in his book *al-Fawā'id*, "The sources of benefit and harm associated with the life to come can only be known through the Law; as for earthly sources of benefit and harm, they can be known through human experience and customs."[11]

(e) Ibn Taymiyyah (d. 728 AH/1327 AC) states:

> God Almighty has created His servants with an inborn nature (*fiṭrah*) by virtue of which they recognize and believe in the truth, and by means of which they likewise recognize untruth and reject it. It is by virtue of this God-given, inborn nature that human beings recognize that which is beneficial and appropriate and accordingly incline thereto, just as they also recognize that which is harmful and incompatible [with their best interests] and respond to it with an instinctive aversion. Hence, whatever is true and existent, human beings will believe in it by nature, and whatever is truly beneficial, they will recognize it as such by nature, cherish it, and find reassurance there-

> in. This is known. As for that which is false and nonexistent, people will disbelieve in it by nature, feel antipathy toward it and spurn it. As God Almighty has declared, [the Prophet] "will enjoin upon them the doing of what is right and forbid them the doing of what is wrong (7:157)."[12]

(f) As for Ibn Taymiyyah's disciple, Ibn al-Qayyim, some of his statements on this topic are well known.

1. He states, for example,

> Islamic Law is structured and founded upon wise purposes and the best interests of God's servants both in this world and the next. The Law is pure justice, pure mercy, pure benefit, pure wisdom. Hence, anything which embodies injustice rather than justice, cruelty rather than mercy, harm rather than benefit, or folly rather than wisdom does not originate from the Law, even if it happens to have been interpolated therein by means of interpretation.[13]

2. Elsewhere in the same work Ibn al-Qayyim declares:

> Indeed, God sent His messengers and revealed His holy scriptures in order that, as a result of them, people would be upholders of equity, namely, the justice upon which the heavens and the earth were founded. If the signs of truth are manifest, if rational proofs thereof are adduced, and if its dawn breaks in any manner whatsoever, then there is God's Law, God's religion, God's good pleasure and God's command. After all, He has not restricted truth's paths, evidences and signs to a single type while invalidating other paths which are more powerful, cogent or plain. Rather, He has made clear by means of the paths He has laid down that His intention (*maqṣūduhu*) is for truth and justice to be established, and for people to uphold equity. Hence, any path by means of which the truth is brought to light and justice is recognized, is a path in accordance with which rulings should be made. Such paths are, in essence, causes and means which are not ends in themselves but which, rather, exist for the sake of their ultimate ends, that is, their *maqāṣid*. However, by means of the paths which God has laid down, He alerts us to their causes and the like. Indeed, you will not find any path which confirms the truth but that it is, itself, a law and a means of pointing to them [its causes and the *maqāṣid* for the sake of which it exists]. And would one expect otherwise of the perfect Law?[14]

(g) Al-Shāṭibī made a number of statements which indicate that he was convinced of the role of reason within certain limits:

1. In his first introduction [to *al-Muwafaqāt*], for example, he states that "if rational evidence is used in this discipline, it is only used in tandem with textual evidence, in support thereof, as a means of confirming the basis [of a legal ruling], and the like. It is not employed independently, as a self-contained guide to meaning, since the consideration of this type of evidence is the consideration of a matter pertaining to Islamic law, and reason is not a Lawgiver, a fact which may be seen clearly in scholastic theology."[15]

2. In his tenth introduction, al-Shāṭibī states, "If textual and rational evidence are in mutual agreement concerning legal questions, the textual evidence must be given priority over the rational; that is to say, reason is to be given only the degree of latitude which the textual evidence allows. Moreover, there are numerous bases for the validity of this statement."[16]

3. In another passage on this topic he states,

> Concerning that which is ascertained on the basis of human experience and custom it may be said: Neither material nor spiritual benefits are achieved by submitting without hesitation to one's caprices and desires or by freely pursuing earthly aims. This is clear given what such a pursuit leads to by way of disorder, strife and destruction, all of which is contrary to these very interests. This is recognized among people based on ongoing experience and human practice. Consequently, they are in mutual agreement that those who submit to their fleshly desires, following them wherever they happen to lead, should be censured. In fact, there are those among our predecessors who had no divinely revealed law or whose law had ceased to exist yet who, nevertheless, adopted this principle, preserving earthly interests by restraining whoever gave free rein to his passions, and this based on a [purely] rational point of view. Moreover, they only agreed on this approach given its validity among them and given the steady advantages which they experienced as a result, including the establishment of earthly prosperity. This is referred to as civil policy, the overall validity of which is attested to by rational and textual evidence alike. As such, it is too clear to require further evidence in its support.[17]

4. Elsewhere al-Shāṭibī states,

> The Lawgiver has spoken at length about the bases (*ʿilal*) and wise purposes (*ḥikam*) which underlie Islamic legal rulings pertaining to customs. Moreover, He most frequently explains such bases in accordance with the principle of 'appropriateness' which, when presented to people's minds, meets with ready acceptance. From this we may conclude that it is the Lawgiver's intention for us to adhere to the meanings [which we are given to comprehend].[18]

5. Al-Shāṭibī continues somewhat later in the same discussion, saying,

> Attention to meanings was a known practice during the period prior to the advent of the Islamic message, and was the approach most frequently adopted by the wise and discerning, whose interests were achieved in this manner. Whether they were among those who devoted themselves to the study of philosophical wisdom or members of the general populace, they applied the universals [which they had derived based on human reason] and found that they were, indeed, applicable to the majority of cases. However, certain details remained unaccounted for by the principles they had formulated until Islamic law came to perfect noble traits of character.[19]

6. However, al-Shāṭibī does not carry this line of thought as far as al-ʿIzz ibn ʿAbd al-Salām. Al-Shāṭibī says:

> The fact that a benefit is a benefit or that a source of harm is a source of harm is determined based on the ruling of the Law. Given the negation of *al-taḥsīn wa al-taqbīḥ*,[20] this is a matter which concerns the Lawgiver alone, and human reason has no role to play in it. If the Lawgiver has issued a ruling concerning a given benefit, it is He who has established it as a benefit; otherwise, it would be possible, logically speaking, for the same entity not to be a benefit. For all things are, in essence, equal, and it would be impossible for reason to declare some things good and others bad. Consequently, the fact that a benefit is a benefit is determined by the Lawgiver alone; this is a reality to which human reason gives assent and which the human soul accepts in tranquility. For benefits, insofar as they are benefits, have been determined through examination to belong to the category of *taʿabbudī*,* and whatever is based upon that which is *taʿabbudī* is, itself, *taʿabbudī*.[21]

7. Al-Shāṭibī responds to al-ʿIzz ibn ʿAbd al-Salām by saying:

> Based on the foregoing, objections might be made to this view. As for his statement that benefits pertaining to the afterlife may only be ascertained through Islamic law, it is as he says. As for the view he expresses concerning earthly benefits, however, it is not as he says in every respect. Rather, his view is accurate in some respects, but not in others. When the Law was revealed after a period of time during which no prophet was sent, it revealed the extent to which people during that era had deviated from true righteousness and their failure to execute justice in their rulings. If things were as he describes them without exception, there would have been no need for the Law to promote anything but the interests which pertain to the life to come. However, this is not the case, since the Law came to establish human affairs both in this life and in the next. Moreover, even if, in promoting earthly interests, the Law's ultimate intent is to promote those of the life to come, this is not inconsistent with the intent of promoting the benefits of this earthly life so that, in this way, people might conduct themselves in a manner which befits the life to come. In this connection, Islamic law has promoted untold numbers of [beneficial] behaviors and eliminated countless forms of corruption which were prevalent at that time.
>
> Common experience thus precludes the possibility that human reason is able to perceive in detail that which is of earthly benefit or harm, unless what this person [i.e., al-ʿIzz ibn ʿAbd al-Salām] means to say is that knowledge of these things is acquired through experience and the like after the Law has established their foundations, since of this there can be no doubt.[22]

Commenting briefly on this statement, Shaykh Abd Allah Darraz states, "This differs significantly from his (that is, al-ʿIzz ibn ʿAbd al-Salām's) statement [quoted earlier] that 'whoever wishes to recognize the occasions for benefit and harm and to identify those which are more or less probable must consult his own reason *if no mention of them is made in the Law...*'"

As I see it, what al-Shāṭibī affirms here is not applicable to the situation of which al-ʿIzz ibn ʿAbd al-Salām is speaking, namely, cases for which Islamic law has not provided an organized framework, or what is referred to by some as a "legislative vacuum." This concept has special significance for the conditions of modern life, in which this "legislative vacuum" is expanding at an ever increasing rate as a result of the tremendous development in the various activities of our lives. This being the case, there is no conflict between a basic reliance on the methods outlined by al-Shāṭibī for arriving at *maqāṣid al-sharīʿah*, and the addition of a supplementary method in the event that the existing methods prove insufficient.

Al-Hasani enumerates the functions of human reason as presented by al-Shāṭibī in the following situations: (a) Those in which rational evidence is combined with textual evidence, as when one premise is rational and the remaining premises are textual. (b) Those in which rational evidence assists in enabling textual evidence to fulfill its purpose, as when the basic evidence is textual, and in order for it to bring about its intended results, recourse is had to rational evidence. (c) Cases in which reason serves to help verify and clarify the situation to which the textual evidence applies.[23]

(h) Allal al-Fasi approaches this issue based on the premise that leaving the assessment of human interests to individually chosen criteria for discerning good from evil and the beneficial from the harmful leads to incoherence, that is, inconsistent appraisals of what true human interests are, and the conflicts which such incoherence inevitably entails. Al-Fasi states that Islam takes this fact into consideration when it makes clear that the criterion for every human interest is the inborn disposition which derives from primordial human nature. This is the moral foundation which has been affirmed by all previous religions and philosophies despite their differing tendencies and temperaments. This, says al-Fasi, is the 'straight path' along which we have been enjoined to seek God's guidance in every one of our daily prayers: the path of those who have been blessed by their Lord and Sustainer, who have not incurred His displeasure, and who have not gone astray.[24]

(i) Ibn Ashur points to inborn human nature:

1. Ibn Ashur holds that the *maqāṣid* are based upon the single most important distinguishing feature of Islamic law, namely, the fact that it answers to inborn human nature (*al-fiṭrah*): "And so, set thy face steadfastly towards the [one ever-true] faith, turning away from all that is false, in accordance with the natural disposition which God has instilled into man (*al-fiṭrah*): [for] not to allow any change to corrupt what God has thus created – this is the [purpose of the one] ever-true faith; but most people know it not" (30:30). The description of Islam as being "in accordance with the natural disposition

which God has instilled into man" means that it is consistent with a rational disposition, since Islam is made up of doctrines and legal rulings, all of which are rational matters, that is, realities which operate in accordance with what is comprehended and attested to by human reason.[25]

2. He does not leave the matter to reason alone; rather, he stipulates that in order for terms used to denote their literal meanings (*al-maʿānī al-ḥaqīqiyyah*) and terms used to denote secondary meanings based on prevailing convention (*al-maʿānī al-ʿurfiyyah al-ʿāmmah*) to be considered legitimate *maqāṣid*, they must be characterized by: (a) *thubūt*,* that is to say, they must be based on texts which have been narrated and passed down in a reliable manner; (b) *ẓuhūr*, i.e., they must bear a meaning which is clear and self-evident; (c) *inḍibāṭ*;* that is, they must be consistent from one person, place, time and circumstance to the next; and (d) *iṭṭirād*,* that is, they must be consistent and regular.[26]

§*Second:* "Clearing the playing field" (*taḥrīr maḥall al-khilāf*)

(a) As will be clear from the foregoing, those who have objected to arguments in favor of appealing to human reason, innate understanding or experience in the absence of a consensus from the Muslim community or a text from the Qur'an or the Sunnah have not, in fact, been opposed to these sources of information.

1. Rather, they have been fighting what might be termed a battle based on illusion: the battle of *al-taḥsīn wa al-taqbīḥ*, that is, the question of whether it is possible through human reason to determine whether a given act is good and praiseworthy, or evil and blameworthy, or whether this can only be determined based on explicit declarations of the Law.

In the original formulation of this issue, it was said that God Almighty is obliged to demonstrate the greatest possible kindness (*al-luṭf wa al-aṣlaḥ, or al-ṣalāḥ wa al-aṣlaḥ*) to His servants.[27]

2. Those who took this wary position toward human reason feared being forced to say that there is no need for Islamic law, since human reason renders it unnecessary. In his book, *Imam al-Shatibi's Theory of the Higher Objectives and Intents of Islamic Law*, Ahmad al-Raysuni presents a thorough

discussion of this question; hence, we refer the reader to what he has written in this connection.[28]

(b) Al-Raysuni clearly enumerates the areas in which reason may be used in the appraisal of human interests, namely: i) interest-based textual interpretation, ii) assessment of changing and conflicting interests, and iii) assessment of unrestricted interests.* He concludes his discussion of these areas with the words:

> As I see it – and God knows best – growth in purity likewise involves the purification of one's mind by developing it, guiding it and putting it to use. This is what the Law does when it works to set our minds in motion and release them from their bonds, freeing them from the delusions and superstitions which impede sound thinking. The Law feeds our minds with its values and precepts, then gives them free rein to work and purify themselves. This is an additional aspect of preservation of the faculty of human reason; after all, the Law's preservation of human reason is not limited to outward measures such as prohibiting intoxicants and imposing penalties for partaking of them. After all, how many a person's mind has been lost without his or her ever having touched a drop of liquor? Indeed, people's minds are lost through ignorance, lethargy, idleness and blind imitation. Consequently, putting the mind to use and giving it a wide berth is not merely an aid toward the assessment and preservation of human interests; rather, it is, itself, one of the most vital human interests, since the mind's proper use ensures its preservation, and its preservation is one of the agreed-upon essentials.[29]

(c) Concerning the role of reason, al-Khadimi states,

> The Islamic legal system, with its rulings, its texts, its teachings, its contexts, its *maqāṣid*, its effective causes, and its bases, was not made manifest in the universe, nor were eternal chastisement and bliss in the presence of the Lord of the Worlds made dependent thereon, nor were entire ways of life and civilizations constructed on the basis thereof but for the purpose of its being comprehended by human reason and in order for it to be a suitable basis for both theory and practice. In order to facilitate such theory and practice, it is necessary to engage in a constructive rational process and in beneficial mental activity. Moreover, such activity must be carried out in an orderly manner which involves coordination among the processes of understanding and

> induction, adjustment and measurement, comparison and contrast, weighing and refining, derivation and incorporation, the identification of roots and branches, as well as other aspects of the mental process and creativity. The concrete effects of such processes are observable in the overall cultural edifice as embodied in the establishment of legal, social and value systems, and in the emergence of a remarkable earthly milieu with its intricate, overlapping cultures, its thriving agriculture, its communications revolution, and its orderly yet varied web of interconnections.
>
> The descent of this system of legal rulings onto life's stage, with its multitudinous facets and problems, is evidence of the intervention of reason in this system's formulation and implementation by virtue of the considerable roles which reason has played in the understanding, collection, organization and coordination of the various sources of evidence, as well as in the coordination between such evidence, the circumstances to which it applies and the people whom it addresses.[30]

§*Third:* The complementarity of the means by which *maqāṣid* may be identified:

(a) The means by which *maqāṣid al-sharīʿah* may be identified is a recognized principle which requires no evidence in its support. As we have seen, Ibn al-Qayyim made a number of well-known statements in this connection, in one of which he writes:

> Islamic Law is structured and founded upon wise purposes and the best interests of God's servants both in this world and the next. The Law is pure justice, pure mercy, pure benefit, pure wisdom. Hence, anything which embodies injustice rather than justice, cruelty rather than mercy, harm rather than benefit or folly rather than wisdom does not originate from the Law even if it happens to have been interpolated therein by means of interpretation.[31]

Elsewhere Ibn al-Qayyim writes and as cited previously in point (f) 2:

> Indeed, God sent His messengers and revealed His holy scriptures in order that, as a result of them, people would be upholders of equity, namely, the justice upon which the heavens and the earth were founded. If the signs of truth are manifest, if rational proofs thereof are adduced, and if its dawn

> breaks in any manner whatsoever, then there is God's Law, God's religion, God's good pleasure and God's command. After all, God has not restricted truth's paths, evidences and signs to a single type while invalidating other paths which are more powerful, cogent or plain. Rather, He has made clear by means of the paths He has laid down that His intention (*maqṣuduhu*) is for truth and justice to be established, and for people to uphold equity. Hence, any path by means of which the truth is brought to light and justice is recognized, is a path in accordance with which rulings should be made. Such paths are, in essence, causes and means which are not ends in themselves but which, rather, exist for the sake of their ultimate ends, that is, their *maqāṣid*. However, by means of the paths which God has laid down, He alerts us to their causes and the like. Indeed, you will not find any path which confirms the truth but that it is, itself, a law and a means of pointing to them [its causes and the *maqāṣid* for the sake of which it exists]. And would one expect otherwise of the perfect Law?[32]

(b) It goes without saying that the source which is to be given priority over all others when seeking evidence of the *maqāṣid* is a definitive text from the Qur'an or the Sunnah. In the absence of such a text, recourse may be had to what is referred to by al-Shafiʿī and al-Juwaynī as *istidlāl*, what al-ʿIzz ibn ʿAbd al-Salām terms reason (*al-ʿaql*), experience (*al-tajribah*) and innate understanding (*al-fiṭrah*), what al-Shāṭibī refers to as inductive reading (*al-istiqrā' al-maʿnawī*), as well as other methods.

(c) The question which arises here is not whether each of these various methods – with the exception of reliance on a definitive text from the Qur'an or the Sunnah[33] – can be treated as an independent guide to knowledge of the *maqāṣid*. Rather, the question of relevance is: What are the conditions which must be met by each of these methods in order for it to be considered such a self-contained guide? The existence of diverse methods for ascertaining the *maqāṣid* and acknowledgement that they cannot be limited to a particular number implies, by necessity, the possibility that any one of the aforementioned methods can operate independently of the others. What remains, then, is to identify these conditions.

(d) An exhaustive enumeration of these conditions would require a separate study; hence, we will point out only some of them here by way of example:

1. There must not be a definitive text [from the Qur'an or the Sunnah] which points to the *maqṣid* being investigated.

2. The *maqṣid* under investigation must not conflict with a definitive text or with another *maqṣid* derived from such a definitive text.

3. In the event that such a conflict exists, appeal must be made to the rules governing textual interpretation and the process of determining which text should be given priority over another.

4. The *maqṣid* under discussion must be characterized by, for example, *thubūt, ẓuhūr, inḍibāṭ and iṭṭirād*.[34]

(e) The plurality of methods by which *maqāṣid* may be determined lends credibility to the results of the process of *istidlāl*, since each of the methods used serves to support the others. At the same time, however, the use of a single method in isolation does not diminish the value of the results obtained thereby.

[THEME 2]

Establishing the Order of the Maqāṣid in Relation to Each Other

A number of texts quoted thus far from the works of al-ʿIzz ibn ʿAbd al-Salām and al-Shāṭibī point to the fact that neither sources of benefit nor sources of harm are all characterized by the same degree of importance, and of this principle many examples can be cited.[35]

§*First:* Although the disparity among the various sources of benefit is a matter of general agreement, the resulting order in which they are to be placed – as a number of modern thinkers have pointed out[36] – is not the subject of agreement, much less consensus.

1. Al-Ghazālī (d. 505 AH/1111 AC) established the order for the universal *maqāṣid* which was to become the most widely accepted thereafter, namely:

religion, followed by human life, the faculty of reason, progeny, and material wealth.[37] Elsewhere al-Ghazālī states:

> Wherever we note disagreement, it is in a situation in which there is a conflict between two different sources of benefit or two intents of the Law, or *maqāṣid*, in which the more vital of the two is to be given priority. Consequently, we have stated definitively that if someone is under duress [that is to say, if someone is threatened with death for failing to comply], this renders it permissible for him or her to utter a word of apostasy, partake of alcoholic beverages, consume others' wealth unjustly, or neglect fasting and prayer, since the proscription against the shedding of blood is more serious than any of these things. By the same token, however, adultery is not rendered permissible by virtue of duress, since one should guard against it just as one must guard against [engaging in] the act of compulsion itself.[38]

This passage presents two difficulties which are due to the order al-Ghazālī has proposed for the *maqāṣid*. The first of these difficulties lies in the giving of priority to human life over religion by deeming it permissible to utter a word of apostasy or neglect fasting and prayer if one's life is threatened for doing otherwise. As for the second difficulty, it lies in giving priority to honor (that is, chastity) over the preservation of human life by judging it not to be permissible to commit adultery even under penalty of death.

2. Al-Rāzī (d. 606 AH/1209 AC) did not adhere to any specific order for these universals. Hence, he would sometimes list them as: human life, material wealth, family lineage, religion and human reason,[39] while at other times he would list them as: human life, the faculty of reason, religion, material wealth and family lineage.[40]

3. Neither al-Ghazālī nor al-Rāzī clarifies the reasons for the order he adheres to. Al-Āmidī (d. 631 AH/1233 AC), however, although he does not adhere to a single order, nevertheless clarifies the reasons behind his decision to favor religion over human life and progeny over the faculty of reason. We will have occasion below to spell out his point of view. As for the order which he adopts, he follows that proposed by al-Ghazālī in one place,[41] but differs with him in another[42] by placing religion over human life, followed by progeny, human reason and material wealth.

4. As for Ibn al-Ḥājib (d. 646 AH/1248 AC), he follows al-Āmidī's chosen order as well as his justification for it.

5. Al-ʿIzz ibn ʿAbd al-Salām (d. 660 AH/1261 AC) neither enumerates the essential *maqāṣid*, nor does he adopt any particular order for them.

6. As for al-Qarrāfī (d. 684 AH/1285 AC), he orders them in the following manner without providing any explanation: human life, religion, progeny, human reason, and material wealth, while noting that some also add honor.[43]

7. Similarly, al-Bayḍāwī (d. 685 AH/1286 AC) places them in the following order – human life, religion, human reason, material wealth, and progeny – without offering any explanation for the order he has chosen.[44]

8. Ibn Taymiyyah expands his enumeration of human interests, including among them the five traditional *maqāṣid*, which he orders as follows without explanation: human life, material wealth, honor, human reason and religion,[45] all of which he considers to be means of averting harm.

9. Al-Isnawī (d. 772 AH/1370 AC), al-Bayḍāwī's commentator, follows the latter's order in two places without comment.[46] Elsewhere,[47] al-Isnawī gives religion priority while retaining family lineage at the end – religion, human life, reason, material wealth, and family lineage – without offering any explanation for this choice of order. In a fourth place,[48] he places family lineage between human life and the faculty of reason in emulation of al-Āmidī, Ibn al-Ḥājib and others, likewise without explanation, thereby causing the order to be as follows: religion, then human life, then family lineage, then human reason, then material wealth. One notes here that he has used the particle *thumma* ('then'), which serves to stress the order; in addition, he uses the term 'family lineage' (*nasab*) rather than al-Āmidī's 'progeny' (*nasl*).

In another of his works,[49] al-Isnawī repeats this last order without explanation and states forthrightly, "Of the five essential *maqāṣid*, the interest embodied in religion is to be given highest priority, followed by human life, then family lineage, then human reason, then material wealth."

10. As for Ibn al-Subkī (d. 771 AH/1369 AC), he orders them as: religion, then human life, then human reason, then family lineage, then material

wealth and honor,[50] where it will be noted that he uses the connecting particle *fā'* which, [like *thumma*], serves to convey the concept of ordinality between all items in the list with the exception of material wealth and honor, which he has simply joined with the particle 'and' (*wāw*).

11. Al-Shāṭibī (d. 790 AH/1388 AC) adheres to no set order for the five essential *maqāṣid*. Hence, he sometimes presents them as: religion, human life, progeny, material wealth and reason,[51] sometimes he presents them as: religion, human life, reason, progeny and material wealth,[52] and at still other times, religion, human life, progeny, reason and material wealth.[53] In none of these places does al-Shāṭibī offer any explanation for the order he has chosen, the only exception being his statement that religion is the most important of all. This being the case, human life, material wealth and all other human interests are to be treated as of secondary importance in comparison with that of religion. And since human life is ranked as second in importance to religion, the human interests embodied in the preservation of progeny, human reason and material wealth are to be treated as of subordinate importance in comparison with human life. In consequence of this, one group of scholars hold that if someone were compelled to commit adultery under threat of death, it would be permissible for him to do so in order to protect himself.[54]

12. Al-Zarkashī (d. 794 AH/1391 AC) lists the five essential *maqāṣid* as: human life, material wealth, progeny, religion and human reason, while some thinkers who came after him added a sixth, namely, the preservation of honor.[55] Al-Zarkashī makes reference elsewhere to rules for assigning priority to one interest over another when there is some conflict between them, and which we will have occasion to mention later in this discussion.[56]

13. Ibn Farḥūn (d. 799 AH/1396 AC) offers an expanded listing of the essential *maqāṣid*, including within his classification the five traditional ones (with the addition of honor), the basis for this being that the aim behind the essential *maqāṣid* is guidance and restraint, with the exception of the Islamic forms of worship, whose purpose he identifies as that of taming the soul. Along with other *maqāṣid*, Ibn Farḥūn lists the essential *maqāṣid* in the following order: religion, human survival, family lineage, honor, material wealth, and reason,[57] an order for which he provides no explanation.

14. As for al-Badakhshī (a scholar of the 10th Century AH), he orders the *maqāṣid* in his commentary on al-Bayḍāwī[58] as follows: religion, human life, family lineage, human reason, and material wealth. That is to say, he differs with al-Bayḍāwī with respect to the position of religion and family lineage; however, he offers an explanation for his disagreement which will be discussed below.

15. Shaykh Ibn Ashur (d. 1393 AH/1973 AC) adds nothing but to say, "al-Ghazālī in *al-Mustaṣfā*, Ibn al-Ḥājib, al-Qarrāfī and al-Shāṭibī represented this essential set of interests as the preservation of religion, human life, human reason, material wealth, and progeny."[59] However, it will be clear from what we have presented thus far that this order was not adhered to by any of the thinkers named here; rather, it is one of the choices proposed by al-Isnawī. Ibn Ashur does not specify his own choice, though perhaps the order he attributes here to al-Ghazāli, Ibn al-Ḥājib, al-Qarrāfī and al-Shāṭibī is actually his own undeclared preference.

16. Wahbah al-Zuhayli has written a book on the theory of legal necessity in Islam; similarly, al-Alim devotes a section[60] of his book, *al-Maqāṣid al-ʿĀmmah* to the theme of [legal] necessity, where he discusses the criteria for such necessity, representative cases, and their influence on the transition from a fundamental ruling (*ḥukm aṣlī*) to an emergency ruling (*ḥukm ṭārī'*). It is this transition in the event of legal necessity that explains the problematic cases which arise in connection with establishing the order of the *maqāṣid*.

17. After presenting the views of a number of *uṣūl* scholars on this topic, al-Raysuni concludes his discussion by saying, "The most logical order is that proposed by al-Āmidī,"[61] namely: religion, human life, progeny, the faculty of reason, and material wealth.

§*Second:* If we categorize the views presented above into groups and discuss the problems relating to each group with reference to the justifications offered by al-Āmidī, al-Badakhshī and al-Zarkashī for their respective choices, this may help us to arrive at a conclusion on this issue.

(a) Let us begin with the group which gives religion lower priority than any or all of the following: human life, material wealth, family lineage, progeny, honor, and the faculty of reason.[62]

1. Al-Ghazālī states, as quoted earlier: "Wherever we note disagreement, it is in a situation in which there is a conflict between two different sources of benefit or two intents of the Law, or *maqāṣid*, in which the more vital of the two is to be given priority. Consequently, we have stated definitively that if someone is under duress [that is to say, if someone is threatened with death for failing to comply], this renders it permissible for him or her to utter a word of apostasy, partake of alcoholic beverages, consume others' wealth unjustly, or neglect fasting and prayer, since the proscription against the shedding of blood is more serious than any of these things."[63]

2. Al-Zarkashī[64] quotes a statement by Ibn al-Ḥājib which is included by al-Āmidī in the form of a question rather than a statement. The gist of al-Ḥājib's statement is that when there is a conflict between a human interest associated with religion – that is to say, an interest which is spiritual in nature – and another interest associated with some material or earthly concern, the earthly interest should be given priority over the spiritual interest given the fact that human rights are based on deprivation. To this, however, al-Zarkashī responds by saying that the spiritual or religious interest should be given priority in such a case, since its fruit is the eternal happiness to which nothing else can compare, pointing out that al-Rāzī and al-Āmidī both affirm the same thing unequivocally.

3. If we review al-Rāzī's position, we find that it differs from what al-Zarkashī attributes to him. In two places in his book in which he discusses the order of the essential *maqāṣid*, he gives the preservation of religion lower priority than other *maqāṣid*. In the first of these places, he gives it lower priority than the preservation of human life, material wealth and family lineage,[65] while in the second, he places religion after human life and reason.[66] If what al-Zarkashī means by his quotation from al-Rāzī is that "what serves as an appropriate basis for an interest associated with the life to come is the wise purposes mentioned in connection with the discipline of the soul and the refinement of morals, since its benefit consists in the happiness to be attained in the afterlife,"[67] then this statement – as becomes clear from its wider context – has to do with the category of 'enhancements' (*al-taḥsīniyyāt*), which he describes as having to do with instilling noble morals and character traits.[68] Prior to this he states, "A given basis will be appropriate either for an interest having to do with earthly concerns or for an interest having to do

with the life to come. As for the former...", whereupon he makes mention of the five essential *maqāṣid* in the order which we have mentioned.

4. As for what al-Zarkashī attributes to al-Āmidī, it is correct. In al-Āmidī's discussion of *tarjīḥāt*, that is, decisions relating to which of two interests to give greater weight based on their *ᶜillah*, or basis, al-Āmidī says in *tarjīḥ* No. 17:

> If the intent underlying one of the two bases is the preservation of the essence of the religion, and if the intent underlying the other is any of the other essential *maqāṣid*, then the one whose aim is the preservation of the essence of the religion should be given greater weight in view of its intent and its outcome, namely, the attainment of eternal happiness in the presence of the Lord of the Worlds. As for other *maqāṣid* such as the preservation of human life, the faculty of reason, material wealth, etc., these are all intended for the sake of this one ultimate aim. As God Almighty declares, "I have not created the invisible beings and men to any end other than that they may [know and] worship Me" (51:56).
>
> To this someone might object, saying, "Rather, that which leads to the preservation of human life should be given greater weight. The reason for this is that the preservation of the religion is God's right, whereas the preservation of other things is human beings' right. Moreover, duty to human beings' has precedence over duty to God, since human beings' rights are based on deprivation and affliction, whereas God's rights are based on forbearance and compassion. We say this because God Almighty suffers no harm if His right is forfeited; hence, the preservation of [the creature's right] is of greater importance than preserving the right of One who will suffer no harm should his right be forfeited. This is why we hold that one's duty towards fellow human beings has priority over one's duty of pure worship to God. For example, murder is more of a grievous sin than rejecting the faith – according to scholars – since murder is jeopardising a human's life while disbelief is jeopardising a personal value. In addition, we give higher priority to human life than to the interests of the religion, since we alleviate hardship for those who are on a journey by allowing them to shorten their prayers to two *rakᶜahs*, we exempt travelers from having to fast, and we allow someone who is ill to pray while sitting or prostrate and to forego fasting. Similarly, we give higher priority to the preservation of human life than we do to prayer by

allowing someone who is praying to interrupt his prayer in order to rescue someone who is drowning.

Even more serious is the fact that we give higher priority to preserving material wealth than we do to the interests of the religion by making it permissible to leave the Friday communal prayer out of consideration for the need to preserve the slightest amount of material wealth. Similarly, we give higher priority to protecting the *dhimmīs*[69] living among the Muslims than we do to the interests of the religion, as evidenced by the fact that we guarantee the safety of *dhimmīs*' lives and possessions despite the fact that their presence among Muslims entails the presence of overt unbelief."

In response to these objections we say: As for [the preservation of] human life, just as it is based on human beings' rights with respect to certain legal rulings, it is based on God's rights with respect to other rulings. Consequently, an individual is forbidden to kill himself or to conduct himself in a manner which leads to his own destruction. The decision to place higher priority [on the divine right or the human right] is based on considerations relating to one or both of these rights. Thus, it would not be impossible to give [both] God's right and humans' right precedence based on that which is solely to a divine right. After all, the intent of preserving the religion is fulfilled through the legitimacy of killing,[70] since the act of putting to death is in order to fulfill the threat of doing so. The intent (*maqṣūd*) behind the law of retribution is to satisfy the thirst for revenge. However, this intent cannot be fulfilled on behalf of the [murdered individuals'] heirs merely by virtue of the law which sanctions the act of putting the murderer to death; rather, the law must be actually enforced, a fact which is attested to by prevailing custom. Hence fulfilling both rights [the human and the divine] is preferable to forfeiting either of them. Indeed, giving priority to the human right here through bodily punishment[71] in no way leads to the forfeiture of God's right, since the punishment to be suffered in the afterlife still remains, whereas giving priority to God's right does lead to the forfeiture of the human right as manifested in the infliction of bodily punishment.[72] Hence, this [that is, the realization of both the divine and human rights] is to be preferred.

As for the matter of alleviating the hardship faced by those who are ill or on a journey, this does not give the preservation of human life priority over the preservation of the root of the religion (that is, its fundamentals) but rather, over the preservation of its branches (subsidiary aspects). And the branches of something are not the same as its root. Besides, it should be noted that the hardship involved in performing two *rakᶜahs* while one is on a journey is equivalent to the hardship entailed by performing four *rakᶜahs* under normal circumstances; the same is true of the prayer performed by a sick person while seated as compared to the prayer he would perform from a standing position if he were in good health. In both of these situations, the intent, or *maqṣūd*, remains unchanged. As for the exemption from fasting for those who are ill or on a journey, this exemption is only temporary, after which such persons will be required to fast other days to make up for the ones they missed on account of their travel or illness. The same consideration serves to refute the objections raised above in connection with the fact that someone who is praying would be permitted to interrupt his prayer in order to rescue someone who was drowning, or in relation to leaving the Friday communal prayer for the sake of protecting one's material wealth. As for allowing the *dhimmī* to remain within the Muslim community with the guarantee that his life and possessions will be protected, this is done in order to acquaint the *dhimmī* with the beauties of Islamic law and the principles of the Islamic religion in order that, as a consequence, it will be easier to guide him aright and ensure his obedience and cooperation. All of this, moreover, serves the interests of the religion alone. And just as the intent of preserving the religion is to be given priority over all other essential *maqāṣid*, the intent of preserving human life, insofar as it relates to the preservation of religion, is likewise to be given priority over all others.[73]

5. According to al-ᶜIzz ibn ᶜAbd al-Salām, apostasy in either word or deed is rendered permissible for someone who is forced into it [by a threat on his or her life], provided that the person concerned has certain faith in his/her heart. (As for unbelief in the heart, this could not be forced.) Similarly with respect to other religious obligations such as prayer, fasting, the payment of zakah, engaging in jihad, enjoining the doing of what is right and forbidding the doing of what is wrong, these must be abandoned if one is threatened with death for engaging in them. He also holds that if a Muslim invader realizes that he is in danger of being killed without thereby inflicting damage on those who deny the truth, he should admit defeat.[74] In all of this we find that the preservation of human life is being given priority over the preservation of the religion; moreover, some of the responses by al-Āmidī cited above may be of relevance here.

6. Tāj al-Dīn al-Subkī comments on this issue, saying:

> An essential human interest might be spiritual in nature, or material. When a spiritual interest and a material interest come into conflict, some scholars hold that the spiritual interest should be given priority over the material interest, since the former results in eternal happiness, while the latter results in a happiness which is fleeting and evanescent. Other scholars, by contrast, affirm the view that essential interests relating to earthly needs should be given precedence over those related to spiritual or religious needs, since human beings' rights are based on deprivation and affliction, while God Almighty's rights are based on forbearance and compassion. This, they say, is why the human right is to be given precedence over the divine right in situations in which it is impossible to accommodate them both. In this view, the sin of theft is more grievous than the sin of not paying zakah.
>
> As for us, we favor giving precedence to God's right in accordance with the words of the Prophet, "God's religion is most worthy of implementation." As for putting to death [the apostate][75] and amputating the thief's hand, the Law's intention in this connection is to eliminate the harm brought about by apostasy [and theft]. The Law's purpose is not to kill; however, if it serves as a means of eliminating the harm [caused by apostasy], then the Law affirms it. When the human right and the divine right are in harmony and there is no conflict between divine and human purposes – since the human purpose is simply to satisfy the thirst for revenge – we leave the matter up to the person to whom the bloodwit is to be paid in order for him to receive his due. In this way, then, both the human and divine purposes are fulfilled rather than precedence being given to the human right over the divine right. And the same applies to the view on the amputation of a thief's hand.[76]

7. Quoting from al-Āmidī, al-Badakhshī summarizes the objection to giving precedence to the preservation of religion and the response thereto; hence, there is no need to repeat what he says here.[77]

8. In his commentary on al-Shāṭibī's *al-Muwāfaqāt*, Darraz states, "When preservation of the religion is given precedence over the preservation of human life, this is only in order to preserve the root (that is, the fundamentals) of the religion. However, in relation to its branches (i.e., subsidiary aspects thereof), we find that the Lawgiver often exempts human beings

from religious obligations for the sake of preserving human life, as in the case of illness. In cases such as this, religious considerations are not given priority over human life, nor even over material wealth in all situations."[78] In a statement of al-Āmidī's quoted above, he likewise makes reference to the root and branches of the religion, a distinction which Shaykh Darraz draws upon in order to resolve this difficulty.

9. Similarly, Ali Jumah draws a distinction between the preservation of the religion as a religion, and the piety of individuals who follow the religion. Based on this consideration he ranks individual piety in third place, that is, after human life, which is preserved through people's actions and via the faculty of reason on the basis of which we are held accountable before the divine law.[79] This is a sound point of view which likewise resolves the difficulty despite the fact that Jumʿah does not clarify where the preservation of the fundamentals of the religion are ranked on the scale of priorities.

10. Yahya Muhammad observes that treating religion as one among a number of other components of the essential *maqāṣid* leads to a separation between religion and the areas of life represented by the other essentials. He notes that when *maqāṣid* scholars speak of religion in this way, they are referring not to the religion in its entirety, but only to its worship-related aspects.[80] Consequently, he says, it would be more appropriate to use the term 'worship' specifically [to refer to this aspect of the religion as distinct from the other *maqāṣid*], and to reserve the term 'religion' to speak of Islam in its broader sense, which includes not only doctrinal knowledge but, in addition, comprehensive knowledge of the many and varied spheres of life, and among which all of the essential *maqāṣid* are included.[81]

11. Ahmad al-Rifayah[82] draws a distinction between the level of the individual and the level of the Ummah, or wider Muslim community. On the level of the individual, higher priority is given to the preservation of human life than is given to the preservation of the religion (as in the cases of special allowances [such as provisions for allowing those who are on a journey to shorten their prayers and refrain from fasting] and cases of necessity). On the level of the Ummah, by contrast, preservation of the religion is given priority over preservation of human life (as illustrated by legislation relating to jihad). Here, then, we have a conflict between two interests – the overall

interest of the Ummah, and the particular interest of individuals. However, when weighed in the balance of *maqāṣid al-sharīᶜah* and their various categories, it becomes clear that the interest of the Ummah is to be given priority over the interest of individuals.

12. In the categorization of universals discussed in Chapter Two of this book, and which we treat in the context of the four realms of the individual, the family, the Ummah and humanity, the priority assigned to the preservation of religion and individual piety differs from one realm to another. However, it does not head the list of priorities in any of the realms mentioned; rather, it comes in third with respect to the individual, fifth with respect to the family, fourth with respect to the Ummah, and fifth (tentatively) with respect to wider humanity (otherwise, it would have come in first) for reasons which we will clarify in Chapter Two.

(b) We now come to the group[83] which gives lower priority to the preservation of human reason than it does to any or all of the following: material wealth, progeny/family lineage, and honor.

1. Following the text we quoted earlier concerning the matter of giving the preservation of religion lower priority than other *maqāṣid*, al-Āmidī presents his view on the priority to be given to the preservation of human reason. Moreover, given the close connection between his view on the faculty of reason and his view on family lineage, we quote below what he has to say about both of these matters:[84]

> And just as the intent of preserving the religion is to be given priority over all other essential *maqāṣid*, the intent of preserving human life, insofar as it relates to the preservation of religion, is likewise to be given priority over all others. As for the preservation of family lineage, it should receive lower priority because it is not intended for its own sake, but rather, for the sake of protecting children lest they be lost and deprived of a caretaker. Hence, the preservation of family lineage is sought not for its own sake, but in order for children to be well cared for and able to enjoy life's blessings to the fullest, and in order that they might be able to carry out the obligations required of them under the Law and to bear the burdens which worship entails.
>
> With regard to the preservation of the faculty of reason, it should be borne in mind that human life is the root, or that which is most fundamental,

whereas the faculty of reason is a branch, or that which is subordinate or secondary. Of course, the preservation of what is fundamental takes priority over the preservation of that which is secondary (by which he means to justify giving priority to the preservation of human life over the preservation of human reason), because whatever leads to the loss of human life as a result of judging something else to be of greater value causes it to be lost absolutely (by which he appears to mean death, which includes the resultant loss of the faculty of human reason). As for what leads to the loss of the faculty of reason, such as imbibing intoxicants, this does not lead to its loss absolutely (perhaps he means that the loss is temporary, lasting only as long as the effect of the intoxicant). Hence, preserving the prohibition against whatever would lead to its loss absolutely should receive higher priority (all of which is to justify giving the preservation of human life higher priority than the preservation of human reason).

In keeping with the foregoing, the preservation of family lineage should receive higher priority than the preservation of human reason (here he draws a link between the preservation of human reason and the preservation of family lineage based on what he stated earlier about the preservation of family lineage; however, this is not self-evident, since he stated earlier that the preservation of family lineage is not sought for its own sake but, rather, for the sake of protecting children lest they be lost and in order for them to enjoy ease, luxury and life's blessings to the fullest, none of which may be considered to be among the essentials, as will be clear). It [human reason] should likewise be given priority over the preservation of material wealth since, unlike material wealth, reason serves as the means by which human beings are able to bear the trust given them by their Maker and is the foundation for human beings' ability to carry out the responsibilities which are theirs under the Law. Moreover, unlike material wealth, the faculty of reason is required in itself for worship without any intermediary. (This is self-evident, and supports the validity of giving human reason priority over material wealth). It is for this reason that these categories differ in terms of the punishments associated with them, just as they differ amongst themselves. (This is a new, general argument, the gist of which is that the arrangement of the various categories or ranks of *maqāṣid* is based on the arrangement of their associated punishments, a view which is rejected by Ibn Ashur.[85]) And just as there exists a disparity among these ranks of *maqāṣid*, so also is there a disparity among their complements.[86]

In sum, it may be said that al-Āmidī's justifications for giving human life priority over human reason and human reason priority over material wealth are both acceptable. As for his justification for giving family lineage priority over human reason, it is not convincing. We might also note here that he uses the term *nasab* (family lineage) rather than the term *nasl* (progeny); in fact, had he used the latter term as he does in his arrangement of the essential *maqāṣid*, his argument would have had nothing to support it in the first place.

2. After presenting a summary of al-Āmidī's view in favor of giving the preservation of religion priority over other essential *maqāṣid*, al-Badakhshī makes a number of statements, some of which are quotations from al-Āmidī and others of which are new. Hence, given the overlap between his own contributions and those of al-Āmidī, we present them in full below:

> Among the four [that is, the four essential *maqāṣid* which follow religion in terms of priority], the interest which is to be given highest priority following religion is the preservation of human life, since it is by virtue of this that it is possible to perform acts of worship. This is followed by the preservation of family lineage, since this serves to further human survival given the fact that it was provided for in the Law for the sake of protecting children lest they be lost or without a caretaker. Next in order of priority is human reason, which is given priority over material wealth because, unlike material wealth, the faculty of reason is the means by which we acquire knowledge and understanding, it serves as the basis for human beings' accountability before the divine law, and it is required in itself for worship without any intermediary.
>
> Someone might object, saying: What you have said here about [the preservation of family lineage] serving to further human survival is actually a basis for giving family lineage lower, rather than higher, priority than human reason and material wealth, since material wealth also furthers human survival.
>
> In reply to this objection we say: The preservation of family lineage is dedicated solely to furthering human survival, unlike material wealth, which also serves other interests which go beyond mere survival, including the provision of ease, luxury, adornment and the like. According to al-Muḥaqqiq, the preservation of human reason should be given priority given the fact that in its absence, human life will be forfeited as well, while al-Fāḍil states that the apparent sense of this argument is invalid, since the opposite is actually true. Therefore, al-ʿAllāmah holds that the preservation of human reason is

> subordinate to the preservation of human life given the fact that if human life is lost, so also is the faculty of reason, whereas the opposite affirmation [namely, that if human reason is lost, human life is lost as well] is not true. Therefore, it is preferable to maintain a prohibition against whatever would lead to its absolute loss. This is the same meaning conveyed by what al-Āmidī states as well. [In any case,] the most that can be said is that with the loss of human reason, human life is lost as well insofar as that which preserves human life from certain evils has ceased to exist. However, there is nothing in what has been said here which would indicate that the preservation of family lineage should be given priority over that of human reason. They have said that the preservation of family lineage should receive higher priority than either human reason or material wealth, since unlike the latter two, the preservation of family lineage is related to human survival. In sum, then, religious/spiritual necessity is given higher priority than earthly/material necessity of whatever sort it happens to be, and in the order which we have mentioned.[87]

The passage just quoted may be summarized in the following points:

- The justification for giving priority to the preservation of human life is that it is by virtue of human life that the performance of the various forms of worship is made possible. (This is unquestionable with respect to its conclusion.)
- The preservation of human reason should be given priority over the preservation of material wealth for the reasons previously enumerated by al-Āmidī (this is beyond dispute; moreover, it represents a response to al-Rāzī, Ibn Taymiyyah, al-Shāṭibī and Ibn Farḥūn, who give material wealth priority over human reason).
- The justification for placing the preservation of family lineage next in line after the preservation of human life is that it serves to further human survival (which is the same position affirmed by al-Āmidī, and which was discussed earlier).
- Al-Badakhshī adds a question pertaining specifically to the faculty of reason and material wealth; he then answers the question by addressing the part specific to material wealth and disregarding the part specific to human reason. Following this he cites statements which he attributes to individuals whom he refers to as al-Muḥaqqiq, al-Fāḍil and al-ʿAllāmah,

all of which have to do with giving human life priority over human reason, the validity of which is uncontested.

- Lastly, he notes that "there is nothing in what has been said here which would indicate that the preservation of family lineage should be given priority over that of human reason" (and herein lies the main point). He then offers a thorough, frank response having to do with human reason and material wealth in which he states, "They have said that the preservation of family lineage should receive higher priority than either human reason or material wealth, since unlike the latter two, the preservation of family lineage is related to human survival." (In other words, the reason family lineage is given priority over human reason is that the former furthers human survival whereas the latter does not.)

In sum, then, al-Badakhshī does not discuss the matter of giving family lineage in particular priority over human reason in particular. Rather, he treats family lineage as an adjunct to human life and, as a consequence, assigns it higher priority than he does to human reason. He does cite the view according to which, "with the loss of human reason, human life is lost as well insofar as that which preserves human life from certain evils has ceased to exist." However, although this view serves as a justification for treating human reason as an adjunct to human life and, as a consequence, assigning it higher priority than the preservation of family lineage, he offers no response to it. This difficulty, therefore, remains unresolved.

3. As we see it, the assignment of lower priority to the preservation of human reason than to the preservation of progeny, family lineage, honor or even material wealth on the part of this sizeable number of *uṣūl* scholars may be attributed to the fact that, as we have had occasion to observe, their view of human reason is limited to that of preventing intoxication and goes no further than this. However, Chapter Two of this study includes a discussion of the preservation of human reason in four broad spheres of life with their many and varied dimensions, which will serve to clarify the true significance of human reason and its place among the universals [of Islamic law].

(c) We now proceed to a discussion of a third group[88] who give material wealth higher priority than family lineage and honor. None of these scholars gives a justification for giving material wealth priority over family lineage and honor; hence, there is no possibility of discussing their arguments in favor of this position. However, al-Āmidī's and al-Badakhshī's discussions in favor of assigning higher priority to family lineage than to human reason and material wealth contain a response to the implied argument [for the opposite position]. In our view, it is preferable to consider family lineage, honor and human reason as adjuncts and supports to the preservation of human life, thereby giving them priority over material wealth. After all, material wealth is a mere servant to human beings and external to their nature, whereas the preservation of family lineage, honor (and the faculty of reason) are intrinsic to the makeup of human beings, whom God has honored and favored above all other creatures, and to whom He has made the rest of the creation subservient.

(d) Lastly, to the aforementioned difficulties we add two additional difficulties which have to do with assigning the preservation of human life lower priority than the preservation of honor and material wealth.

1. The difficulty that arises as a result of assigning human life lower priority than honor is based on the Prophetic hadith which states, "Anyone who is killed for the sake of his family is a martyr."[89] If we understand this hadith to be referring to a defense of one's family's lives, then it presents no problem. If however, we understand it to include the defense of one's family's honor, we will thereby have placed the preservation of honor over the preservation of human life by encouraging people to sacrifice their lives in defense of honor.

Imam al-Juwaynī supports this point of view when he states, "Many an act considered reprehensible by the Law cannot be justified even by necessity. Rather, the Law requires that one be willing to perish rather than to engage in such acts, such as murder and adultery, if one is being forced into them under threat of death."[90]

Al-Ghazālī expresses a similar view in the words, "Adultery is not rendered permissible thereby (that is, by virtue of outward compulsion or threat), since one should guard against it just as one must guard against [engaging in] the act of compulsion itself."[91]

Similarly, al-ʿIzz ibn ʿAbd al-Salām states, "Neither adultery nor homosexuality is rendered permissible by virtue of compulsion or threat."[92]

Al-Shāṭibī, however, continues to adhere to the principle of giving precedence to the preservation of human life, saying, "...then human life, in comparison with which the preservation of progeny, human reason and material wealth are all to be treated as of secondary importance. In consequence of this, one group of scholars hold that if someone were compelled to commit adultery under threat of death, it would be permissible for him to do so in order to protect himself. And in the case of a woman in dire straits who fears death and finds that no one will be willing to feed her unless she sacrifices her chastity, it is permissible for her to do so."[93]

This issue is thus a controversial one, and by adopting the view of al-Juwaynī, al-Ghazālī, and al-ᶜIzz ibn ᶜAbd al-Salām, one forfeits the traditional arrangement in which human life is given precedence over honor.

2. As for the difficulty related to assigning human life lower priority than material wealth, it is likewise based on a Prophetic hadith which states, "Anyone who is killed for the sake of his material wealth is a martyr,"[94] since in this case, the preservation of material wealth is given precedence over the preservation of human life by encouraging people to sacrifice their lives in defense of their possessions. Here also, then, we have a departure from the traditional order between human life and honor.

3. According to al-Ghazālī, one of the principles of the Islamic religion is embodied in the words, "and who, whenever tyranny afflicts them, defend themselves" (42:39). Hence, in adherence to my religion, I will spurn tyranny even if I should die (in the cases of defending honor and material wealth). However, this is not to be considered giving precedence to material wealth and honor over human life but, rather, a means of defending the religion against all else.[95]

§*Third:* Some modern thinkers have added the following foundational perspectives on this theme.

(a) That *maqāṣid al-sharīᶜah* are closely interrelated in the sense that the existence of some of them depends on the existence of others.[96] In keeping with this affirmation it may be said that "if religion ceased to exist, the hoped-for reward [for righteous deeds] would cease to follow as a result. If there were no human beings held accountable before the Law, there would be no one capable of experiencing true piety. If there were no faculty of reason, piety would cease to have any meaning; if there were no progeny, there would be no survival for the most part; and if there were no material wealth, there would remain no possibility of life."[97] In other words, the *maqāṣid* overlap and mutually influence one another. Consequently, the preservation of any one of them will reflect automatically on the preservation of the others, just as the violation of any one of them will have an effect on the others. They are like links in a single chain, or like interlocking hands.[98]

This notion, expressed long ago by al-Shāṭibī and picked up on by certain modern scholars, has now been taken a step further. For example, Fu'ad Abu Hatab declares with respect to the arrangement of priorities:

> We have before us three different methods of classification: We can deal with all of these priorities as separate blocs arranged alongside one another. According to this conceptualization, each of the priorities is independent of the others; hence, we can begin however and wherever we choose. However, this is a system which I do not believe to be in harmony with the logic that underlies the fundamental arrangement of the *maqāṣid*.
>
> As was indicated by our mentor and imam, Shaykh al-Ghazālī, we can view them in light of the idea that there are essentials which are included within still other essentials. These essentials can be conceptualized as concentric circles: vast, spacious circles inside of which are circles of ever decreasing size, with the circle of religion being the largest and most inclusive of all.
>
> There is also, of course, the hierarchical conceptualization of the *maqāṣid* which begins with a broad, basic foundation. Once this foundation has been established, we ascend to the next step, then the next step, and so on until we reach the top of the ladder.[99]

In a seminar held recently at Azhar University[100] to discuss the draft of this study, Ahmad al-Mahdi Abd al-Halim expressed the view that we do not need to arrange the *maqāṣid* in the same manner proposed by earlier scholars but that, instead, we would do well to adopt the image of concentric circles, which is likewise the choice preferred by Fuad Hatab himself.

(b) The question of how the *maqāṣid* are to be arranged applies not only to what are termed the universal *maqāṣid* (*al-maqāṣid al-kulliyyah*) but, in addition, to what are referred to as the 'higher' *maqāṣid* (*al-maqāṣid al-ʿāliyah*).

1. Muhammad Umarah states:

> In dealing with the question of priorities [among the *maqāṣid*], we are given a model by Ibn Taymiyyah, who lived in a Mamluk society replete with injustice and problems. In fact, the situation led to Ibn Taymiyyah's death in a Mamluk prison after he had been persecuted in that society. However, when we read what Ibn Taymiyyah wrote about the rule of the Mamluks, who were malefactors and despots, we find him extolling this Mamluk power and saying, "If this band should perish, Islam will be lost and so will the Ummah." The reason for this is that during Ibn Taymiyyah's era, the highest priority was that of preserving the Ummah's existence. The Ummah's very survival in the face of the Tatars and the Crusaders was a priority in and of itself. Consequently, it was possible for concerns such as freedom, participation, consultation and social justice to be relegated to places of lower priority, overshadowed as they were by the concern to ensure the Ummah's ongoing existence. This position, which was fleshed out by Ibn Taymiyyah so ingeniously in the context of that history, is something which we ourselves can identify with today in the age of invasion, an age in which the Islamic Ummah is being invaded, whether by means of Christian proselytizing, economic indenture, military subjugation, cultural infiltration, intellectual encroachment, or all of the above. What I wish to say here is that the issue of sovereignty and the implementation of an autonomous project for the Ummah is a top priority the importance of which must be recognized in the programs of thinkers, movements, the Ummah as a whole, and in the context of the Islamic call, since we are confronted today by a danger which threatens the Ummah's very existence.[101]

2. According to Yahya Muhammad, the higher *maqāṣid* – or what he terms the ultimate *maqāṣid* (*al-maqāṣid al-ghā'iyyah*) – impact one another in a functional relationship by virtue of which human movement becomes integrated and unrestricted given the fact that it strives for the absolute or perfection.[102]

§*Fourth:* The conclusions which emerge from the foregoing discussion may be summarized as follows:

1. The proper arrangement of the five universals (or what are sometimes termed the five essential *maqāṣid*) is a matter of disagreement among scholars.

2. The majority of scholars provide no justification for the arrangement which they choose.

3. Among the justifications cited for giving this or that fundamental higher or lower priority, as well as the objections raised against giving this or that fundamental higher or lower priority, we find that some are more acceptable than others. Indeed, the conflicting arguments can sometimes be confusing.

4. It must be acknowledged that the arrangement posed by al-Ghazālī remains, to this day, the basis of every amendment or objection.

5. This arrangement derives its importance from the fact that in the event of a conflict between two universals or *maqāṣid*, one of the two will be given precedence, while the other will be sacrificed. If, then, the arrangement is not the subject of universal agreement, each scholar of jurisprudence will apply the arrangement which he deems superior, the natural result being conflicting rulings based on the various independent interpretations of the jurists concerned. This type of conflict is illustrated clearly in the differing points of view represented by al-Shāṭibī on one hand and, on the other hand, by al-Juwaynī, al-Ghazālī and al-ʿIzz concerning the ruling on someone who commits adultery under compulsion or threat.

6. There is a certain degree of common ground, or at least, a type of evidence which ought to be agreed upon, namely, cases in which there is an explicit text from the Qur'an or the Sunnah which clarifies the ruling required in the event of a conflict between two universals or *maqāṣid*, such as the texts which address the subject of jihad and which give the preservation of the religion precedence over the preservation of human life. If some researcher were to undertake an inductive reading of such texts in preparation for their classification and analysis, this could help lead to an arrangement which is convincing to all.

7. Al-Shāṭibī's expressed desire to arrive at a set of definitive principles of Islamic law can only be fulfilled by resolving the disagreement over the proper arrangement of the Islamic universals, or *maqāṣid*.

8. The notion of a circular conceptualization of the *maqāṣid* as a substitute for the traditional arrangement is worthy of further investigation.

9. The question of how to arrange the *maqāṣid* is not limited to the universal *maqāṣid* alone, but includes the 'higher' *maqāṣid* (*al-maqāṣid al-ʿāliyah*) as well.

10. Together with al-Raysuni, we call upon scholars to engage in further detailed studies of the categories of *maqāṣid* and of clear criteria for distinguishing among them.[103]

[THEME 3]

Establishing the Order of the Means (Wasā'il) Associated With Each of the Maqāṣid

[*Subtheme* 1]: *The Deterrent Force of Innate Understanding, Religion and External Authority*

In the context of discussing the authority of the Law, Ibn Ashur[104] notes that in order to establish this authority, the Law makes use of varying types of deterrent force, specifically, those embodied in human beings' innate understanding, religion and external authority.

In thus establishing its authority, the Law relies first of all on human beings' innate perception of the benefits which we naturally crave and on cautionaries against those sources of harm from which we have a natural aversion, such as the benefits manifested in seeking out food and clothing and protecting one's progeny. At the same time, there are few references in Islamic law to the safekeeping of one's children except in cases where a particular form of neglect has been prevalent such as the practice of burying female infants alive.

Most Islamic legal precepts depend for their fulfillment on religious motivation, namely, the motivation generated by sound faith which gives rise to the twin emotions of hope and fear. When religious compunctions grow weak during this or that certain historical period, among a particular people, or in circumstances in which there is reason to believe that the impulse to violate the Law is more compelling for people than the force of religious sentiments, recourse is had to the deterrent force of external authority. As ʿUthmān ibn ʿAffān once declared, "God curbs through external authority what He does not curb through the Qur'an." Al-Shāṭibī presents a detailed discussion of this notion as it relates to innate understanding, particularly those things in relation to which consideration is given to human desires and inclinations, and enumerates the consequences which follow from it.

[*Subtheme* 2]*: The Categories of Essentials (Ḍarūriyyāt), Exigencies (Ḥājiyāt) and Enhancements (Taḥsīniyyāt) Have to Do With Means (Wasā'il), Not Intents (Maqāṣid)*

Uṣūl scholars hold that the primary *maqāṣid* are the essentials (*al-ḍarūriyyāt*), while exigencies (*al-ḥājiyāt*) and enhancements (*al-taḥsīniyyāt*) are included among secondary, or subsidiary *maqāṣid*.[105] In addition, they hold that just as each of the essential *maqāṣid* is divided into the categories of primary (*aṣlī*), secondary (*tabaʿī*) and associated complements (*mukammilāt*), so also are exigencies and enhancements divisible into these three sub-categories.[106] However, this overlapping type of division leads to complication and ambiguity.

§*First:* We propose that:

1. The *maqāṣid* are not limited to the category of essentials; rather, they include the categories of exigencies and enhancements in a single unit. Within this scheme, the category of essentials represents the minimum level of the *maqāṣid* concerned. However, Islamic law does not stop at seeking to ensure this minimum level; rather, it goes beyond this to seek its completion to every possible extent.

2. Given the foregoing, it may be concluded that the categories of essentials, exigencies and enhancements are not related to the *maqṣid* itself but, rather, to the means which lead to its fulfillment. And to the extent that a given *maqṣid* is fulfilled by virtue of the means available, it is classified accordingly among the essentials, the exigencies or the enhancements.

The following two examples should help to illustrate what we are saying:

1. Food is one of the means by virtue of which the *maqṣid* of preserving human life is fulfilled. Obtaining an amount of food which is sufficient to keep one alive, however unpalatable or unrefined it happens to be, and without which one would perish, belongs to the category of essentials. Obtaining food in a form which allows for a variety of dishes and balanced

meals prepared in an appetizing way belongs to the category of exigencies. The category of enhancements is represented by the way in which the food is served, the observance of table etiquette, etc. And as for what goes beyond this by way of extravagance and surfeit, it is forbidden.

2. Access to a place to live is also one of the means by which the *maqṣid* of preserving human life is fulfilled. Access to minimal shelter, be it in the form of a cave, a hut or a tent, belongs to the category of essentials. The level of exigencies includes the availability of a house with doors and windows that one can lock securely and which is equipped with water and electricity. As for the level of enhancements, it is attained by having the wherewithal to decorate one's house, to have air-conditioning, a garden, etc.

In both examples cited above, we find that the overall requirement of food or a dwelling represents the legal intent, or *maqṣid*, and that the levels known in Islamic legal parlance as essentials, exigencies and enhancements are determined by the means through which the *maqṣid* is being fulfilled, not by the *maqṣid* itself.

§*Second:* This same meaning is conveyed in the following words by al-ʿIzz ibn ʿAbd al-Salām, although his manner of expressing it is somewhat misleading:

> *The essentials* include such things as food, drink, clothing, spouses, vehicles for transporting foodstuffs, and the like. *The minimal level of such entities is considered to belong to the category of essentials.* As for the same categories of things, but provided in abundant quantities or of the highest quality, such as tasty foods, fine clothing, spacious rooms, large mansions, costly vehicles, attractive spouses..., they belong to the category of extras (that is, enhancements), whereas anything which falls between these two extremes belongs to the category of exigencies.[107]

The two instances of the word 'essentials' placed in italics in the quote above are misleading. The author might have used the phrase "the means by which human life is preserved, such as food...which fulfills this *maqṣid*, and that which meets human needs at the most minimal level, belong to the category of essentials."

§*Third:* As for al-Shāṭibī, what he has to say on this topic is even more misleading, since he asserts the view that the categories of exigencies and enhancements are included within the category of essentials which they, in effect, serve simply to complete and perfect. Similarly, he holds that any disturbance in the realms of exigencies or enhancements will result in hardship and distress in the realm of the essentials as well.[108] In this connection, see "Fourth" on p. 24 [of *al-Muwāfaqāt*], where he describes the conditions and pillars of ritual prayer as serving and reinforcing prayer despite the fact that they are, at the same time, part of prayer and not distinct from it. Al-Shāṭibī refers to the essentials, exigencies and enhancements as a single unit; at the same time, however, he continues referring to this unit with the term 'essentials'. If he had spoken of this unit as the overarching *maqṣid* (intent) or *maṣlaḥah*[109] (interest or source of benefit), it would not have led to such ambiguity. Al-Shāṭibī states,

> Based on this arrangement, essentials function along with exigencies and enhancements. After all, easement (*tawsiʿah*) and the elimination of hardship require, by implication, something in which there might be constriction and hardship, and this, undoubtedly, represents the level of essentials, while the level of enhancements (*taḥsīniyyāt*) is comprised of complements (*mukammilāt*) and auxiliaries (*mutammimāt*). Now, in order for there to be complements and auxiliaries, there must be something which requires complementation or augmentation. After all, the processes of enhancement (*taḥsīn*), completion, or perfection (*takmīl*) and broadening or easing (*tawsīʿ*) require some kind of object which, in the absence of these processes, would be considered lacking in some respect, imperfect and in need of expansion and mitigation; indeed, they would be seen as objectionable, inadequate, constricted and uncomfortable. Hence, these processes must be traced back to something else which is needed and sought after. The process of enhancement and mitigation must follow upon the quest for that which is enhanced and mitigated. This is what we meant by our earlier statement regarding the need for there to be both an ideal that is sought after, and a process by which it is sought after.[110]

§*Fourth:* In his treatment of the various levels of preservation of human life, al-Alim[111] adopts an approach which is consistent with the view that we ourselves are proposing. Although he does not spell out clearly his conceptualization of the problem, he outlines three situations in which the preservation of human life may be observed: The first is the most commonly occurring situation, in which the individual enjoys a degree of comfort, ease and luxury; this is a case in which general legislation is applied. The second is a situation in which the individual is in a state of distress, hardship and difficulty, but has not reached the point of dire need or the essentials; rather, he is still at the level of exigencies. In a situation such as this, God alleviates the person's hardship by means of certain allowances, and it is possible for him to enter the realm of judiciously ambiguous action (*dā'irah al-shubuhāt*).[112] As for the third situation, it is one in which the individual experiences such dire need that it becomes necessary, or at least permissible, for him to engage in certain actions which would otherwise be forbidden, or to refrain from or postpone certain actions which would otherwise be obligatory in order to protect himself from what he has good reason to believe would cause him harm. All such allowances, however, are permitted within the limits of the Law and its basic principles.

§*Fifth:* As we have seen, the means by which the *maqāṣid* are fulfilled are categorized as being either essentials, exigencies or enhancements. However, within each of these categories there are differing degrees of urgency or importance. It is with this fact in mind that al-Shāṭibī states, "If you examine the level of preservation of human life, it will become apparent that not all actions relating thereto are of the same degree of seriousness. After all, amputation of a part of the body is not the same as the cutting of the throat, nor is a scratch the same as amputation of a part of the body..."[113]

[*Subtheme* 3]: *Should There be Three Levels, or Five?*

§*First:* There are five levels [of *maqāṣid*]:

1. Of these five levels, three are legitimate, namely, that which is essential (*al-ḍarūrī*), that which is necessary, or an exigency (*al-ḥājī*), and that which serves to enhance (*al-taḥsīnī*). This, of course, assumes the existence of two other levels which are not legitimate, namely, that which falls short of the

essential (*mā dūn al-ḍarūrī*), and that which goes beyond mere enhancement (*mā warā' al-taḥsīnī*).

2. As for the three legitimate levels of *maqāṣid*, al-Shāṭibi[114] demonstrates mastery and creativity not only in establishing their existence, but in providing proof of their definitive nature by means of an inductive reading of the Law and a careful examination of all textual evidence contained therein, both that which is of universal application and that which applies to particular cases. Al-Shāṭibī's method of undertaking such an inductive reading involves reliance on what is termed *al-tawātur al-maᶜnawī*[115] rather on human reason [alone], *ijmāᶜ*, that is, the consensus of the Muslim community, or texts whose chain of transmission does not fulfill the requirements of *tawātur*.

3. I have no comment to make either on the three-fold division of the *maqāṣid*, or on the evidence for this division. However, what I would like to add is that there is a need to engage in further study of both: (a) situations which fall short of the level of essentials, and (b) situations which involve excess that goes beyond the level of enhancements. These two types of situation need to be recognized in order to make it possible to formulate the legal rulings which they call for. In fact, they should be given priority in view of the need to eliminate them as illegitimate or unsatisfactory situations.

During the discussion of the draft of this study in the context of a recent seminar at Al-Azhar University, Ali Jumah (Grand Mufti of Egypt) drew my attention to a statement made by al-Suyūṭī which may be understood to imply such a five-fold division of the *maqāṣid*. This statement, after the correction of a typographical error, reads as follows:

Lesson: Someone has said[116] that there are five levels: utter necessity (*ḍarūrah*), need or exigency (*ḥājah*), benefit (*manfaᶜah*), adornment or embellishment (*zīnah*) and surfeit (*fuḍūl*).

- Utter necessity (*ḍarūrah*) refers to a situation in which, unless one partakes of what would otherwise be forbidden, one will perish or be on the verge of perishing. This situation, then, renders it permissible to partake of what would otherwise be forbidden. (This corresponds to that which falls short of the essential, or *mā dūn al-ḍarūrī* in my proposed division.)

- Need or exigency (*ḥājah*) refers to the situation of someone who is hungry and who, if he did not find anything to eat, would not perish but would suffer hardship. This situation does not render it permissible to partake of what would otherwise be forbidden; however, it does render it permissible to break one's fast [during Ramadan]. (This corresponds to the level of essentials [*al-ḍarūrī*] in the three-fold division.)
- Benefit (*al-manfaʿah*) refers to a situation in which one has a craving for wheat bread, mutton, and rich foods. (This corresponds to the level of exigencies in the three-fold division.)
- Adornment or embellishment (*al-zīnah*) would be illustrated by someone who has a craving for sweets, sugar, or garments of linen or silk (which corresponds to the level of enhancements, or embellishments (*al-taḥsīniyyāt*) in the three-fold division).
- Surfeit (*al-fuḍūl*) refers to partaking of forbidden foods[117] and other dubious indulgences (which corresponds to 'that which goes beyond enhancements,' *mā warā' al-taḥsīnī*, in my proposed division).[118]

§*Second:* Let us cite a number of examples from modern life:

1. In relation to nutrition and, hence, the preservation of human life, there are millions who die annually as a result of famines and malnutrition and who, therefore, fall short of what is essential. In the realm of housing, there are millions of displaced, homeless persons for whom not enough tents are available and who, as a consequence, are exposed to the bitter cold in winter [and scorching heat in the summer]. At the opposite extreme, namely, what goes beyond that which merely enhances the quality of life, there are millions who live lives of extravagance, wastefulness and surfeit, whether on the level of food, clothing or housing.

2. In relation to the preservation of religion, most people lack even the essentials in that they either have no religion whatsoever, or have a kind of theoretical faith but engage in no kind of worship or devotion. At the other end of the spectrum we see people who, going beyond what could be considered enhancements, take their religion to extremes, espousing rigid points of view and cutting themselves off from [secular] life in the belief that this is what is required of them in order to draw near to God.

3. In the realm of preservation of progeny, there are people whose most essential needs are unmet due to circumstances which prevent them from marrying at all, or who only marry at a late age. Such individuals may seek to compensate for their inability to marry by engaging in illicit sexual practices, or they may simply remain captive to repression and a sense of deprivation. At the same time, there are others who are so preoccupied with sex that they fail to give proper attention to anything else in life, going to excess in illicit relationships, or even in licit ones, which is inconsistent with the balance for which God instituted marriage or to which human beings are naturally disposed. In fact, there are some who go so far as to take a new wife every week in their quest for a kind of sensual pleasure whose flames are extinguished with time and lose their meaning.

And so on in all other areas of life....

§ *Third:* Al-ʿIzz ibn Abd al-Salām[119] cites a number of examples which he prefaces by saying:

> Moderation is a station between two other stations, a degree between two other degrees. There are thus three stations or degrees: (1) negligence in pursuing what is of benefit, (2) excess in this pursuit, and (3) moderation. God Almighty has said, "And neither allow thy hand to remain shackled to thy neck, nor stretch it forth to the utmost limit [of thy capacity], lest thou find thyself blamed [by thy dependents], or even destitute" (17:29). [He likewise praises those] "...who, whenever they spend on others, are neither wasteful nor niggardly but [remember that] there is always a just mean between those [two extremes]" (25:67). He also declares, "O you who have attained to faith! Do not deprive yourselves of the good things of life which God has made lawful to you, but do not transgress the bounds of what is right: verily, God does not love those who transgress the bounds of what is right" (5:87); and, "eat and drink freely, but do not waste: verily, He does not love the wasteful (7:31)."

He also cites numerous other verses from the Qur'an, as well as prophetic hadiths and scores of examples from a variety of areas.

As for al-Shāṭibī, he writes that:

> In its imposition of obligations in accordance with its precepts, Islamic law proceeds along the path of moderation and consummate fairness. It is a path which appropriates both extremes without inclining toward either of them, and which remains within the limits of human capacity, thereby causing us neither hardship nor harm. Indeed, the obligations entailed by the Law of Islam are founded upon an equilibrium which requires that every one of us progress toward perfect moderation. Hence, if a given precept comes into being in order to correct human beings' tendency to diverge from the right path [in this or that area of life], or because there is good reason to believe that we might diverge from the middle way toward this or that extreme, it thereby serves to restore us to the path of moderation and full integrity. However, it performs this function by moving us toward the opposite extreme in order for the desired balance to be restored, just as a compassionate physician makes a patient do what is in the patient's best interest as dictated by his condition, his habits, and the severity of his illness and infirmity so that when he regains his health, he will be prepared to manage his affairs in moderation, and in the way best suited to him in all situations.[120]

He continues elsewhere, saying:

> If you look at a universal of the Law and give it careful thought, you will find that it serves to foster moderation. Hence, if you observe a tendency [in the Law] toward one or another extreme, this is because it is countering some actual or anticipated tendency toward the opposite extreme. The extreme of austerity – and, in general, anything that would fall within the realm of warning, intimidation and rebuke – is intended to confront those who incline towards laxness and decadence in the religion. Conversely, the extreme of lenience or alleviation – and, generally, anything which falls under the rubric of encouragement, enticement and allowances – is intended to respond to those who incline towards severity and inflexibility. In all other situations, however, you will find it to be palpably moderate. This is the foundation to which the Law always returns and the stronghold in which it takes refuge.
>
> Consequently, if you find passages in the writings of recognized religious scholars which indicate a move away from moderation, you can be certain that this is a response on their part to an actual or anticipated tendency

toward an opposite extreme. It is with this principle in mind that we should view matters such as abstinence (*wara*ʿ), renunciation (*zuhd*), and the like, as well as their opposites.

Moderation may be recognized through the Law; it may likewise be recognized through the benefits [which result from this or that course of action], the testimony borne by the majority of the wise and discerning, and [through observation of what results from the extremes of] wastefulness and niggardliness in the realm of monetary expenditure.[121]

§*Fourth:* The importance of highlighting the notions of negligence and excess is based on a number of considerations:

1. They are both transgressions of the bounds set by God, as a result of which concern needs to be demonstrated to eliminate them altogether. And this, in turn, requires that we define them and clarify the rulings on them and the proper manner of dealing with them.

2. Delineation of the realm of *mā dūn al-ḍarūrī* (that which falls short of the essential) requires that we define the boundary between this realm and the realm of the essential (that is, the minimum of what is to be considered essential); similarly, delineating the realm of what goes beyond that which enhances (*mā warā' al-taḥsīnī*) requires that we define the boundary between this and the realm of enhancements.

3. The wealth, energy and time which are squandered in extravagant living would be sufficient to put an end to abject need, after which efforts could be expended to meet essential needs, followed by efforts to provide satisfaction on the levels of exigencies and enhancements to the extent possible.

4. There is a need to clarify the role of the state in observing the dual limits of negligence and excess, and this in two respects: (1) with respect to the use of a combined carrot-and-stick approach toward those who transgress these limits, and (2) with respect to the state's responsibility to provide for people's essential needs.

5. Those who have renounced the world for spiritual/religious reasons content themselves with the bare essentials, while some of them may content themselves with even less than this in the belief that this is an expression of

perfect devotion.[122] Consequently, it is important to define the limits of legitimate renunciation in order to distinguish it from niggardliness, negligence and the violation of one's own rights (in keeping with the truth, "Your body has rights over you").

[*Subtheme* 4]: *The Criterion on the Basis of Which a Given Ruling or Means is to be Placed in the Category of Essentials, Exigencies or Enhancements*[123]

Is this criterion the type of legal ruling with which the interest, or *maṣlaḥah* is associated? If so, this means that if the legal ruling concerned is an emphatic command or prohibition, that is, one which points to an action which is either obligatory (*wājib*) or forbidden (*muḥarram*), then the interest with which it is associated is to be classified among the essentials, and that if it is a non-emphatic command or prohibition, that is, one which points to an action which is either recommended (*mandūb*) or undesirable (*makrūh*), it is to be classified among the exigencies, and that if it is an action which is simply permitted (*mubāḥ*), it is to be classified among the enhancements. In this case, we will have adopted a formalistic criterion.

Or is the criterion an objective one, based on the degree of benefit or harm associated with the legal ruling concerned? If so, then if the legal ruling is associated with a significant benefit or harm, it is classified among the essentials; if it is associated with only minor benefit or harm, it is classified among the enhancements, and if it falls somewhere in between these two, it is classified among the exigencies.

Or should the criterion represent a combination of these two measures?

§*First:* Let us see how early scholars of *uṣūl al-fiqh** dealt with this question.

1. Al-ʿIzz ibn ʿAbd al-Salām states:

> Sources of benefit and harm associated with this life and the life to come are characterized by varying degrees of importance. Hence, there are some that are of highest priority, others that are of lowest priority, and still others which fall somewhere in the middle. Moreover, sources of benefit are of three types: i) benefits associated with permissible actions, ii) benefits associated with recommended actions, and iii) benefits associated with obligatory actions. As

for sources of harm, they are divided into two types: i) those associated with undesirable actions, and ii) those associated with forbidden actions.[124]

In the passage below he combines the two types of criteria:

> In essence, the Law's injunction to perform the most significant acts of obedience is framed in the same way as its injunction to carry out the most insignificant or lowly of them. Similarly, its command that we refrain from the most serious acts of disobedience is framed in the same way as its command that we refrain from the less serious of them. There is no difference between one command and another [in terms of outward formulation].
>
> Rather, the difference among commands and prohibitions lies in the disparity among the benefits they are meant to bring and the sources of harm they are meant to avert. For this reason, acts of obedience have been divided into 'noble' (*al-fāḍil*) and 'more noble' (*al-afḍal*) based on the division of their benefits into 'perfect' (*al-kāmil*) and 'more perfect' (*al-akmal*). Similarly, acts of disobedience have been divided into 'major' (*al-kabīr*) and 'more major' (*al-akbar*) in keeping with the division of the harm they bring into 'serious' (*al-radhīl*) and 'more serious' (*al-ardhal*).[125]

In this passage al-ʿIzz ibn ʿAbd al-Salām rejects the formalistic criterion and adopts the objective criterion instead, since the wording or formulation of a command or a prohibition reveals no difference between one and another.

In another passage on the various ranks of human interests, al-ʿIzz divides them into two types, saying:

> The first type consists of interests which God has made obligatory out of compassion for His servants. These interests are characterized by differing degrees of importance, being divided into 'noble' and 'more noble', as well as degrees between these two. The most noble of the human interests are those which are meritorious in and of themselves. As for the second type of interest, it consists of those which God has recommended that we pursue as a means of refining our characters. The highest rank among the interests which God has recommended that we pursue remains lower than the lowest of the ranks among those which He has made obligatory. Such gradations continue down to increasingly minor interests, including those classified as permissible. Similarly in the case of acts which are recommended on the communal

level, they vary [in degrees of importance] according to the disparities among the interests they promote and the virtues with which they are associated.[126]

In still another passage [also quoted above], al-ʿIzz explicitly adopts a formalistic criterion. He writes:

Whoever investigates the intents of the Law (*maqāṣid al-sharʿ*), which are there to achieve benefit and prevent harm, will arrive at a conviction or recognition that this or that benefit must not be neglected and that this or that source of harm must be avoided. For even if there is no consensus, text or analogy which deals specifically and explicitly with the source of benefit or harm in question, an understanding of the Law itself necessitates such a conclusion. The situation might be likened to one in which someone has lived in close communion with a companion of virtue, wisdom and discernment and gained an understanding of this companion's likes and dislikes in all sorts of situations. If this person is then presented with a source of benefit or harm about which he or she has never heard his/her companion express an opinion, he or she will nevertheless – based on his or her accumulated experience of this companion's manner of thinking and habits – know that this companion would incline toward a particular benefit and be averse to a particular source of harm.

Moreover, if we investigate the *maqāṣid* manifested in the Qur'an and the Sunnah, we will realize that God has enjoined all that is good, from the most trifling to the most momentous, and that He has forbidden all that is evil, from the most minor to the most heinous. In speaking of 'good,' He is referring to the pursuit of benefit and the prevention of harm, and in speaking of 'evil,' He is referring to the pursuit of harm and the prevention of what is beneficial. As He has declared, may He be Exalted, "And so, he who shall have done an atom's weight of good, shall behold it; and he who shall have done an atom's weight of evil, shall behold it" (99:7-8).

This may be seen easily in cases of pure goodness and unmitigated evil. The difficulty arises when it is not known which is the greater of two goods or which is the greater of two evils, or when we do not know whether a given benefit is of greater weight than a corresponding source of harm, or whether the source of harm is of greater weight than the corresponding benefit; or, alternatively, when we do not know which things are of benefit and which are harmful. There are some sources of benefit and harm which can only be recognized by those with sound understanding and virtuous character, by means of which they are able to discern the fine gradations of what is beneficial and what is harmful, from the most negligible to the most significant and which of these should be given greater weight. People differ in their capacity for such discernment depending on the factors I have just mentioned. Hence, an intelligent, 'superior' person might fail to be aware of some things which are clearly discernible to a stupid, 'inferior' person, few though they may be.

> The Qur'anic verse which is most inclusive in terms of its exhortation to all that is beneficial and its proscription of all that is harmful declares, "And behold, God enjoins justice, and the doing of good, and generosity towards [one's] fellow-men; and He forbids all that is shameful and all that runs counter to reason, as well as envy; [and] He exhorts you [repeatedly] so that you might bear [all this] in mind" (16:90).[127]

In this passage, then, we find that he gives precedence to the objective criterion, especially in situations in which, as he puts it, "there is no consensus, text or analogy which deals specifically and explicitly with the source of benefit or harm in question."

In another book, al-ʿIzz returns to the adoption of a formalistic criterion, saying:

> The processes of achieving benefit and averting harm may be divided into a number of categories, namely, essentials, exigencies, and enhancements. The essential acts of obedience which have a bearing on the afterlife include the performance of religious obligations and abstention from what is forbidden. Exigencies with a bearing on the afterlife consist of emphatically enjoined emulations of the prophetic Sunnah and clearly established religious rites. And as for enhancements with a bearing on the afterlife, they include recommended practices other than Islamic religious rites.
>
> Essentials with a bearing on this life only include such things as food, drink, clothing and sexual fulfillment. Enhancements with a bearing on this life alone include the enjoyment of appetizing food and drink, sumptuous dwellings and chambers, spacious suites, and the like. And as for exigencies that pertain solely to earthly existence, they consist of things that fall somewhere in between the categories of earthly essentials and earthly enhancements.[128]

Elsewhere in the same book, al-ʿIzz talks about varying levels of benefit, saying,

> Benefits associated with obligatory acts are more noble than those associated with acts which are recommended, just as benefits which result from acts which are recommended are more noble than those that result from acts which are [simply] permissible. Similarly, sources of harm that relate to acts which are forbidden are more ignoble than those that relate to acts which are [simply] undesirable.[129]

2. Al-Shāṭibī deals with the same theme in a number of different passages:

In the first he states:

> It should also be noted that with respect to the way in which they are worded, commands and prohibitions all convey equally a message of obligation. Hence, it is not possible to determine from the text alone whether an act being enjoined is obligatory (*wājib*) or recommended (*mandūb*), or whether an act being forbidden is utterly prohibited (*muḥarram*) or merely undesirable (*makrūh*). It might be possible to make this determination in some cases, but in most cases it is not. Rather, the distinction among them only becomes apparent through attention to the meanings of the text, consideration of the human interests involved and to which categories they belong, and an inductive reading of a number of different representative texts. As for the wording of the text, we cannot rely on this alone. Otherwise, the commands contained by the Law would have to be of a single type, rather than of various types. And the same would apply to the Law's prohibitions. Rather, we hold that when dealing with the Arabs' speech in general, consideration must be given to the meaning of the context in order to understand this or that manner of phrasing [a thought, a command, a prohibition, etc.]. Otherwise, it [the process of textual interpretation] would be a farce. Have you never heard anyone say, for example, 'So-and-so is a lion, or a donkey,' or 'of great ashes' (*aẓīm al-ramād*), or 'has a timid dog' (*jabān al-kalb*)?[130,131]

In a second passage he writes:

> It may be seen on the basis of this arrangement that the commands found in the Law are not all equally emphatic, nor do they all have the same aim or intent. Commands having to do with the essentials differ from those having

to do with exigencies or enhancements. Similarly, complements[132] to the essentials differ from the essentials themselves, and the disparity between them is a known fact. Indeed, even the essentials themselves are not all of the same degree of importance or urgency. We find, for example, that actions relating to the preservation of the faith are enjoined more emphatically than those relating to the preservation of human life, while those relating to the preservation of human life are enjoined more emphatically than those relating to the preservation of human reason. And the same gradation will be observed among all other essentials, as well as the exigencies. Hence, commands relating to licit pleasures against which no objection could be raised will differ from those relating to actions against which some objection might be raised, like the enjoyment of licit pleasures by virtue of a loan one has received, payment in advance, crop sharing, and the like. The pursuit of things such as these is not the same as availing oneself of allowances without which one would be likely to suffer hardship. Nor is the enjoyment of these things the same as availing oneself of things which, were one to forego them, one would be obliged to engage in actions which are beyond one's capacity to bear. And the same is true on the level of enhancements,[133] down to the last detail...

Hence, the possibility of making an unconditional statement about the Law to the effect that a command points to an obligatory action, a recommended action, a permissible action, to something common among them, or to anything else to which consideration is given in order to settle the dispute over the question, depends on the aforementioned considerations. For they say that a command is to be understood as referring to an obligatory action so long as there is no evidence to indicate otherwise, in which case the meaning of the command is determined on the basis of evidence found within the command itself; if this is the case, then the meaning is based on what is actually mentioned. However, making an unconditional statement concerning something for which there is no clear evidence is difficult. The school of thought whose position on this question is most convincing is *al-wāqifiyyah*.* However, there is nothing in the Arabs' speech which would lead one to recognize one of these points of view to the exclusion of the others.

Hence, in order to make a decision on this matter, one must examine each command individually and ask: Does it reflect a primary intent, or a secondary intent? If it reflects a primary intent, it is to be given the highest rank of its type, whereas if it reflects a secondary intent, one should ask: Is it possible to establish the existence of the essential interest in question without it? Or can the action be referred to as the essential itself? If not [i.e., if it is not possible to establish the essential interest in question apart from the action concerned], then the action enjoined by the command in question serves as a pillar and as a particular which is necessary for the existence of the essential in question. If, on the other hand, it is possible to apply the name to it [the essential] without it [the action being enjoined],[134] then the action called for by the command is not a pillar; rather, it is a complement or accessory, either to the exigencies or to the enhancements. Hence, the levels or ranks [of a command] are examined based on the aforementioned arrangement or something similar thereto, depending on the results yielded by an inductive reading of the Law in every part thereof.[135]

Al-Shāṭibī thus agrees with al-ʿIzz that in order to determine if a given command refers to an action that is obligatory, recommended or permissible, it is not sufficient to rely on the wording of the command itself; rather, it is necessary to engage in further inquiry. However, al-Shāṭibī clarifies the mechanism by which such an inquiry is to be undertaken, whereas al-ʿIzz leaves it unspecified, referring only to the need to assess the degrees of benefit and harm involved. In the text quoted above, al-Shāṭibī mentions one element of this mechanism, namely, the recognition of whether the command reflects a primary intent or a secondary intent, and whether it is a fundamental (that is, an essential), or whether it is a pillar or a complement to such a fundamental. As for other elements of this mechanism, and which we shall have occasion to mention later in this discussion, he deals with them elsewhere in *al-Muwāfaqāt*.

In a third passage from al-Shāṭibī's writings, he comes close to adopting al-ʿIzz's approach to arranging sources of benefit and harm. Al-Shāṭibī draws attention to two inquiries involved in this process: (1) An inquiry into the warnings and legally prescribed punishments to be carried out against those who violate them [i.e., the prescriptions of Islamic law], and (2) an inquiry into whether a given entity or ruling brings benefit or harm to people in general and on the level of their essential interests, or whether it serves simply to perfect such a benefit or exacerbate such harm. However, although the first inquiry is a valid one, the second leads to circular thinking. The reason for this is that what we want to determine is what is universal and essential. How, then, can we employ knowledge of the universal and essential to acquaint ourselves with what is universal and essential,[136] unless we are speaking in general, unqualified terms as al-ʿIzz does? And if we are speaking in such general terms, then al-Shāṭibī has not really added a new mechanism in this connection. The following is the passage in question:

> It is understood from what the Lawgiver has established that the virtue of an act of obedience increases in proportion to the magnitude of the benefit it brings and that, conversely, the seriousness of an act of disobedience increases in proportion to the magnitude of the harm it causes. It is also known based on the Law that the greatest benefits are embodied in the five essentials recognized by every religion, and that the greatest sources of harm are embodied in those things which undermine these five essentials. Evidence for this may be found in the warnings [found in the Law] against those who violate any of the five essentials, as we see in the cases of rejection of the truth (*kufr*), the taking of human life and the evils attributable to it, sexual misconduct, stealing, and partaking of intoxicants and the evils attributable to it. For all these violations there is a prescribed punishment. The same is not true, however, of violations relating to the realms of exigencies and enhancements; rather, such violations in and of themselves are not associated with warnings with particular prescribed punishments. And if, in any case, they are connected with such a warning or punishment, this is because of their association with one or more of the essentials. This truth is evident based on an inductive reading of the Law; hence, there is no need to present evidence in its support.
>
> However, sources of benefit and harm are of two types: (1) those which entail well-being or harm for people overall, such as preserving human life in the realm of benefits and taking life in the realm of harm, and (2) those which serve to complete or perfect such well-being or exacerbate such harm. The sources of benefit and harm which belong to each of these two types are characterized by various degrees of importance or seriousness. If we look to the first type, for example, we will find that preservation of the religion is the greatest source of benefit, as a result of which, by comparison with this benefit, secondary importance is assigned to the preservation of human life, material wealth, and others. This is followed in order of priority by the

> preservation of human life, in comparison with which the preservation of progeny, human reason and material wealth are all treated as of secondary importance. Hence, one group of scholars hold that if someone were compelled to commit adultery under threat of death, it would be permissible for him to do so in order to protect himself.
>
> If we look at the practice of *bay*ᶜ *al-gharar**, for example, we find varying degrees of potential harm involved depending on the situation. The harm involved in the sale of *ḥabl al-ḥabalah* (that is, the unborn offspring of a fetus now present in the womb of a pregnant animal) is not the same as the harm entailed by the sale of a fetus in the womb of its mother which is physically present at the time of the sale. Nor is the sale of an as-yet-unseen fetus the same as the sale of merchandise which is not present at the moment of sale but for which a description has been provided and which can be examined without undue hardship. And the same is true of the benefits to be derived from guarding against such sources of harm. This being the case, then, if a given act of obedience or disobedience produces benefit or harm which can be categorized as universal and essential, then the act of obedience concerned is to be considered commensurate with a pillar of the religion, while the act of disobedience is to be considered a major sin. If, on the other hand, the act concerned leads to an outcome with no implications beyond the realm of the particular, then the act of obedience is to be classified along with voluntary acts of devotion and associated virtues, while the corresponding act of disobedience is to be classed as a minor sin. Yet not all major sins are equally serious, nor are all pillars of the religion of equal significance. Similarly, particulars relating to obedience and disobedience differ in their degree of importance; hence, each of them has a station and degree appropriate to itself.[137]

In the first passage quoted above, al-Shāṭibī seeks to ascertain the degrees of obligation involved in legal prescriptions – that is, by identifying the actions called for as obligatory, recommended, or permissible – in order to be able thereby to classify them appropriately among the essentials, exigencies and enhancements. However, he reverses this approach in another passage, in which he classifies an action as obligatory based on the fact that the interest it serves belongs among the essentials. He states:

> Generally speaking, the determination that a given action serves a primary intent of the Law is reason for classifying the action in question as obligatory. The primary intents are related to the ruling that this or that action is obligatory, since they revolve around the preservation of the agreed-upon essentials of the religion. And if this is the case, then actions which fall outside the realm of human interest will have to do with general affairs. As we have seen, actions which are not obligatory on an individual level [may] become obligatory on the communal level. Similarly, an action may be recommended or permissible on the individual level, yet be obligatory on the communal level such that [life's] order will be disturbed if it is violated. As for building on secondary intents, it is related to particular inclinations and desires. However, that which is particular does not necessitate obligation; it follows, therefore, that building on secondary intents does not neces- sitate obligation. Thus, a given action might be permissible on the individual level, permissible on both the individual and collective levels, or permissible on the individual level while being undesirable or forbidden on the collective level.[138]

Elsewhere al-Shāṭibī states, "When an action fulfills the primary intents of the Law (*al-maqāṣid al-aṣliyyah*), the resulting obedience is all the more vital, and when it violates them, the resulting disobedience is all the more blameworthy."[139]

Al-Shāṭibī also clarifies another element of the mechanism by which sources of benefit and harm may be placed in the proper arrangement. This element, like the one just discussed, is based on the distinction on which al-Shāṭibī places such great importance, namely, the distinction between what he refers to as the primary and secondary intents of the Law. The passage in which al-Shāṭibī explains this element is too lengthy to quote; however, I will attempt to summarize it here, since it draws a distinction between two types of essential interests:

The first of these two types includes those things in relation to which human beings have an immediate, conscious interest, such as an individual's pursuit of his own needs and those of his family by obtaining food and clothing, taking a wife and finding a place to live, all of them being things which people have a powerful, even compelling inward motivation to seek out. As a consequence, the Lawmaker enjoins the pursuit of these things as a recommended, but not an obligatory action; in fact, many such commands are on the level of what is simply permissible, which is a recognition on the Lawgiver's part of incentives which arise from our inborn nature.

As for the second type of essentials, it includes things in relation to which people have no immediate, conscious interest, whether they be individual duties such as the obligatory acts of worship, or collective duties such as public posts involving the exercise of sovereign powers, including the caliphate, the judiciary, engaging in jihad and teaching. In the case of individual duties, the Lawgiver has affirmed the intention that they should be fulfilled by issuing binding commands, and the intention that actions which impede their fulfillment should be refrained from by issuing binding prohibitions; in addition, He has established prescribed punishments for the violation of such commands and prohibitions. In relation to collective duties, allowances are made for natural human inclinations and yearnings through the Law's secondary intents (*al-maqāṣid al-tabaʿiyyah*) since, although such duties were not legislated in order for human beings to achieve the glory and renown that come with power, the dignity and pride that accompany sovereign authority, or the honor of issuing commands and prohibitions, the fact is that practically speaking, these are the benefits which are gained as a result of their fulfillment.[140]

What we observe here is that al-Shāṭibī contradicts an earlier statement of his about a necessary correlation between the classification of a command as obligatory and the classification of the benefit with which it is associated as being among the essentials (whether the former leads to the latter, or the latter to the former). That is to say, he now associates essential interests in relation to which there is no consideration for human desires or inclinations with obligatory commands, while associating other essential interests – those in regard to which there is consideration for human enjoyment or inclinations – with commands that enjoin either recommended or permissible actions.

3. As for Ibn Ashur, he adopts the objective criterion. This may be seen clearly in his discussion of whether to classify the preservation of honor as an essential and his response to al-Subkī and others who drew a connection between the prescribed punishment for *qadhf** and the consideration of *qadhf* as one of the essentials. He declares, "We are not persuaded of the view according to which, if the forfeiture of something entails the enforcement of a legally prescribed punishment according to Islamic law, it must therefore

be classified as one of the essentials. Indeed, neither al-Ghazālī nor Ibn al-Ḥājib considered it [that is, *qadhf*] to be among the essentials."[141]

§*Second:* Summary and conclusion

From the foregoing we may draw the following conclusions:

(a) Al-ʿIzz ibn ʿAbd al-Salām adopts the formalistic criterion in one place, in a second place he adopts the objective criterion, in a third place he combines the two, and in a fourth place he gives the objective criterion precedence, considering it to be the deciding factor, particularly if there is no consensus, text or analogy which deals specifically and explicitly with the source of benefit or harm in question.

(b) Al-Shāṭibī agrees with al-ʿIzz that in order to determine if a given command refers to an action that is obligatory, recommended or permissible, it is not sufficient to rely on the wording of the command itself. In other words, he rules out the formalistic criterion. However, he does not adopt the objective criterion unconditionally as al-ʿIzz does; rather, he attempts to establish a mechanism for further inquiry:

1. He distinguishes between commands which reflect a primary intent (which are to be given the highest rank of their type) and those that reflect a secondary intent (which are to be given a lower rank).

2. In one place he considers a command obligatory if it reflects a primary intent, and [merely] recommended if it reflects a secondary intent, which contrasts with the previous view.[142]

3. He considers the warnings and prescribed punishments for violating a command as a criterion for determining the importance of the benefit to be achieved or the seriousness of the harm to be averted [by adherence to the command in question].

4. He inquires into whether the command in question is related to a universal, be it essential or non-essential, an approach we have criticized due to the fact that it leads to circular thinking.

5. Within the category of essentials, he distinguishes between those in regard to which human beings have an immediate, conscious interest (actions

related to which he categorizes as either recommended or permissible) and those in regard to which human beings have no immediate, conscious interest (actions in relation to which he classifies as obligatory, either on the individual or collective level). In so saying, al-Shāṭibī contradicts earlier statements according to which there is a necessary correlation between the classification of a command as obligatory and the classification of the benefit with which it is associated as being among the essentials.

(c) Ibn Ashur adopts the objective criterion.

(d) Based on the foregoing analysis, we propose following al-ʿIzz ibn ʿAbd al-Salām's thinking in the place where he adopts the objective criterion [for determining whether a given ruling or means is to be placed in the category of essentials, exigencies, or enhancements] if there is no consensus, text or analogy which deals specifically and explicitly with the ruling or means in question.

[*Subtheme* 5]: *Practical Observations*

In the course of doing my research, my attention was arrested by a number of examples which call for discussion:

(a) The unconditional categorization of ritual purity among the enhancements. We find that in nearly all writings on this subject, ritual purity (*al-ṭahārah*) is cited frequently as an example of the category of enhancements (*al-taḥsīniyyāt*).

1. Al-Juwaynī cites the example of ritual purity as an illustration of the category of enhancements. He concludes that in discussing this category of human interests, it is impermissible to engage in *qiyās*,* that is, to draw analogies between one ruling and another. Moreover, given the fact that the context of al-Juwaynī's discussion is the divisions of *ʿilal* (that is, the bases of Islamic legal rulings) and principles as they relate to *qiyās*, it is not the proper place in which to distinguish between the ritual purity required for prayer, namely, ritual ablutions (*wuḍū'*), and other forms of ritual purity.[143]

2. After defining the term 'enhancements', al-Shāṭibī states, "in the area of Islamic expressions of worship, [the enhancements may be illustrated by] the

removal of impurity – and, in general, all forms of ritual purity – as well as the concealment of one's private parts."[144]

In this statement, al-Shāṭibī is speaking in general terms, and hence makes no distinction between ritual purity as manifested in the performance of ritual ablutions, which are a condition for the validity of prayer, and ritual purity in a more general sense. However, he does refer to this distinction in his discussion of the relation between means (*wasā'il*) and intents (*maqāṣid*); in this context he cites the example of ritual purity with prayer, saying that ritual purity is only required so long as prayer is required, unless there is evidence to indicate the requirement of continuous ritual purity. For it is possible for someone not to be required to pray, yet for the performance of ritual ablutions nevertheless to be desirable, since there is nothing to prevent something from being desirable for its own sake and, based on a separate consideration, required as a means to some other end.[145]

Hence, in speaking of the relationship between ritual ablutions and prayer as a means related to an end, al-Shāṭibī draws attention to the negative side, namely, a situation in which the intent (namely, prayer) is absent and its effect upon the ruling concerning the means (namely, ritual ablutions). In the first passage (p. 11), however, he disregards the positive side of this relationship, namely, that as a means of achieving an intent, ritual ablutions become subject to the same ruling that applies to the intent itself based on the principle which states, "those things without which an obligation cannot be fulfilled are themselves obligatory."[146] Hence, it is necessary to distinguish this situation [from others involving ritual purity] based on the fact that ritual ablutions are a means of fulfilling the obligation to perform prayer, by virtue of which they should not be classified among the enhancements, whereas ritual purity in general [considered apart from obligatory prayer],[147] as well as ritual ablutions which are performed in preparation for voluntary prayer, do belong among the enhancements.

3. In the course of discussing the confluence of sources of benefit and harm, al-ʿIzz ibn ʿAbd al-Salām draws attention to this distinction, saying,

> The performance of prayer when one is contaminated with impurities is a source of harm which should be avoided. The reason for this is that the worshipper is sitting with his Lord and confiding in Him his inmost thoughts. Hence, as a way of showing Him the proper reverence, one should only

> approach Him in the best possible condition. If, for some cogent reason, it is a cause of hardship to avoid such impurities, such as traces of excrement which remain after cleaning oneself with stones, flea blood, mud from the streets, or blood from ulcers or pustules, then one's prayer is still acceptable out of compassion for God's servants. Similarly, if it is so difficult to avoid such contamination that ritual impurity is impossible to achieve, one's prayer will still be valid, properly speaking, since the achievement of the most sublime intents of prayer is more important than ensuring ritual purity, which is an auxiliary or complement to prayer. And in fact, scholars disagree on whether it should be stipulated as a condition for prayer.[148]

Al-ʿIzz thus draws a connection here between the consideration of ritual purity as a complement or auxiliary to prayer, and the disagreement among scholars as to whether it should be stipulated as a condition for prayer.

(b) Categorizing obligatory forms of worship among the exigencies (*al-ḥājiyāt*). Yusuf al-Alim, in discussing the matter of preserving the ongoing existence of the religion, states,

> The human interests embodied in the preservation of the religion differ in degree and rank. Some interests are ranked among the essentials and fundamentals in relation to all others. This rank includes belief and recognition of the existence of the Supreme Reality, faith in God and the Last Day.
>
> Other such interests, which are ranked among the exigencies, include worship and action based on definitive commands. This rank includes those things which follow from faith and serve to fulfill its intents, such as prayer, zakah, fasting, and the pilgrimage to Makkah.
>
> Still other such interests, which serve to adorn and enhance the religion, include voluntary acts of worship and virtue, and all actions based on non-definitive commands. This rank is subordinate and complementary to the second rank, and includes things such as voluntary prayers and charity.[149]

Al-Alim then speaks further about the level of faith, followed by the second level, namely, that of obligatory acts of worship,[150] which is followed in turn by the third level, namely, that of voluntary acts of worship and virtue.[151]

Of particular concern to us here is the content of the level of exigencies, on which al-Alim has placed obligatory acts of worship. As I see it, however, obligatory acts of worship should be placed, alongside faith, on the level of essentials. After all, obligatory acts of worship are, like faith, the pillars and mainstays of Islam, while in an Islamic conceptualization of faith, faith and action are inseparable.[152]

If we say that faith is the root while acts of worship are its branches or offshoots,[153] this justifies dividing the rank of essentials into sub-levels characterized by differing degrees of importance or urgency. However, it does not justify demoting obligatory acts of worship from the rank of essentials to that of exigencies. Moreover, if there is some question about the rank of exigencies, it would be possible to place emphatically enjoined practices in emulation of the prophetic Sunnah in this rank, while leaving non-emphatically enjoined voluntary acts of worship and virtue on the level of enhancements.

(c) In accordance with the intent of preserving human life, the prohibition against the shedding of blood is a recognized fundamental with respect to both Muslims and non-Muslims ("do not take any human being's life – [the life] which God has declared to be sacred – otherwise than in the pursuit of justice" [6:151]) which belongs to the rank of essentials. If this prohibition is lifted with respect to enemy combatants, and if exceptions to this prohibition go into effect for specific groups by virtue of an explicit text in the Law, this still takes place on the basis of the fundamental prohibition, and is by no means a mere enhancement. Rather, like texts pertaining to the sanctity of human life and the punishment of those who violate this sanctity, such exceptions also belong to the category of essentials.

(d) The classification of knowledge, culture, preaching, and social and legal services. Writing on the term, "enhancement-related interests," Dr. Ismail al-Hasani provides a definition (which he clarifies in a footnote) and examples thereof, including

> ...the dissemination of knowledge, preaching and exhortation, cultivating people's minds through a program of comprehensive education, the provision of shelters with adjoining kitchens, parks and recreation areas, and health and legal services, all of which belong within the realm of public interests. As for individual interests, examples of them may be drawn from areas

involving the cultivation of noble morals, chivalry, generosity, honor, and adherence to inborn virtues.[154]

[One might ask, however]: Viewed from the perspective of public interests, how can the dissemination of knowledge, preaching to people about the tenets of the religion, the cultivation of people's minds, and the provision of health and legal services, be classified as [mere] enhancements? Specifically:

1. Aren't the dissemination of knowledge and the cultivation of people's minds among the necessary means of preserving the faculty of reason? Or has the example traditionally cited to illustrate this interest, namely, the prohibition of intoxicants, so thoroughly monopolized the rank of necessities relating to the preservation of human reason that all others have been relegated to the ranks of exigencies and enhancements?

2. With regard to exhorting people to be faithful to the tenets of the religion, I ask: Aren't the enjoining of what is right and the prohibition of what is wrong among the central conditions for the goodness of the Muslim community? As God declares, "You are indeed the best community that has ever been brought forth for [the good of] mankind: you enjoin the doing of what is right and forbid the doing of what is wrong, and you believe in God" (3:110). If so, then how is it that this condition, which is given priority in this Qur'anic verse even over faith itself, can be reduced to the level of enhancements, especially if we are speaking about public interests? And if this step is taken, what are we to classify as essential for the preservation of public interests?

3. In regard to legal services – whether this term is used to refer to the judicial system (the appointment of judges), services which assist in the execution of justice such as the police force and the public prosecutor (those who aid judges in their task), or even what is termed judicial assistance, such as state-sponsored legal counsels to defend suspects unable to provide lawyers for themselves – all of these are basic to the judicial system as a means of establishing justice. Justice is, in fact, the intent of the divinely revealed messages ("so that men might behave with equity" [57:25]) and, together with belief in the divine unity, the hallmark of Islam: "the religion of divine unity and justice."

4. And as for health services: How are these to be classified as mere enhancements despite the fact that they represent the first step toward rescuing those who are in danger of dying, or who suffer injuries, broken bones, heart attacks and other health-related problems? Aren't these among the necessity means of preserving human life?

Whether we adopt the formalistic criterion, the objective criterion, or a combination of both, these illustrations should suffice, I think, as evidence in favor of calling for a reconsideration of the practical examples generally cited to clarify [Islamic] principles and rules – especially given the fact that our concern here is the realization of *maqāṣid al-sharīʿah*.

[THEME 4]

The Specification and Categorization of Means Based on Considerations of Place, Time, Persons and Circumstances

The division of the universals of Islamic law into the categories of essentials, exigencies and enhancements is the fixed framework within which these universals have come to be conceptualized, and it is within this framework that they are categorized into one of these three ranks. However, this categorization is not fixed; rather, it varies based on considerations of time, place, persons and circumstances, and this is what is meant by the term 'relativity of application.'

§*First:* Before discussing the relativity which characterizes the categorization of the universals of Islamic law, reference needs to be made to another aspect of this relativity, namely, the relativity of theorization:

1. Those things which serve as complements to the essentials, exigencies and enhancements are not on the same level as the essentials, exigencies and enhancements which they serve to complement.

2. Interests which are classified within each of the categories of essentials, exigencies and enhancements, as well as those things classified as their complements, differ from each other [in importance].[155]

3. From the point of view of Islamic law, a given action is evaluated in light of the benefit or harm which it brings. This may be seen from the way in which Islamic law distinguishes between actions which result in great benefit and which are termed pillars (*arkān*, singular, *rukn*), and those which result in great harm and which are termed major sins (*kabā'ir*, singular, *kabīrah*). Similarly, it distinguishes between acts which result in lesser benefit and which are termed virtues (*iḥsān*), and those which result in lesser harm and which are termed minor sins (*ṣaghā'ir*, sing., *ṣaghīrah*).[156]

4. However, not all major sins are of equal gravity, nor are all pillars of equal merit.

5. Similarly, particular acts of obedience or disobedience are not all of equal weight; rather, each one has a rank specific to itself.[157]

6. With regard to actions which the Lawgiver deems permissible (i.e., actions which may either be engaged in or not engaged in to equal effect), the legal rulings applicable to them may be affected by their attendant circumstances, which may cause them to become either praiseworthy or blameworthy.

7. More important than this is the fact that permissible actions which are not affected by attendant circumstances are divided by al-Shāṭibī into four types, for each of which he cites illustrative examples to be discussed below.[158]

8. In addition to the foregoing, it should be noted that the listing of universals themselves is subject to change according to time, place, persons and circumstances.[159]

§*Second:* This notion of relativity is not new; indeed, we find clear examples of it in the writings of traditional *uṣūl* scholars, though they do not refer to it by this name.

Al-ʿIzz ibn ʿAbd al-Salām

Al-ʿIzz ibn ʿAbd al-Salām states:

> The covering of one's body is obligatory; moreover, it is one of the most virtuous, commendable practices, particularly for women. However, it is permissible to expose some parts in cases of necessity or need. As for the

> situations in which such a need exists, they include spouses looking at each other; a witness's looking at [someone's private parts] given the necessity of offering testimony; a physician's looking at parts of the body for purposes of treatment; and looking at a woman one hopes to marry before the marriage contract has been signed. Similarly, it is permissible to look at someone's private parts in order to carry out religious rites such as circumcision or to carry out the prescribed legal penalty against adulterers. However, if someone who has seen two people engaged in the act of adultery has confirmed that the glans of the man's penis entered the woman's vagina, it is forbidden for him to look any longer, since there is no need to do so. Likewise, once a witness has seen someone's private parts [for purposes of giving testimony] or once a physician has seen the area of a patient's body affected by illness, he is not permitted to continue looking, since there is no need to do so. After all, what is rendered permissible by virtue of necessity or need is permitted only to the extent of such necessity or need and, by the same token, ceases to be permissible once the necessity or need has ceased to exist.
>
> And as for necessities, they include such things as banning lethal or injurious commodities and treating fatal or serious injuries.
>
> Due to the shamefulness of the private parts, the urgency of the need required to justify looking at them is greater than that required to justify looking at other private parts of the body. Moreover, for fear of the temptation which might result from looking at them, the urgency of the necessity and need required to justify looking at a woman's private parts is greater than that required to justify looking at a man's. Similarly, looking at the area of the thigh immediately above the knee is not the same as looking at the buttocks.[160]

The fundamental principle being affirmed here is that concealing one's genitalia and other private parts is, as al-ᶜIzz states, "one of the most virtuous, commendable practices." That is to say, he classifies this practice among the enhancements. It bears noting in this connection that al-ᶜIzz does not draw a connection between an action's being obligatory under Islamic law and its being classified among the enhancements (rather than among the essentials). In other words, he has adopted the objective criterion.

Al-Shāṭibī

Al-Shāṭibī presents lengthy, detailed discussions of various factors and their effect upon the *maqāṣid* and Islamic legal rulings. Such factors include: (1)

that which is permissible (*al-mubāḥ*) and its various types,[161] (2) hardship (*al-mashaqqah*) and its types,[162] (3) human desires and inclinations,[163] (4) individual and collective obligations, (5) God's rights and human rights, and others.

Al-Shāṭibī's discussions of these factors result in a highly ramified, if not tangled, network of interconnected systems, which serves to confirm the notion of relativity with which we are concerned here.

However, lest we go too far afield, we will content ourselves with a presentation of only one of the factors addressed by al-Shāṭibī, namely, the category of what is permissible, or *al-mubāḥ*. Acts which are classified as permissible are those which, as far as the Lawgiver's intention is concerned, one is free either to engage in or refrain from. This description applies to acts which are permissible in and of themselves apart from the influence of any and all external factors which might render them praiseworthy or blameworthy, in which case they cease to be classified as permissible.

On the basis of considerations such as these, al-Shāṭibī divides permissible actions into four categories: (1) permissible individually, recommended collectively (2) permissible individually, obligatory collectively, (3) permissible in moderation, undesirable in excess, and (4) permissible in moderation, forbidden in excess. In addition, al-Shāṭibī offers a detailed discussion, complete with illustrative examples, of the legal rulings on these categories of the permissible – with the attendant circumstances that exert an influence on them – in the realms of essentials, exigencies and enhancements. He also touches upon points on which he differs with other scholars, such as Ibn al-ʿArabī.[164]

Ibn Ashur

Whereas al-ʿIzz and al-Shāṭibī focus their attention on the varying effects of persons and circumstances [on the classification of human interests within the framework of Islamic law and its priorities], Ibn Ashur adds time and place to the list of variables. In this connection, the following observations are in order:

1. Unlike *uṣūl* scholars before him, Ibn Ashur highlights what relates to the Muslim community, or Ummah, alongside what relates to the individual, thereby opening the way for a consideration of the role played by the

deterrent [and motivating] force of external authority alongside religion and innate human understanding.

2. This shift initiated by Ibn Ashur served to alert his commentator, Ismail al-Hasani, to the fact that, "The identification of essential human interests in society is subject to what is dynamic in society and not to what is static, to what is variable and changing and not to what is constant or unchanging.[165] In other words, the determination of the essentials in Islamic society is based on a comprehensive understanding of and full attention to recent, unexpected developments and changes in Islamic society in particular, and in the broader human society in general." What this means is that in establishing the basis of essential interests, researchers cannot rely solely on the declarations of the Law; rather, they must attend to the changing circumstances in which such declarations are made. This understanding calls for the recognition of the historically determined nature of the decision to restrict human beings' essential interests – as set forth in the writing of early *uṣūl* scholars – to nothing but the preservation of religion, human life, the faculty of reason, progeny and material wealth. As such, it likewise calls for the recognition that these essentials include other interests as well, interests which Islamic society needs to preserve more at the present time:[166] the right to free expression and freedom of political association, the right to elect and change our rulers, the right to employment, sufficient food, housing and clothing, the right to medical care, as well as a long list of other rights which, like those mentioned here, are aptly considered to be essential to human existence in modern society.[167]

Yusuf al-Alim

Yusuf al-Alim[168] points out that some types of contracts may be classified among the essentials while others may be placed among the exigencies. A covenant of protection, for example (Arabic, *ijārah*), might be considered an essential, as might be the hiring of a wet nurse for a child, the provision of housing to protect the child from cold and heat or hiring someone to protect his money from loss or theft if no one were available to do this voluntarily.

In addition, he notes the view expressed by al-Juwaynī in *al-Burhān*, according to which if selling [and buying] are viewed in relation to society as a whole, they fall into the category of essentials. After all, if buying and selling were not declared legitimate, this would lead to hardship in view of the fact that not everyone has all the things he needs in order to live. However, if viewed on the individual level, they are not an essential, since not everyone is obliged to buy and sell.

Yusuf al-Qaradawi

In more than one place Yusuf al-Qaradawi has pointed out the need to show greater concern for the *maqāṣid* which relate to society as a whole, such as freedom, equality, justice, brotherhood, solidarity and dignity, as well as to reconsider the terminology used in discussing the *maqāṣid*. One example of such terminology is *uṣūl* scholars' habit of illustrating the preservation of human reason with the example of the punishment prescribed for imbibing intoxicants, as if this were the entire extent of Islam's concern for the human mind. Where, he asks, is the emphasis on establishing a scientific mindset, the pursuit of learning, the commendation of scholars and affirmation of the value of knowledge?[169]

Ahmad al-Raysuni

As for Ahmad al-Raysuni, he notes the need for further detailed study in order to clarify the degree of constancy and variability in the categories of human interests.[170]

§*Third:* As noted in the beginning of this section, what we have termed the relativity of application includes the enumeration of the universals of Islamic law [that is, human interests] and their classification into three groups. We have devoted Chapter Two of this book to their enumeration; now, however, we turn to the matter of their classification.

As we had occasion to note in an earlier section, the universal intent, or *maqṣid* with its three levels of essentials, exigencies and enhancements, constitutes a single unit, while the various levels may be understood in terms of the means by which the overall intent is achieved. The present discussion, then, has to do with the classification of these means into the various levels. Our aim here is not to investigate all aspects of this topic; rather, we will content ourselves with some examples which will clarify what we mean to convey. In relation to the intent of preserving human life, we will take examples from the areas of nutrition, housing and transportation. This will be followed by a discussion of the preservation of human reason, in the context of which we will consider examples relating to individual duties, collective duties and the pursuit of knowledge.

1. DIET

The diet essential for the preservation of life differs from one environment to another. Among the Bedouins, for example, dates and yogurt suffice for this purpose, in the countryside a slice of bread and a piece of cheese meet the need, while a large sector of those living in urban areas live on bread, rice and other staples. However, with the development of urban life and the nutritional sciences, it has come to be recognized that people's daily diets need to fulfill certain conditions in terms of the balance of elements needed by the body, the amount of each element needed every day, and the types of food that contain the required amounts of these elements. All of these matters, of course, are for food specialists to determine.

(a) What has been described here constitutes the level of essentials in relation to nutrition; this level also includes refraining from eating those things which are not permissible to eat and from drinking things that are not permissible to drink if to do so would result in death or severe harm.

(b) A lack of these elements or the proper amounts thereof lowers our classification of the situation from the level of essentials to the level of the sub-essential (*mā dūn al-ḍarūrī*), which leads to malnutrition and resulting diseases. Even worse is the absence of nutrition altogether, that is, famine, as a result of which millions of people die every year.

(c) As for the level of exigencies, it consists in the availability of a variety of foods such that people are not obliged to subsist on a single type to the point of tedium. In also includes having regular meal times, which helps to facilitate proper digestion, and the preparation of food in a way that is appetizing, easy to eat, and easily digested.

(d) As for the level of enhancements, it includes the way in which food is served and arranged on the table, the utensils used – such as dishes, spoons, forks and the like – as well as table manners, which range from washing one's hands and mouth before eating to saying a pre-meal blessing, eating only what is directly before you, giving others the first opportunity to eat the most appetizing things on the table, and conversing during the meal so as to break the silence and dispel feelings of loneliness.

(e) As for what goes beyond the level of enhancements, it consists in luxury and excess, the use of gold and silver utensils, etc. It is important to define where the legitimate enjoyment of gastronomic pleasures ends and where luxury and excess begin, bearing in mind that answers to this question will differ from one person to another according to each one's means.

2. HOUSING

(a) What used to be considered essential housing was nothing more than a hut or tent, as compared with the sub-essential level of living in caves, in the open air or on sidewalks, or in public parks or subway stations.

(b) However, with the development of urban life, huts and caves came to be classified on the level of the sub-essential, to be replaced by scattered dwellings with doors and windows yet lacking any added facilities, in which beds were piled up in a single room and to which water was brought from a public pump along the road or somewhere in the neighborhood, a situation in which people would dispose of their human waste in open areas and along the banks of waterways.

(c) The level of exigencies, then, was reserved for dwellings with running water and electricity. However, again with the development of urban life, dwellings with running water and electricity were raised to the level of essentials, while the level of exigencies came to include dwellings with a refrigerator, washing machine and telephone, as well as even an elevator leading up to flats located higher than a certain floor.

(d) Until recently, appliances and services such as those just mentioned were classified as enhancements, which now include – in addition to the things classified on the level of exigencies – the availability of an elevator even for the lower floors, and air-conditioning; this is the minimum (as in the case of an apartment within a larger building), with the maximum including an independent dwelling with a yard, garden, etc.

(e) Still another factor that enters into such a classification is that of floor area; hence, on the level of essentials it suffices for the floor area to be 10 to 25 square meters per person, with the area increasing on the level of exigencies to somewhere between 25 and 50 square meters per person, whereas on the level of enhancements, it may range from 50 to 75 square meters, all of these estimates being bound to vary according to people's financial status and needs.[171]

(f) It should be noted that what matters is not that a person own a dwelling with these specifications except, perhaps, on the level of enhancements. On the levels of essentials and exigencies, renting is sufficient. However, a distinction should also be made between these two levels such that on the level of exigencies, the rent will be consistent with market prices, whereas on the level of essentials, it will be subsidized by the government as a way of enabling [those in low-income brackets] to obtain housing of this quality.

(g) As for the level of that which goes beyond enhancements (*mā warā' al-taḥsīnī*), it includes what we hear about by way of flats that cover an area of 2,000 square meters, with special lifts that bring the owner's car upstairs, and each of which is fitted out with a private swimming pool, not to mention towering mansions whose proprietors also own numerous other dwellings in the city, in the countryside, on the seashore, and abroad, all of which falls in the category of extravagance and wastefulness.

3. MEANS OF TRANSPORTATION

(a) In the past, a mount met essential transportation needs, and some writers translate the term 'mount' into modern language as the equivalent of the car. On this point, the following observation is in order. The legal intent of relevance here is achieved by providing public transportation characterized by regularity, comfort (a seat for every passenger), cleanliness, and the ability to take the passengers wherever they need to go. It also includes the provision of transportation by government institutions and companies for their employees and by schools for their students.

(b) The level of exigencies would include, in addition to the aforementioned, the availability of privately owned cars for those who, like physicians, for example, practice particular professions which require such.

(c) As for the level of enhancements, it includes the availability of a privately owned vehicle and (in some families), more than one. (It should also be noted that, as was mentioned under 'First' above, each of these levels is characterized by internal gradations relating to the specifications of the car itself.)

THE PRESERVATION OF HUMAN REASON

When discussing the preservation of the faculty of reason, earlier scholars of *uṣūl al-fiqh* contented themselves with a focus on the Islamic prohibition against intoxicants, with some of them also adding the requirement that one obtain whatever religious learning is essential for the performance of obligatory acts of worship. Some of them might also add the necessity of learning arithmetic in order to be able to calculate inheritances and zakah. Yusuf al-Qaradawi holds that it should be obligatory to learn to read and write,[172] as well as to learn astronomy in order to be able to identify the times of prayer and fasting.

(a) The custom of linking the types of knowledge required of Muslims solely to matters pertaining to worship has its roots in a narrow view of religion which limits it to the realm of ritual and devotion alone. However, if we understand religion in its comprehensive sense, it will be natural for us to place it where it belongs, namely, within an integrated educational system. The initial phase of such an education will include – along with the study of Islamic doctrine and forms of worship – the Arabic language (with its basic sciences), mathematics (arithmetic, algebra and geometry), history, geography, physics, chemistry, the principles of Islamic sciences (the Qur'an, the Sunnah and the life of the Prophet), Islamic jurisprudence in a comprehensive but simplified form, principles of the English language, and computers. This initial phase constitutes the essential [that is, minimum] degree of knowledge to be required of everyone without exception in our modern age. As such, it constitutes an individual duty for Muslims, men, women and children. With respect to children, it represents the initial, mandatory phase of their public education, which may last up to six years.

(b) On the level of exigencies, this educational phase is supported by an integrated cultural network of school and public libraries, audio-visual media, specialized periodicals, general and specialized reference works, clubs and societies.

(c) The level of enhancements relating to the preservation of human reason has to do with nurturing outstanding, creative students who have been discovered through the levels of essentials and exigencies and to whom the state devotes special attention. Al-Shāṭibī draws attention to the variety of gifts, talents and abilities with which people have been endowed. In addition, he formulates this notion in legal and educational terms. One person has an aptitude for academic pursuits, another for leadership and management, another for industry or agriculture, and still another for struggle. What is required, then, is to educate and nurture each individual in those things for which he has an aptitude in order to enable each one to excel in those areas in which he or she has strengths or for which he or she has a special inclination. He states,

> In this manner, education and training are provided for every action which is a collective duty of this or that community. The reason for this is that it is, first of all, a march along a shared path. Hence, when a traveler stops and is unable to proceed further, he has stopped at a level for which there is a need, generally speaking.[173] If, on the other hand, the traveler has the strength needed to proceed further, he moves on until he reaches the furthest limits of collective duties.[174] In this way, the foundations of this earthly life are preserved and, at the same time, the actions performed for the sake of the world to come fulfill their intended purposes.[175]

(d) This brings us to a discussion of collective obligations as they pertain to knowledge and learning as a means of achieving the intent of preserving the faculty of human reason. As we have had occasion to note, the preservation of human reason is not confined to the level of individual interests but, rather, affects the interests of the entire community. In relation to the former [individual interests], the knowledge and skills needed to populate and develop the Earth and earn a living are acquired through specializing in this or that profession or trade, whereas in relation to the latter [that is, the interests of the community], the Ummah strives to achieve self-sufficiency in all areas of life, on the levels of essentials, exigencies and enhancements alike. Given this religious motivation, human potentials are released; for while some people's intellectual capabilities are more limited, others' potentials make it possible for them to advance along the path of knowledge and creative interpretation in a variety of areas.

1. The starting point for achieving this intent in our present situation is to undertake a fundamental review of the currently prevailing system of vocational and university education, in which the situation is the reverse [of what is intended]: The numbers of those with vocational training are not sufficient to meet development needs, while university graduates pour forth only to suffer, for the most part, both declared and undeclared unemployment. The first step, then, is to define society's needs of whatever type in each area, then to direct students into the areas of need by determining their abilities during their years of preparatory school as well as in programs for exceptional and creative students. In addition, students' test grades should constitute only one of a number of evaluative elements not to exceed 10-20 percent of the total evaluation, and not 100 percent as is the case at present. (This represents the level of essentials.)

2. The level of exigencies includes demonstrating concern for academic research by establishing research institutes and centers and earmarking the necessary funding for their budgets, cooperating with the private sector in this area, benefiting from the system of religious endowments which sponsored this type of pursuit in the brightest eras of Islamic renewal, and investing the outputs of such research in the relevant practical areas (rather than shelving them, as is the practice now) and publishing them for the benefit of specialists in the relevant fields.

3. As for the level of enhancements, it consists in encouraging academic research by offering prizes and grants to researchers, as well as offering them the use of facilities, publication services, libraries, laboratories, exhibition halls, museums, etc.

In conclusion, it should be noted that the aforementioned examples are by no means exhaustive, since the present study does not aim at a thorough treatment of the *maqāṣid*. Rather, I wish simply to illustrate the notion of relativity as it applies to identifying the means that lead to their fulfillment and their classification among the various levels.

CHAPTER TWO

A New Conceptualization of *Maqāṣid*

[THEME 1]

Whether 'Essential' Maqāṣid Should be Limited to Five

§*First:* Early *uṣūl* scholars limited the category of essential *maqāṣid* to five, namely, the preservation of religion, human life, the faculty of reason, progeny and material wealth. This consensus was established from the time when they were identified by Imam al-Ghazālī, who refined them in his book *al-Mustaṣfā*, after which the restriction of the essentials to five (or six) was subject to question to a certain degree.

(a) The essentials of Islamic law were enumerated by al-Ghazālī, then by al-Rāzī, neither of whom stated explicitly that they should be limited to a particular number. Somewhat later, however, al-Āmidī declared expressly that they were limited to five, which he justified by saying that as a rule, reality [itself] serves as evidence of there being no other essential intent of the Law.[1] Hence, apart from the addition of the intent to preserve honor (chastity), which brings the total number of essentials to six rather than five, scholars of *uṣūl al-fiqh* continued for the most part to restrict them to five only.

(b) Despite the details provided on this question by al-ʿIzz ibn ʿAbd al-Salām, he does not limit universal interests to a particular number. However, he categorizes them sometimes into obligatory, recommended, and permissible,[2] at other times into otherworldly and this-worldly or immediate and long-term,[3] and at other times into ends (*maqāṣid*) and means (*wasā'il*).[4] He divides the categories of obligatory, Sunnah-based and permissible into graduated ranks.[5] In addition, he divides them into divine rights[6] versus creaturely rights,[7] which he further subdivides into human beings' rights over themselves and their rights over one another (both during their lifetimes and after their deaths) and animals' rights over human beings.[8] In addition, he divides interests pertaining to this life and the next into essentials, exigencies and enhancements,[9] just as he draws distinctions among different types of worship[10] and different types of mundane transactions.[11] Al-ʿIzz may have seen no need to discuss the matter of whether the essential interests safeguarded by Islamic law should be set at five, since the divisions and examples which he cites thereof provide a sufficient response to the position that it is possible to limit them to a particular number.

(c) As for Ibn Taymiyyah, he views the five essentials (or universals) as ways of averting harm, and holds that human interests consist in achieving benefit and preventing harm:

1. The achievement of benefit may be either material (earthly) or spiritual (otherworldly). Earthly benefits may be achieved through certain types of transactions and actions which are said to serve people's interests without conflicting with any legal prohibition. As for otherworldly benefits, they may be attained through various types of gnosis, spiritual states, forms of worship and ascetic practices which are said to serve people's interests, likewise without violating any legal prohibition.[12]

Ibn Taymiyyah draws attention to the various types of experiential knowledge of God, His angels, His books and His messengers, as well as the states and movements of the heart, such as love for God and fear of God, sincere devotion to God and reliance upon Him, and hope in His mercy and blessing. He also devotes attention to a number of other interests that pertain to both this world and the next.

In addition, Ibn Taymiyyah discusses what God has legislated by way of faithfulness to covenants, preservation of family ties, respect for the rights of slaves (*mamālīk*) and neighbors, Muslims' rights over one another, as well as other things which God has enjoined and prohibited in order to preserve lofty principles and refined morals, all of which may be seen to be among the interests attained through Islamic law.[13]

2. As we have seen, some people have restricted the interests which Islamic law is intended to protect to prevention of harm through the preservation of human life, material wealth, honor, human reason and religion. However, anyone who restricts these interests to the punishments which serve to ward off harm relating thereto in order to preserve the body alone is guilty of negligence.[14]

3. In connection with this classification Ibn Taymiyyah draws attention to the various forms of worship, virtues, noble character traits, human rights, and their importance in relation to the *maqāṣid*. In addition, he notes: (1) that the five universals (essentials) proposed by his predecessors are derived from the punishments imposed on those who violate them, as a result of which he classes them as means of averting harm; (2) that limiting human interests to the five essentials fails to do justice to Islamic law; and (3) that the *maqāṣid* which he (Ibn Taymiyyah) has added include some which fall within the category of higher intents (*al-maqāṣid al-ʿāliyah*), and others that fall within the class of universal intents (*al-maqāṣid al-kulliyyah*).

(d) Despite the fact that he restricts the universals of the Law to the traditional five, al-Shāṭibī nevertheless opens the door to a discussion of the interests of the Islamic community as a whole. He states:

> The essentials are divided into individual and collective [obligations]; however, individual obligations only apply in conjunction with collective ones. The reason for this is that collective obligations have to do with general interests which affect all people without exception; what is enjoined on the level of collective obligations remains collective in nature, since it is not decreed on the basis of a private interest alone. Otherwise, it would be an individual obligation. Rather, collective obligations are for the purpose of establishing and preserving the existence [of the human race]. Human beings serve as God's vicegerents among His servants in accordance with their abilities and relevant potentials. No one individual is able to look after himself and, in addition, take responsibility for all of his family, his tribe, and the interests of everyone on earth. As a consequence, God has appointed people as vicegerents [throughout the earth] to look after public needs so that order may prevail on earth.[15]

However, al-Shāṭibī stops here rather than following the idea through to its conclusion by specifying *maqāṣid* for the community at large alongside *maqāṣid* for the individual.

(e) Ibn Farḥūn expands the range of *maqāṣid al-sharīʿah* by dividing them into five categories, namely: (1) that which has been legislated for the purpose of subduing the ego, such as obligatory acts of worship, (2) that which has been legislated in order to further human survival, such as the sanctioning of permissible activities which serve to provide comfort and ease, including [the enjoyment of] food, clothing, shelter, sexual intercourse and the like, (3) that which has been legislated in order to meet needs, such as buying and selling, renting, sleeping partnerships (*al-qirāḍ**) and crop-sharing due to the fact that people lack some of the specific items which they require in order to live, and given the necessity of hiring others in order to achieve their interests, (4) that which has been legislated in order to foster noble actions and character traits, such as urging people to share their earthly possessions and offer others assistance and support, to free slaves, to give gifts and alms and set aside religious endowments, as well as other acts of virtue, and (5) that which has been legislated for the purpose of guidance and restraint, which is, in turn, divided into six types:

1. that which has been legislated to preserve human life, such as the law of retribution,
2. that which has been legislated to preserve progeny, such as the legally prescribed punishment for adultery,
3. that which has been legislated to preserve honor, such as the legally prescribed punishment for *qadhf* and discretionary punishments meted out for slander and otherwise harming others with one's words,
4. that which has been legislated in order to protect material wealth, such as the legally prescribed punishments for theft and highway robbery, and discretionary punishments meted out against usurpers and their like,
5. that which has been legislated in order to preserve the faculty of reason, such as the legally prescribed punishment for imbibing intoxicants, and
6. that which has been legislated for the sake of deterrence and for the sake of punishment.[16]

The following observations might be made about the classification of Ibn Farḥūn:

1. He sets aside a separate category for acts of worship without referring to them with the term 'religion,' explaining them as being for the purpose of subduing the ego. In so doing, he differs with those who hold that acts of worship cannot be explained in terms of a logical purpose or that their purpose is to teach people obedience, reverence, awe and subservience, none of which serves as a valid basis on which to draw analogies between acts of worship and other actions.[17]

2. In speaking of the preservation of human life (*ḥifẓ al-nafs*), he uses the term 'human survival' (*baqā' al insān*).

3. In speaking of the category of exigencies (*al-ḥājiyāt*), he uses the term 'meeting of needs' (*daf ͨal-ḍarūrāt*).

4. In speaking of enhancements (*al-taḥsīniyyāt*), he uses the phrase, 'noble character traits and deeds' (*makārim al-akhlāq*).

5. Like Ibn Taymiyyah, Ibn Farḥūn devotes attention to the penal aspect of the five traditional universals, to which he refers as 'guidance and restraint' (*al-siyāsah wa al-zajr*). He also draws a distinction between the preservation of family lineage (*al-nasab*) and honor (*al-ͨirḍ*). However he makes no reference to what has been legislated in order to preserve the religion, such as jihad or commanding the doing of what is right and prohibiting the doing of what is wrong. At the same time, he opens the door to consideration of other types of punishment (discretionary punishments, or *taͨzīr*) and deterrent measures.

(f) Ibn Ashur touches upon a relatively new aspect of the discussion of *maqāṣid*, namely, their social dimension:

1. Ibn Ashur states that the overall intent of Islamic legislation is to preserve the order of the Ummah and perpetuate its well-being and integrity through the well-being and integrity of those who safeguard this order, namely, the human race. People's well-being includes the well-being of their minds and the soundness and integrity of their actions in relation to the world around them.[18] Elsewhere Ibn Ashur states, "The preservation of these universals pertains to the individual members of the Ummah and, even more importantly, to the Ummah as a whole. Hence, each of these *maqāṣid* has one aspect that pertains to individuals and another that pertains to the Muslim community."[19] In a third passage, he states that:

> Just as the achievement of this intent relates to doctrine and actions, so also does it relate to people's social conditions and affairs, the reason for this being that the betterment being referred to here aims for well-being and integrity in the individual, collective and civilizational realms. On the level of individual well-being and integrity, what matters most is soundness of belief, since belief is the source of one's social graces and way of thinking. As for communal well-being and integrity, they are attained first of all on the basis of individual well-being and integrity, as well as through the regulation of people's conduct, otherwise known as the science of transactions (*ʿilm al-muʿāmalāt*). And as for civilizational well-being and integrity, they are more inclusive than this, since they involve preserving the order of the entire Islamic world and regulating the conduct of groups and regions in relation to one another in a manner which safeguards the best interests of all, protects universal Islamic interests, and guarantees the collective interest when individual interests come in conflict with it.[20]

In a fourth passage Ibn Ashur writes,

> There can be no doubt on the part of the observer that the most important intent, or *maqṣid*, of legislation under Islamic law is regulation of the Ummah's affairs, achieving benefit for it and protecting it from harm and corruption. All scholars of Islamic jurisprudence have perceived this truth with regard to the well-being and uprightness of individuals; however, they have not gone on to elucidate and demonstrate it with respect to the well-being and uprightness of the entire community.[21]

2. Ibn Ashur likewise discusses equality, saying that it is a principle which applies in all situations unless there is something to prevent it from doing so.[22]

3. He holds that it is a primary intent of the Law for all individual members of the Ummah to have equal opportunity to conduct themselves as they see fit, which is what is meant by freedom.[23]

4. Elsewhere he states that the intent of the Law is to identify the various types of rights for the groups of people who are entitled to them.[24] Moreover, the concept of right is connected with the concept of justice, since justice consists in identifying what someone's right is and enabling him or her to enjoy that right.[25]

5. Ibn Ashur speaks of the concepts of inborn human nature (*al-fiṭrah*) and benevolence (*al-samāḥah*) as *maqāṣid*.[26]

(g) Among modern thinkers, reference to this theme has been made by Muhammad al-Ghazali in some of his unpublished statements, Ahmad al-Khamlishi,[27] Yusuf al-Qaradawi,[28] Ahmad al-Raysuni,[29] Ismail al-Hasani,[30] and others, all of whom propose listing justice, equality, freedom, and social, economic and political rights among the higher intents of the Law, especially given the fact that limiting them to five is nothing more than a personal interpretation put forth by Abū Ḥāmid al Ghazālī, who based his enumeration on the prescribed punishments in Islam which were instituted for the purpose of safeguarding these *maqāṣid*:

1. In a seminar on the theme of "Islamic Legal Priorities," Shaykh Muhammad al-Ghazali commented,

> There need to be additions to the five essentials of the Law. After all, why should I not benefit from the accumulated experience of fourteen centuries of Islamic history? Corrupt rule over the centuries has led to baneful outcomes. Hence, to the five essentials I could add freedom and justice, especially in view of the fact that I have the Qur'an, which states, "Indeed, [even aforetime] did We send forth Our apostles with all evidence of [this] truth; and through them We bestowed revelation from on high, and [thus gave you] a balance [wherewith to weigh right and wrong], so that men might behave with equity" (57:25). Hence, justice appears to be an intent of all the prophetic messages. The five essentials might serve as criteria for [ruling on] secondary issues which we face; however, in order to regulate the order of the state, there has to be a guarantee of freedoms.[31]

2. During the same seminar, the following comment was made by the late Muhammad Abd al-Hadi Abu Ridah:

> One cannot help but note the absence of the notion of the state which possesses authority and which guards and implements the religion, and this in spite of its appearance in the writings of ethicists. Hence, might it be possible, alongside the notions of freedom and justice, the recognized religion, comprehensive justice and broad hope, to add the authority of the state which brings everyone into submission as we find in al-Māwardī's *Adab al-Dunyā*

> *wa al-Dīn*? In this valuable study, al-Māwardī brings together numerous considerations which he arranges according to what applies to the circumstances of the individual and what applies to the conditions of society as a whole, which is a commendable thing.[32]

3. As for Muhammad Siraj, he adds equality as well, his view being that equality ranks only slightly lower than justice and freedom. The starting point, of course, is justice and equality; however, justice is not possible without equality, and there are texts which confirm also that equality is independent of justice, a concept which has practical applications.[33]

4. Al-Khamlishi states:

> There can be no doubt that the *maqāṣid*, or the five higher interests, enumerated by al-Ghazālī are no longer sufficient as the sole point of reference in ordering society's affairs and relations among its members. Don't the higher intents of the Law include, for example, justice in both its individual and collective senses, equality, individual freedom and the individual's social, economic and political rights, including the right to participate in directing public affairs ("whose rule [in all matters of common concern] is consultation among themselves" [42:38]). The adoption of *maqāṣid* such as these as an authoritative point of reference at the present time would enable Islamic thought to take part meaningfully in many aspects of social planning from which it has thus far been absent.[34]

5. Yusuf al-Qaradawi states,

> I believe that there is a type of *maqāṣid* which has not been given its due, namely, those which have to do with society at large. For if most of the *maqāṣid* are related to the individual, such as the preservation of the individual's religion, faculty of reason, life, material wealth, etc., then where are freedom, equality and justice and of what value are they? This also calls for reconsideration.[35]

Writing on the theme of, "The Breadth and Inclusiveness of Human Interests in the View of Islamic Law," al-Qaradawi proposes expanding the number of *maqāṣid*, saying:

> In this way we come to see the inclusiveness of the human interests which Islamic law intends to establish and safeguard. After all, they are not simply earthly interests as the opponents of religion would like to claim; nor are they merely material interests as the enemies of spirituality allege, nor individual interests alone as is claimed by supporters of Existentialism and Capitalism, nor the interests of the collective or the proletariat as claimed by the proponents of Marxist and Communist schools of thought. Nor are they racist regional interests as the proponents of bigotry would have us believe, nor the fleeting interests of the current generation alone as imagined by certain superficial views. Rather, the interests upon which Islamic law is founded in both its universals and its particulars, and which are taken into consideration in its rulings overall, encompass both this world and the next, both matter and spirit. Such interests represent the quest to achieve balance between the individual and society, between the class and the Ummah, between particular national interests and the common interests of humanity, and between the interests of the present generation and those of generations to come.[36]

Given the way in which early *uṣūl* scholars spoke about *maqāṣid* and human interests, one might be led to the conclusion that their primary concern was for human beings as individuals and that they were not concerned sufficiently about society and the Ummah. If this is the case, then perhaps their excuse is that societies are made up of individuals; hence, if the individual members of a society are sound and upright, the same will be true of the societies of which they are a part. Moreover, individual members of a society will only be sound and upright if we preserve both the religious/spiritual and earthly/material elements of their lives.

Whatever excuse such thinkers may have had, it must be affirmed that the Law of Islam does indeed concern itself with society just as it concerns itself with the individual. As such, it seeks to establish a balance between the individual and the communal in all spheres of life.

There can be no doubt that Islamic law sets great store by higher social values and classes them among its fundamental intents, evidence for which can be found in texts [from the Qur'an and the Sunnah] which qualify to be classified as *mutawātirah** and in rulings too abundant to enumerate. These values include: (1) justice or equity, (2) brotherhood, (3) solidarity, (4) freedom and (5) dignity.[37]

Supporting his discussion with textual evidence from within Islamic law, al-Qaradawi presents a detailed discussion of human dignity and human rights in general and the rights of the weak and oppressed in particular, the protection of which he classes among the *maqāṣid* of the Holy Qur'an.[38]

6. In the context of discussing the theme of limiting the essential *maqāṣid* to five, Ahmad al-Raysuni presents the views of Ibn Taymiyyah and Ibn Farḥūn and calls for:

> a reconsideration of the matter of whether the 'essentials' of Islamic law should be limited to the five recognized at present. These essentials have, rightly, acquired a special standing and authority. However, there are other vital interests whose importance the religion has affirmed and which may well be no less significant and inclusive than some of the five presently recognized essentials. Hence, we should not deprive such interests of a similar rank and recognition.... It should be borne in mind that, as we have seen, the existing list of essentials is based on ijtihad and that the idea of increasing their number has been a valid possibility from times of old. It is not my desire to make any decisions which would be premature or out of place. However, I urge that this topic be opened up for discussion, subject to recognized standards of academic integrity and evidence which meets such standards.[39]

7. In the course of establishing the political grounding of human interests in the thought of Ibn Ashur, Ismail al-Hasani points out that the identification of the essential human interests in society is subject to what is dynamic in society and not to what is static, to what is variable and not to what is constant. This understanding, he says, leads to the recognition of the historically determined nature of the decision by early *uṣūl* scholars to restrict human beings' essential interests [to nothing but the preservation of religion, human life, the faculty of reason, progeny and material wealth]. Al-Hasani proposes the addition of the right to freedom of expression, the right to political association, the right to elect and remove rulers, the right to employment, food, housing and clothing, and the right to medical treatment. And in support of this perspective, he cites the views of Muhammad Abid al-Jabiri.[40]

8. In his study entitled, "The Theory of *Maqāṣid* and Reality," Yahya Muhammad states that "the current number of levels of human interests is not sufficient to meet the need, since it is clear that there are two types of

rulings which are not included within them. The first of these is what al-Juwaynī refers to as *taᶜabbudī*,* that is, rulings for which there is no rationally discernible purpose, which serve no known human interest and which, as a consequence, call for unquestioning submission. As for the second type, which we term judicial interests (*al-maṣāliḥ al-ḥuqūqiyyah*), no mention is made of them in discussions of the traditional levels, be they general interests or particular ones." At the same time, Muhammad holds that the five universals (*al-kulliyyāt*) have to do with people's material needs, whereas the true *maqāṣid* are those which he terms ultimate intents (*al-maqāṣid al-ghā'iyyah*), the most prominent of which are: worship and devotion (*al-taᶜabbud*), prudence (*al-taᶜaqqul*), emancipation (*al-taḥarrur*), assuming the traits [of the Divine] (*al-takhalluq*), unification (*al-tawaḥḥud*), and perfection (*al-takammul*).[41]

§*Second:* We for our part affirm the view that the universals of Islamic law cannot, as a matter of principle, be restricted to a particular number. As for their application, a discussion of this may be found in Theme 3 of this chapter, which presents the details of our proposal entitled, "From the Five Universals to the Four Realms" and in which we add a number of *maqāṣid*, bringing their total from five to twenty-four.

In regard to the *maqāṣid* whose addition is being suggested by other modern thinkers, namely, justice, freedom, equality, and human rights, I offer the following observations:

(a) I have added justice to the *maqāṣid* which belong to the realm of the Ummah and wider humanity.

(b) As for freedom on the individual level, I view it – along with human dignity – as the non-material aspect of the preservation of human life, which I do not restrict to the physical or material aspect alone. In addition, I locate individual freedom in the realm of the preservation of honor, which I do not restrict to the sexual aspect alone.

(c) As for freedom on the level of the Ummah, I view it as an outcome of safeguarding the Ummah's foreign security. Moreover, neither individual nor communal freedom is, in fact, an absolute value; rather, it is a relative value governed by legal and social considerations.

The absolute freedom spoken of by European Enlightenment philosophers, and which served as the basis for the French Revolution and individualism, quickly revealed itself to be a concept that leads to injustice, since it is exploited by the powerful and wealthy in order to oppress the weak and indigent. Consequently, the individualist school came to be opposed by the collectivist school (whose applications include Communism and Socialism), which concerned itself with equality even at the expense of freedom.

It was only in the early part of the 20th Century that people were led to embrace the moderate socialist school, which holds that although freedom and other human rights are not absolute, they nevertheless have a social function. This is also the approach of moderate Islam as described by Ibn Ashur, who defines freedom as the individual's ability to dispose of his own affairs and person however he chooses within the limits set by Islamic law. The clearest manifestations of this include freedom of belief, freedom of speech and freedom of action, whether in relation to oneself or in relation to someone else's actions.

Ibn Ashur makes clear that Islamic Law has rights over its adherents which accordingly restrict the freedom with which they conduct themselves, and that the violation of people's freedom is a type of injustice which must be dealt with by those in power, who have been appointed to carry out justice for the oppressed by examining the degree of freedom granted to human beings under the Law. Similarly, Islamic law encloses freedom of action within the protective wall of *sadd al-dharā'iʿ** through many of its rulings, precisely in order to prevent the breach of such freedom.[42]

This is the concept of freedom in Islamic law which, in Ibn Ashur's view, arises from inborn human nature and which, according to Allal al-Fasi, is inseparable from responsibility and accountability before the Law. Such responsibility and accountability grow, in turn, out of belief in the divine oneness (*al-tawḥīd*), which delivers human beings from servitude to all that is not God. From this concept Ibn Ashur derives the various forms of freedom, including freedom of belief, national freedom, individual freedom, political freedom, the freedom to engage in scientific research, and freedom of action.[43]

(d) As for equality, it is likewise not an absolute value, for although there is equality in our accountability before the Law, we also find that:

1. Equality does not apply to divine reward and punishment; after all, there is no equality between those who do good and those who do evil. Similarly, it does not apply to things which are acquired in life; hence, there cannot be said to be equality between those who know and those who do not. Rather, God's ways are manifested in the order of life: "[Nay, as] it is We who distribute their means of livelihood among them in the life of this world, and raise some of them by degrees above others, to the end that they might avail themselves of one another's help – [so, too, it is We who bestow gifts of the spirit upon whomever We will]: and this thy Sustainer's grace is better than all [the worldly] wealth that they may amass" (43:32).

2. In his book, *al-Fawā'id*, al-ʿIzz ibn ʿAbd al-Salām devotes a chapter to the enumeration of those things in which people are equal and those in which they differ from each other. He states, "Human beings are equal with respect to the means of acquiring knowledge and forming convictions concerning questions on the fundamentals of the religion, while they differ on the level of traits and characteristics on the basis which different things are required of them. Such differences among people include, for example, inability vs. ability, masculinity vs. femininity, presence vs. absence, slavehood vs. freedom, power vs. weakness, distance vs. nearness, wealth vs. poverty, want vs. abundance, etc., since for all those to whom such differences apply, God Almighty has established rulings suitable to who they are and appropriate to their particular state and circumstances."[44]

3. In his discussion of this theme, Allal al-Fasi concludes that the kind of equality acceptable within an Islamic framework is equivalence with respect to absolute justice,[45] which means that equality is subject to justice.

4. As for Ibn Ashur, he holds that equality in Islamic legislation is a principle which applies in all situations unless there is some factor which would render it inapplicable. He regards innate human understanding as a criterion in this respect; hence, everything in relation to which innate human understanding perceives that there should be equality, Islamic legislation imposes equality in relation thereto, whereas in relation to those things in which innate human understanding perceives that there ought to be distinctions among human beings, Islamic law refrains from imposing equality given the existence of preventative factors, be they legal, social, political, or related to people's natural dispositions.[46]

5. In our view, equality should not be regarded as an all-inclusive principle which applies to all situations but, rather, one which pertains specifically to situations concerning which Islamic legal rulings call for equality.

(e) Lastly, with regard to human rights, they are numerous and overlapping within the various branches and rulings of Islamic law. Moreover, not all human rights are on the same level of priority; hence, the right to life, freedom of ownership, education, etc., are so important that they are closely tied to the preservation of human life, material wealth, and the faculty of reason. Other rights, however, such as the rights due to neighbors, guests, those who knock at one's door and friends, pertain specifically and solely to a particular part of one of the branches of the Law. Consequently, it is sufficient, in order to guarantee such rights, to affirm the general principle of the sovereignty of the Law which we had occasion to mention in the course of discussing the *maqṣid* of the Ummah's institutional organization.

[THEME 2]

The Types and Categories of Maqāṣid

It is not our intention here to repeat what has already been said on this particular topic; what we hope to do is simply to eliminate the ambiguities which have arisen from the plethora of overlapping categorizations, terms and definitions which have come to be used in discussing *maqāṣid*. To this end, we will briefly expound our view on the following subthemes:

(1) The *maqāṣid* of creation (*maqāṣid al-khalq*),
(2) the higher *maqāṣid* of the Law (*maqāṣid al-sharīʿah al-ʿāliyah*),
(3) the universal *maqāṣid* of the Law (*maqāṣid al-sharīʿah al-kulliyyah*),
(4) special *maqāṣid* of the Law (*maqāṣid al-sharīʿah al-khāṣṣah*),
(5) the particular *maqāṣid* of the Law (*maqāṣid al-sharīʿah al-juz'iyyah*), and
(6) human *maqāṣid* (*maqāṣid al-mukallafīn*).

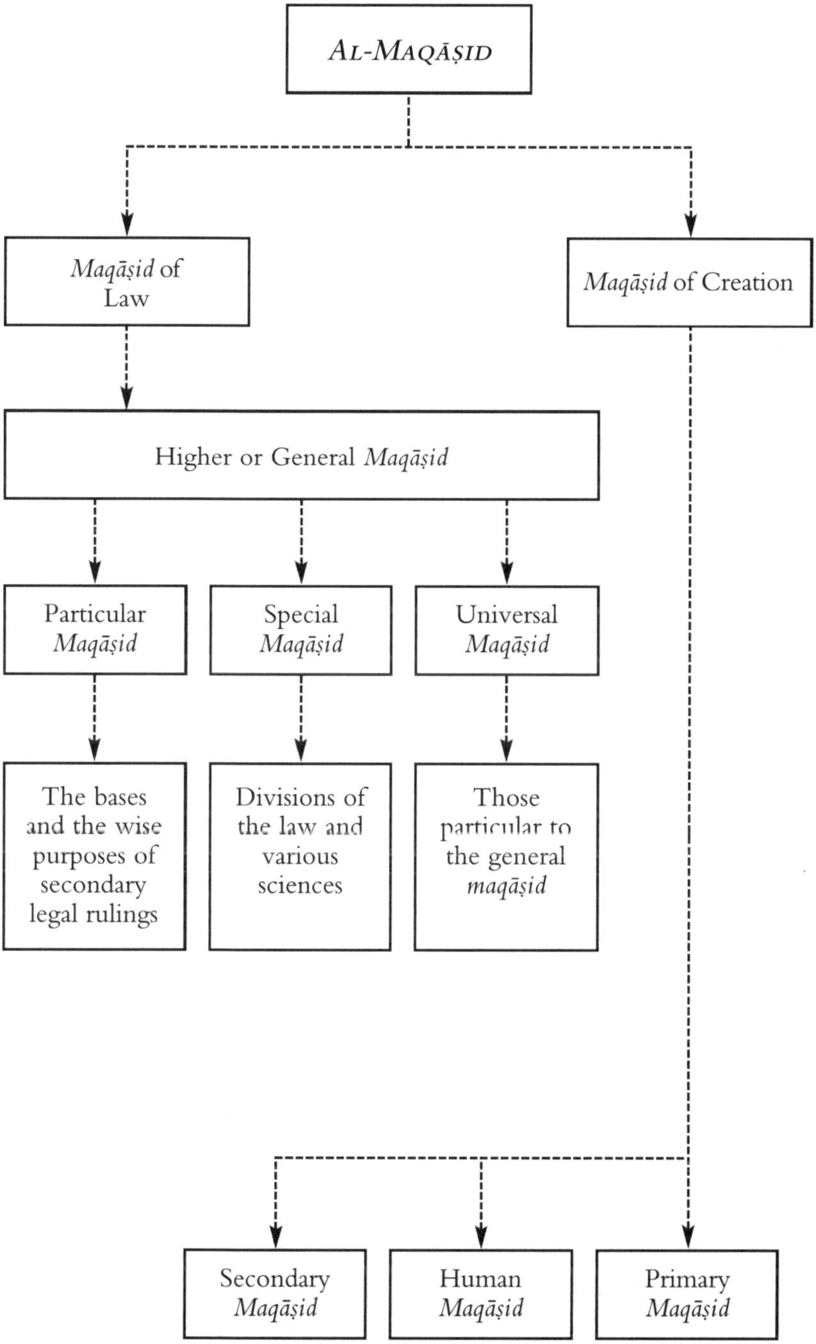
AL-MAQĀṢID
Maqāṣid of Law
Maqāṣid of Creation
Higher or General Maqāṣid
Particular Maqāṣid
Special Maqāṣid
Universal Maqāṣid
The bases and the wise purposes of secondary legal rulings
Divisions of the law and various sciences
Those particular to the general maqāṣid
Secondary Maqāṣid
Human Maqāṣid
Primary Maqāṣid

[*Subtheme* 1]*: The Maqāṣid of Creation*

We must first draw a distinction between the intents behind the command to create (*maqāṣid al-'amr al-takwīnī*) – that is, the intents or purposes of creation – and the intents which underlie commands that impose obligations on us as God's creatures (*maqāṣid al-'amr al-taklīfī*), that is, the intents of Islamic law (*maqāṣid al-sharīʿah*). These two categories of *maqāṣid* are connected, yet distinct, as we hope to show in what follows.

Al-Shāṭibī notes that "a legal intent is one thing, and a creational intent is another; moreover, one can be present without the other, and vice-versa."[47] Elsewhere[48] he clarifies his view somewhat as it relates to scholastic theology. However, space does not permit a presentation of this discussion; rather, our concern here is with two aspects of legal and creational intents.

§*First:*

(a) The first aspect is illustrated in the following words from the Holy Qur'an, where God declares:

1. "I have not created the invisible beings and men to any end other than that they may [know and] worship Me" (51:56).

2. "Behold, I am about to establish on earth one who shall inherit it (*khalīfah*)" (2:30).

3. "Verily, We did offer the trust [of reason and volition] to the heavens, and the earth, and the mountains: but they refused to bear it because they were afraid of it. Yet man took it up – for, verily, he has always been prone to be most wicked, most foolish" (33:72).

4. "Did you, then, think that We created you in mere idle play, and that you would not have to return to Us?" (23:115)

5. "We have not created the heaven and the earth and all that is between them without meaning and purpose" (38:27).

6. "We have not created the heavens and the earth and all that is between them in mere idle play; none of this have We created without [an inner] truth, but most of them understand it not" (44:38-39).

7. "And He it is who has created the heavens and the earth in six aeons; and [ever since He has willed to create life,] the throne of His almightiness has rested upon water. [God reminds you of your dependence on Him] in order to test you [and thus to make manifest] which of you is best in conduct" (11:7).

8. "Hallowed be He in whose hand all dominion rests, since He has the power to will anything; He who has created death as well as life, so that He might put you to a test [and thus show] which of you is best in conduct" (67:1–2).

These and many similar passages from the Qur'an clearly have to do with the intent of creation (*al-qaṣd al-khalqī*), though this does not preclude their shedding light on the intent of the Law (*al-qaṣd al-taklīfī*). Shaykh Abd Allah Darraz, the commentator on al-Shāṭibī's *al-Muwāfaqāt*, believes that passages 4, 5 and 6 above bear a connection to the establishment of Islamic law rather than to the origin of creation.[49] As we see it, however, they establish a link between the former and the latter.

(b) The following examples may serve to clarify the relationship between *al-qaṣd al-khalqī* and *al-qaṣd al-taklīfī*.

1. Qur'anic verses pertaining to worship as one of the purposes of creation have their parallel in the purposes of the Law. This parallel is spoken of by al-Shāṭibī when he writes, "The intent underlying the establishment of the Law is to deliver human beings from enslavement to their selfish whims and desires in order that they might be God's servants by choice just as they are His servants out of necessity."[50] In other words, the Law was established in order to enable human beings to seek God in all circumstances and submit to His judgments at all times; this is the meaning of devotion to God.[51]

It should also be noted here that, as will be seen below, this is among the higher intents of the law, and not the intent referred to as preservation of the religion.

2. Similarly, human beings' role as vicegerents on earth – as one of the purposes of creation – is paralleled in the purposes of the Law by the fact that to the best of their ability and in accordance with their particular skills and gifts, human beings represent the One who established them as vicegerents by executing His judgments, fulfilling His purposes, and safeguarding the

interests which the Lawgiver intends to preserve. The role of vicegerent is both public and private, general and specific, as may be seen from the words of the Prophet, "Each of you is a shepherd, and each of you is responsible for his/her flock."[52] As will be seen in Theme 3 of this chapter, this is included among *maqāṣid al-sharīʿah* as they pertain to the Ummah and to humanity as a whole.

(c) Both types of intents (the intents of creation and the intents of the Law) may also be reflected in the same Qur'anic verses.

1. This may be seen in the words of God Almighty in the Qur'an, "Behold, We have created you all out of a male and a female, and have made you into nations and tribes, so that you might come to know one another" (49:13). The process of coming to know one another serves as an intent of the creation, just as it serves as a purpose of the Law, without any conflict between the two meanings.

2. The same applies to the verses which speak of human beings' call to populate and develop the earth.

§*Second:* The second aspect, having to do with God's ways in relation to His creation, is revealed in the words, "For, He it is who has made you inherit the earth, and has raised some of you by degrees above others, so that He might try you by means of what He has bestowed upon you" (6:165), as well as in numerous other verses having to do with the natural disposition and instincts which God has instilled within human beings.

1. One example of such God-given dispositions is the sexual instinct which ensures the preservation of the species and which is found not only in human beings, but in animals and plants as well. Such observations lead to the conclusion that the preservation of the [various] species is among the intents of creation. This intent of creation is paralleled in the intents of the Law by the restriction of sexual relationships to the context of marriage, the encouragement of procreation, the granting of sympathy, affection and compassion [between spouses], as well as the safeguarding of family lineage and honor, which are dealt with in detail in the context of our discussion of the realms of the individual and the family.

2. Another example of such God-given dispositions is found in the fact that God has brought the creation into existence and caused some creatures to need others in order to ensure that each group looks out for the interests of others.[53] This, then, is among the intents of creation which, in the realm of the Law, finds its parallel in the intents of cooperation and exchange of benefits, whether on the level of the Ummah or that of wider humanity, as well as what such cooperation requires by way of the allowance of contracts and the requirement that they be faithfully adhered to.

These examples should suffice to clarify the distinction between the intents of the creation and the intents of the Law.

[*Subtheme* 2]: *The Higher Maqāṣid of Islamic Law and Foundational Concepts*

Referred to by some as the general *maqāṣid* of Islamic law, they are ranked highest among the legal intents with respect to abstractness, theoreticality and brevity.

§*First:* There are a number of different perspectives on how to identify these *maqāṣid*:

1. Some favor deriving them from verses from the Holy Qur'an which clarify the intention behind the sending of God's messengers and the revelation of the divine messages. Such a derivation yields a set of *maqāṣid* which includes right guidance, instruction, uprightness, illumination, truth, compassion, justice,[54] equality,[55] the strengthening of the Ummah, as well as prudence, emancipation, assuming the traits [of the Divine], unification, and perfection.[56]

2. Some devote special attention to the worship of God, serving as His vicegerent, and populating and developing the earth.[57]

3. Others focus on the achievement of benefit and the prevention of harm.

4. The process of comparing and contrasting obedience-based intents (*maqāṣid al-ṭāʿah*) and human interest-based intents (*maqāṣid al-maṣlaḥah*) has led some to ask: Were human beings created for the sake of worship, or was worship instituted for the sake of human beings?[58]

5. Still others have listed among the *maqāṣid* concepts, distinguishing features, means, and mechanisms such as alleviation (*al-taysīr*) and the elimination of hardship, allowing for inborn human dispositions, beneficence and compassion, prohibitions against the use of legal artifices (*man*ᶜ *al-taḥāyul*), making allowance for evasive legal devices (*murā*ᶜ*āt al-dharā'i*ᶜ) and respect for the Law.[59]

§*Second:* And now, from brevity to detail:

(a) Many verses of the Holy Qur'an clarify the purpose behind the sending of God's messengers and the revelation of His inspired messages. For example:

1. The phrase, "those who believe and work righteousness" is repeated so frequently throughout the Qur'an that it draws attention to the importance, as well as the inseparability, of faith and righteous action. Indeed, the Qur'an states explicitly that "all who believe in God and the Last Day and do righteous deeds shall have their reward with their Sustainer; no fear need they have, and neither shall they grieve" (2:62), thereby confirming that these are the principle elements of all [valid] sects and religions.[60]

2. "And thus [O Prophet], We have sent thee as [evidence of Our] grace towards all the worlds" (21:107).

3. "...a guidance for all the God-conscious" (2:2).

4. "*Alif, lām, rā'*. A Divine writ [is this – a revelation] which We have bestowed upon thee from on high in order that thou might bring forth all mankind, by their Sustainer's leave, out of the depths of darkness into the light: onto the way that leads to the Almighty, the One to whom all praise is due" (14:1).

5. "Indeed, God bestowed a favor upon the believers when he raised up in their midst an apostle from among themselves, to convey His messages unto them, and to cause them to grow in purity, and to impart unto them the divine writ as well as wisdom – whereas before they were indeed, most obviously, lost in error" (3:164).[61]

(b) The Messenger of God would occasionally utter concise statements such as, (1) "Say, 'I have believed in God', then straighten your path;" (2) "I was only sent to perfect noble character traits,"[62] and (3) "I am a mercy given."

(c) This is the way in which the Companions were accustomed to understanding the universals of Islam. Rubᶜī ibn ᶜĀmir, who was the courier for Saᶜd, the Muslim commander during the Battle of al-Qādisiyyah, was asked by Rustum, commander of the Persians, "What brings you here?" Rubᶜī replied, "God has sent us to deliver whomever wills to be delivered from the worship of [God's] servants to the worship of God [Himself], from the constriction of this earthly existence to its broad expanses, and from the injustice of religions to the justice of surrender to God, that is, Islam. Hence, we have been sent to bid God's creatures to embrace His religion."[63]

(d) Imam al-Ghazālī states clearly that in its origin, the term *maṣlaḥah*, or interest refers to the achievement of benefit and the prevention of harm; these, of course, are human intents, the achievement of which is vital for human well-being. However, what is meant by the term 'interest' as used here is, specifically, the safeguarding of the intent of the Law, and the intent of the Law where human beings are concerned consists of five elements, namely, the preservation of their religion, lives, faculty of reason, progeny and material wealth.

Hence, whatever includes the preservation of these five fundamentals is an interest [in the sense of a benefit], and whatever leads to their loss or forfeiture is a source of harm, the prevention of which is likewise a benefit (*maṣlaḥah*).[64] Hence, al-Ghazālī defines the term 'interest' as the preservation of the intent(s) of the Law, after which he defines the intents of the Law as these five fundamentals. In addition, he identifies the means of ascertaining the intents of the Law as the Qur'an, the Sunnah and the consensus of the Muslim community.

(e) Ibn Rushd the grandson (d. 595 AH/1198 AC) did not write specifically on the subject of *maqāṣid al-sharīᶜah*. However, in the conclusion to his book, *Bidāyat al-Mujtahid*, he identifies the intents of acts which are performed in accordance with the Law as being the achievement of moral and spiritual virtues, such as gratitude, chastity, justice, and generosity. Similarly, we read in his book *Faṣl al-Maqāl* that the intent of the Law is simply to teach the truth and how to act in truth. In the view of al-Raysuni, Ibn Rushd is drawing our attention through these statements to highly significant aspects of the higher intents of Islamic Law (*al-maqāṣid al-ᶜulyā li al-sharīᶜah al-islāmiyyah*), namely, the educational and moral aspects to which reference is made in the words of God Almighty, "He it is Who has sent unto the unlettered people an apostle from among themselves, to convey unto them His messages, and to cause them to grow in purity, and to impart unto them the divine writ as well as wisdom – whereas before that they were indeed, most obviously, lost in error..." (62:2).[65]

(f) Later, in the course of defining the concept of the appropriateness of the *ᶜillah*, that is, the basis [for this or that legal ruling], al-Rāzī declares,

> 'That which is appropriate' (*al-munāsib**) is that which leads to what is suitable for human beings with respect to attainment (*taḥṣīl*) and perpetuation (*ibqā'*). Attainment might be defined as the achievement of benefit, while perpetuation might be defined as the prevention of harm, since in relation to what one intends to perpetuate, its elimination would cause harm, while its perpetuation would bring benefit. Moreover, this attainment and perpetuation might be based either on knowledge, or on reasonable certainty. In either of these two cases, it may be either earthly/material or otherworldly/spiritual in nature. Benefit (*manfaᶜah*) may be said to be the equivalent of pleasure or whatever leads thereto, while harm (*maḍarrah*) may be said to be the equivalent of pain or whatever leads thereto. Pleasure has also been defined as the realization of what is appropriate, while pain has been defined as the realization of what is unsuitable. As I see it, however, neither pleasure nor pain should be defined, since they are among the most clearly perceptible of all things to a living being, which of necessity perceives the difference between them, the difference between them and other things, as well as that which would be difficult or impossible to define in terms of anything more evident [than itself].[66]

Here, then, we find that whereas al-Ghazālī links interest (*maṣlaḥah*) with Islamic law, al-Rāzi links interest (benefit, or *manfaᶜah*) with pleasure, and harm (*maḍarrah*) with pain. However, he then rejects the notion of defining pleasure and pain as the realization of what is suitable and unsuitable respectively. In fact, he rejects the notion of defining them at all, since they are 'the most clearly perceptible of all things [experienced by] a living being.' In so saying, al-Rāzī seems to be speaking of what Ibn Sīnā (d. 428 AH/1036 AC) termed innate human understanding (*al-fiṭrah*).

(g) As for al-ʿIzz ibn ʿAbd al-Salām, he asserts in his book, *al-Qawāʿid* that "Islamic law in its entirety consists of [human beings' best] interests, either by warding off harm or bringing benefit."[67] Moreover, he opens his book, *al-Fawā'id* by saying, in explanation of the nature of benefit and harm, "God sent His messengers and revealed His holy scriptures in order to bring that which is beneficial and to prevent what is harmful both in this world and the next." He then proceeds to define what he means by benefit and harm, saying, "Benefit is equivalent to pleasure or its cause, or happiness or its cause, while harm is equivalent to pain or its[68] cause, or sorrow or its cause."

In this definition, al-ʿIzz follows al-Rāzī in avoiding a link between interest (*maṣlaḥah*) and *maqāṣid al-sharīʿah*. Instead, he defines *maṣlaḥah* in terms of the general linguistic import of the word, an import which can be recognized – as was explained earlier – through reason, human experience and custom. At the same time, however, al-ʿIzz later stipulates that *maṣlaḥah* not lead to harm, be it immediate or delayed, which brings in its wake even greater harm. For indeed, "Many a moment's pleasure has given rise to untold grief and calamitous affliction."[69]

(h) The intimate link between *maṣlaḥah*, or 'interest', and Islamic law was later restored by Ibn Taymiyyah and his disciple Ibn al-Qayyim (d. 751 AH/1350 AC). Ibn Taymiyyah asserts that innate human understanding is the basis for recognizing truth and benefit (*al-nāfiʿ*) – which is the equivalent of what the Qur'an refers to as *al-maʿrūf*, that is, 'the doing of what is right' (3:104) enjoined by the Law of Islam – as well as falsehood (*al-bāṭil*), and harm (*al-ḍārr*) – which are the equivalent of *al-munkar*, or 'the doing of what is wrong' which Islamic law prohibits.

(i) As for Ibn al-Qayyim, he made the well-known statement quoted earlier in which he asserts that "Islamic Law is structured and founded upon wise purposes and the best interests of God's servants both in this world and the next."

(j) In the case of al-Shāṭibī, he makes reference to four intents of the Lawgiver (*maqāṣid al-shāriʿ*) as well as human intents (*maqāṣid al-mukallafīn*), which will be discussed elsewhere. As for the intents of the Lawgiver, only the first and fourth of those specified by al-Shāṭibī can actually be viewed as *maqāṣid*. The second, which has to do with the establishment of the Law for people's understanding, is discussed by al-Shāṭibī in terms of the Law's having been revealed to an unlettered people whose language was Arabic; whereas the third, which has to do with the establishment of the Law as a standard of conduct, he discusses in relation to human capacity and hardship.

The first and fourth intents of the Lawgiver, which are in fact the only two which bear a connection to *maqāṣid al-shāriᶜ*, are also closely interconnected:

1. Concerning the first intent, al-Shāṭibī states that Islamic law was established for the sake of safeguarding human beings' best interests both in this life and in the life to come, and that its requirements are based on the achievement of its *maqāṣid* for the creation ('creation' being used here in the sense of human beings).[70]

2. As for the fourth intent, he terms it the Lawgiver's intent to bring human beings under the Law's jurisdiction, saying that God's intention is "to deliver human beings from enslavement to their selfish whims and desires in order that they might be God's servants by choice just as they are His servants out of necessity."[71] It is clear that this intent of the Law parallels worship as an intent of creation (in the sense of the command to bring the creation into existence).

3. With respect to the link between these two types of intent, Shaykh Abd Allah Darraz states that "the first type means the establishment of an order which guarantees happiness both in this world and the next for those who adhere to it, while the fourth is that the Lawgiver calls upon His servants to place themselves in subjection to this order, and not to their whims and desires."[72]

4. One may easily perceive the link here between human interests and the intents of the Law in what may be viewed as a return to al-Ghazālī's conceptualization of this theme.

(k) Coming to Ibn Ashur we find that:

1. He refers to this level of *maqāṣid* sometimes as general intents (*al-maqāṣid al-ᶜāmmah*), the general intent (*al-maqṣid al-ᶜāmm*), the supreme intent (*al-maqṣid al-aᶜẓam*), or overall intents (*maqāṣid fī al-jumlah*), and at other times higher intents (*al-maqāṣid al-ᶜāliyah*), from which we ourselves have taken this term. With respect to common characteristics among similar rulings, Ibn Ashur states, "If these characteristics are secondary (*farᶜiyyah*) and easily

discernible (*qarībah*), we refer to them as *ʿilal*, that is, bases, such as the capacity to intoxicate. If, on the other hand, they are universals, we refer to them as immediate intents (*maqāṣid qarībah*), such as the preservation of the faculty of reason; and if they are higher universals, we refer to them as higher intents (*maqāṣid ʿāliyah*), of which there are two types: sources of benefit, and sources of harm."[73]

2. In relation to higher intents, we find that Ibn Ashur makes no distinction between the terms *maqāṣid* (intents), *mafāhīm* (concepts), and *khaṣā'iṣ* (features). Thus, for example, he speaks about the concepts of innate human understanding, benevolence and compassion, rights, equality, and freedom, for which he sometimes uses the term *maqāṣid*, and at others, other terms. The intents of the Law (*maqāṣid al-sharīʿah*) are, in his understanding, based on the most central foundation of the Law, namely, *al-fiṭrah*, that is, innate human understanding or disposition.[74] Benevolence (*al-samāḥah*) is the most prominent feature of Islamic law and its most central intent.[75] As for equality it is a principle which applies in all situations unless there is some cause or consideration which renders it inapplicable, while the equality among the various members of the Ummah with respect to the ability to conduct themselves as they see fit – in other words, freedom[76] – is a fundamental intent of the Law.[77] And where rights are concerned, he holds that it is the intent of the Law to identify the various types of rights and those to whom they are due.[78]

3. With regard to *maqāṣid* in particular, Ibn Ashur states,

> An inductive reading of numerous pieces of textual evidence from the Qur'an and the authentic Sunnah leads inevitably to the certainty that the rulings of Islamic law are founded upon wise purposes and bases which are, themselves, founded upon [the intent of achieving] the overall well-being of society and its individual members, as shall be seen. Moreover, it is our aim here to demonstrate that the Law has overall intents (*maqāṣid fīal-jumlah*), while leaving the specification of their details to future discussions.[79]

Ibn Ashur defines the general intents of the Law as:

> the meanings and wise purposes on the part of the Lawgiver which can be discerned in most or all of the situations to which the Law applies such that

> they can be seen not to be associated exclusively with a particular type of ruling. Included here are the features of the Law, its overall intent, and the meanings which can be discerned throughout it. It likewise includes [wise] purposes which are not observable in all types of rulings, although they are observable in many of them.[80]

In a third passage, Ibn Ashur discusses what he terms the general intent (*al-maqṣid al-ᶜāmm*) of Islamic legislation, noting that it is "to preserve the order of the Ummah and perpetuate its well-being and integrity through the well-being and integrity of those who safeguard this order, namely, the human race."[81]

In a fourth passage, Ibn Ashur states that "the supreme intent" (*al-maqṣid al-aᶜẓam*) of Islamic law is "to achieve well-being and integrity and to prevent harm and corruption."[82]

In a fifth passage, he observes that "the intent of Islamic law is to preserve world order and to regulate people's conduct in a way which protects against the spread of corruption and weakness. This, in turn, can only come about by achieving benefit and warding off harm in the true senses of these words."[83]

What can be concluded from the foregoing is that Islamic legislation has two functions: (1) "to reform corrupt conditions and to declare the fact that they are corrupt...," and (2) to affirm wholesome, ethical forms of conduct, namely, those referred to as *al-maᶜrūf*, or the doing of what is right. As God Almighty declares concerning the Prophet, he "will enjoin upon them the doing of what is right (*al-maᶜrūf*) (7:157)."[84]

Thus, Ibn Ashur specifies the overall intent [of the Law] as that of achieving benefit and preventing harm for society and its members. Moreover, his interest in the societal aspect of this intent leads him to state that the preservation of the order of the Ummah/world is the intent, and that achievement of interests is the means to fulfill this intent.

(l) As for Allal al-Fasi, he identifies the general intent of the Law as

> to develop and populate the earth and preserve the order of peaceful coexistence therein; to ensure the earth's ongoing well-being and usefulness through the piety of those who have been placed there as God's vicegerents; to ensure that people conduct themselves justly, with moral probity and with

integrity in thought and action, and that they reform that which needs reform on earth, tap its resources, and plan for the good of all.[85]

This statement by Allal al-Fasi indicates that populating and developing the earth and preserving the order of peaceful coexistence therein are the intent, or *maqṣid*, and that the well-being and piety of those who have been placed on earth as God's vicegerents are the means to achieve this intent.

In light of the foregoing it might be asked: Are these statements by Ibn Ashur and Allal al-Fasi an attempt to further abstract the higher intents of the Law by making the notion of benefit and harm nothing but a means, and by highlighting the concepts of the Ummah, the world, and populating and developing the Earth? Perhaps...[86]

(m) Similar to this trend, yet more explicit and clearly defined, is the conceptualization offered by Yahya Muhammad, who holds that the five universals are related only to human beings' material needs and that, as a consequence, they are not essential *maqāṣid*. At the same time, however, he acknowledges them to be among the necessary conditions for the achievement of the true *maqāṣid*. In other words, he holds that they are conditional *maqāṣid* whose purpose is to achieve other, true *maqāṣid*. According to this conceptualization, it is these other, true *maqāṣid* (also termed ultimate intents, or *al-maqāṣid al-ghā'iyyah*) which constitute the ultimate end of Islamic legislation, which seeks to achieve happiness for human beings. These ultimate intents are a set of values, the most prominent of which are: worship or devotion, prudence, emancipation, assuming the traits [of the Divine], unification and perfection, each of which has both an outward dimension and an inward dimension. Muhammad also notes the absence of legal interests (*al-maṣāliḥ al-ḥuqūqiyyah*) from the [traditional] list of essentials.[87]

(n) Before presenting my own perspective, I would like to offer a number of considerations:

1. Given that our concern is a discussion of *maqāṣid*, it is necessary to exclude those things which, although they are related to the *maqāṣid* in some way or another and might tend to be confused with them, actually belong to a different category. What I am referring to here are things such as the foundational concepts which served as a starting point for some in their discussions

of *maqāṣid*, such as innate human disposition or understanding (*al-fiṭrah*) and beneficence (*al-samāḥah*), distinguishing features [of the Law] such as alleviation and the elimination of hardship, means and mechanisms such as the prohibition against legal subterfuges, closing and/or opening the door to legal artifices (*sadd al-dharā'iᶜ wa fatḥuhā*) and respect for Islamic legislation,[88] as well as major values of relevance, the sum total of which goes to make up 'the philosophy of legislation.'

2. Given that our concern is with a discussion of *maqāṣid al-sharīᶜah*, that is, the intents of the Law, and not with *maqāṣid al-mukallafīn*, that is, human intents, it is necessary to adhere to the criterion laid down by al-Ghazālī, namely, the search for human interests recognized by the Law, and not human interests in their non-restricted sense as understood by human beings without reference to the Law.

3. Of the human interests recognized by the Law, some are religious/spiritual in nature, while others are earthly/material in nature. Hence, adherence to the Law does not require that we restrict ourselves solely to so-called religious interests, since Islam does not recognize this type of distinction between the sacred and the worldly. Rather, *maqāṣid* relating to pure worship and devotion, *maqāṣid* relating to pure human interest, and those which are common to both, are all included within *maqāṣid al-sharᶜ*, that is, the intents of the Law, in a single, integrated system which encompasses the realm of what has come to be termed human rights.

4. It makes no sense, therefore, to ask whether human beings were created for the sake of worship, or whether worship was instituted for the sake of human beings. Rather, the dual *maqāṣid* of obedience and preservation of human interests are fundamental and interconnected.[89]

5. The search for the higher intents of Islamic law requires a certain degree of abstraction and comprehensiveness. However, this does not mean that we must err in the direction of excessive brevity, as when we restrict them to the achievement of benefit and the prevention of harm[90] without an explanation which serves to distinguish Islamic law from pragmatism, for example.[91]

6. At the same time, such a search requires that a distinction be made between the abstract level and the practical level, which finds its place among

the universal intents of the Law (to be discussed below) such as education, prudence, assuming the traits [of the Divine], unification, strengthening the Ummah, etc. And thus we find that what we are seeking is a set of higher values which fulfill the intents of creation (*maqāṣid al-khalq*) and which are translated in practical terms into the universal *maqāṣid*.[92]

7. This does not mean that we will necessarily be able to deduce logical, geometric or mathematically precise relationships among these values, or between these values and the intents of creation and the universal *maqāṣid*, since such values are interconnected and overlapping and, taken together, constitute an integrated network or system.

8. It should also be remembered that any conceptualization of this system is merely a human attempt to depict absolute values. And how can the merely relative account fully for the absolute? Rather, the most we can hope for is to formulate, not the one correct conceptualization but, rather, a number of possible conceptualizations, one of which may be the notion of the divine unity and justice which was championed of old.

9. In light of the foregoing, my own conceptualization of the higher *maqāṣid* is as follows: The higher intents of the Law are embodied in the worship of God, acting as His vicegerents on earth, and populating and developing the earth through faith and its requirements. Such requirements of faith include righteous action which achieves happiness both in this life and the next, which encompasses both the material and spiritual aspects of existence, and which strikes a balance between the interests of the individual and those of society, between particular national interests and the interests of humanity at large, and between the interests of the current generations and those of generations to come. All such intents, moreover, find their expression on the respective levels of the individual, the family, the Ummah and all of humanity.

§*Third:*

(a) At this level of abstraction, there is a near merging of the ideas of intents (*maqāṣid*) and rules (*qawāʿid*). And there has, in fact, been a blending of *maqāṣid* with rules pertaining to the fundamentals of jurisprudence (*al-qawāʿid al-uṣūliyyah*) and universal rules (*al-qawāʿid al-kulliyyah*). We will postpone our discussion of this subject to the upcoming subtheme, contenting ourselves here with a reference to two successful attempts at deriving rules relating to *maqāṣid*. The first of these two attempts is that made by al-Raysuni based on al-Shāṭibī's books, *al-Muwāfaqāt* and *al-Iʿtiṣām*,[93] and in the course of which he derives 54 rules; the second is that made by al-Hasani based on Ibn Ashur's book entitled, *Maqāṣid al-Sharīʿah*,[94] which yields 34 rules. Al-Raysuni divides these rules into three groups, namely: (1) intents of the Lawgiver, (2) human intents, and (3) how the intents of the Lawgiver may be ascertained. Al-Hasani also divides them into three categories namely: (1) rules pertaining to general intents, (2) rules pertaining to specific intents, and (3) rules for corroborating intents of the Law.

(b) What follows is a listing of al-Shāṭibī's rules of relevance to the higher intents:[95]

1. Divinely revealed laws have been established in order to serve human beings' best interests both in this world and the next.

2. An inductive reading of the various types of textual evidence found in the Law – both those of universal import and those which apply to particular situations – confirms conclusively that the Lawgiver intends to preserve human interests, including those which are classified as essentials, exigencies and enhancements.

3. The creation of the earthly realm is based on God's bestowal of blessings on His servants in order that they might receive them, enjoy them and give thanks to God for them, and that He, in turn, might reward them in the life to come; these two intents are among the most central intents of Islamic law.

4. The purpose for which the Law was established is to deliver human beings from enslavement to their whims and selfish desires so that they might become God's servants by choice just as they are already His servants out of necessity.

5. The Law was established to the end that human beings' inclinations and desires should be subject to God's intention therein. However, God has granted human beings latitude in relation to their desires, passions and enjoyments to a degree that leads neither to corruption nor to hardship.

(c) According to Ibn Ashur:[96]

1. The wise purposes and bases of Islamic law are based on the pursuit of overall well-being for both society and its individual members.

2. The *maqāṣid* are based upon innate human perceptions and dispositions.

3. Benevolence (*al-samāḥah*) is the primary feature of the Law and its most central intent.

4. The general intent of Islamic legislation is the preservation of world order and the perpetuation of its well-being and integrity through the well-being and integrity of human beings.

5. The general intent of doctrine, action and social affairs involves an all-inclusive pursuit of well-being and integrity.

6. The highest intent is the achievement of benefit and the prevention of harm.

[*Subtheme* 3]*: The Universal Maqāṣid of Islamic Law* (*al-Maqāṣid al-Kulliyyah*)

The universal *maqāṣid* are those which, when the word 'intents' or *maqāṣid* is mentioned, are the first to come to mind, namely, the preservation of religion, human life, the faculty of reason, progeny and material wealth as in the listing proposed by al-Ghazālī and later by al-Juwaynī. Those who came after al-Ghazālī and al-Juwaynī added to and subtracted from these original five; moreover, as we have made clear elsewhere, they also differed over the order in which they are to be arranged.

These universal *maqāṣid* are less abstract than the higher intents (*al-maqāṣid al-ʿāliyah*) which we discussed in the previous section; they are also more inclusive than the specific intents (*al-maqāṣid al-khāṣṣah*) and the particular intents (*al-maqāṣid al-juz'iyyah*) which will be taken up in the following two sections.

Al-Shāṭibī concerns himself with investigating the roots of these *maqāṣid* in the Qur'an and the Sunnah. He explains that the root of each of them may be traced back to the Makkan period of Islamic law, after which particular, detailed rulings were issued during the Madinan period[97] which, as will become clear below, was likewise characterized by *maqāṣid* on the particular level. The discussion of these universal *maqāṣid* raises a number of issues, to some of which we have devoted other sections of this study. These issues are:

1. The role of reason, innate human understanding and experience in identifying and verifying the *maqāṣid* (see Chapter One, Theme 1).

2. Whether the universal *maqāṣid* should be limited to five, or whether the list should be expanded (see Chapter Two, Theme 1).

3. The enumeration and explanation of the universal *maqāṣid* (Chapter Two, Theme 3).

4. The internal arrangement of the universal *maqāṣid* (Chapter One, Theme 2).

5. The arrangement of the means of achieving each *maqṣid* into the categories of essentials, exigencies and enhancements (Chapter One, Theme 3).

As for the remaining issues, they are: 1) primary and secondary *maqāṣid*, 2) *maqāṣid* and *wasā'il* (ends and means), 3) the categories of essentials, exigencies and enhancements, 4) universal *maqāṣid* and *qawāʿid*, or rules, and 5) universal *maqāṣid* and positive law. And it is to these issues that we now turn:

§*First:* Primary and secondary *maqāṣid*

(a) Universal *maqāṣid* are divided into the categories of primary and secondary. A primary intent is the principle objective of the ruling in question, whereas a secondary intent is a subordinate objective of the same ruling which follows from and completes the principle objective.

(b) There may be evidence which indicates that a given intent is intended for its own sake in addition to being intended for the sake of some other, primary, intent. In such a case, it will be simultaneously a secondary intent and a primary intent, albeit in different respects.[98] That is to say, a single action may be a means of achieving two intents:

An example of this may be seen in marriage, which is legitimate for the primary purpose of procreation. This purpose is accompanied by things such as the desire to find reassurance and repose in another's presence, partnership as a couple, cooperation in the pursuit of worldly and otherworldly interests, including the enjoyment of licit pleasures and looking upon the beauty which God the Creator has made, receiving benefit from the woman's wealth or from the care and nurture she provides for her husband and children, protection against sexual temptation, ever more gratitude for God's blessings, and the like.[99]

This same notion can be illustrated through the example of ritual prayer. We find, for example, that in terms of its primary intent, prayer was established in order to instill in us an attitude of submission and reverence for God Almighty and to teach us to come to Him in sincerity, to stand before Him in submission and humility, and to keep God in constant remembrance. In addition, prayer fulfills certain secondary intents, which al-Shāṭibī describes as: "restraining the person who prays from loathsome deeds and from all that runs counter to reason, seeking refuge in prayer from the world's afflictions, asking God by means of prayer to provide one's daily sustenance and grant one success in one's temporal pursuits (as exemplified in *ṣalāh al-istikhārah** and *ṣalāh al-ḥājah**), and asking for grace to attain Paradise, enter into God's protection, and achieve the most exalted of [spiritual] stations."[100]

§*Second: Maqāṣid* and *Wasā'il* (Ends and Means)

(a) The *maqāṣid* contain within themselves human beings' best interests. As for *wasa'il*, or means, they are the paths that lead to them; in other words, they are the rulings which were instituted for the purpose of fulfilling the *maqāṣid*. As a consequence, *wasā'il* take on the status of *maqāṣid* based on the principle which states that, "Those things without which obligations cannot be fulfilled are themselves obligatory, and cease to be obligatory when such obligations cease to apply."[101] The only situations in which the latter part of this rule ("and cease to be obligatory when such obligations cease to apply") may not be valid are those in which the means in question is a type of secondary intent, as in the case of marriage for the sake of enjoyment of licit pleasures, or as when there is evidence to support a ruling that a certain means continues to be desirable in and of itself despite its being a means to some other end. The performance of ritual ablutions, for example, is an act of worship which is intended for its own sake as well as being a means of fulfilling some other intent, such as the performance of ritual prayer, circumambulating the Kaʿbah, touching the Qur'an, etc. Hence, the performance of ritual ablutions continues to be a desirable practice even when there is no need to circumambulate the Kaʿbah or perform any of the other acts of worship mentioned here.[102]

(b) It is important to guard against allowing means to become ends in themselves, having lost their connection with their original intents. Food, for example, is a means of preserving life; however, it is not acceptable for it to be transformed into an end such that one lives to eat rather than eating to live. The same applies to making money, obtaining housing, transportation, etc., all of which are means that, if people fail to associate them properly with their ends, are in danger of becoming ends in themselves.

(c) This or that means may be a means to something which is itself a means to something else, and so on until we come to the original intent or end:

1. An example of this principle may be seen in the teaching of Islamic legal rulings, which is a means of obtaining or imparting knowledge of such rulings, which is, in turn, a means of encouraging acts of obedience, which are, in turn, means of meriting reward and divine favor.[103]

2. Appointing judges and governors is a means of achieving benefits, the appointment of assistants to judges is a means to another means.[104]

3. In addition, the bearing of testimonies[105] is a means of delivering them, while delivering testimonies is a means of achieving benefits and warding off harm.[106]

In other words, this or that means can become an intent or end with respect to the means which leads to it if there is evidence to show that it is something to be sought for its own sake, as in the case of secondary intents for which there is evidence that they are desirable in and of themselves.

(d) Not all means are of the same type:

1. Some means are only resorted to in particular circumstances, such as the prescribed and discretionary punishments under Islamic law; the same is true for legitimate defense in the event of aggression against people's lives, honor, material wealth, and so on.

2. Other means are required on an ongoing basis, such as food, clothing and shelter for the preservation of human life.

3. Still other means are called for by people's innate dispositions and needs, such as food for the maintenance of life, sexual contact for the preservation of progeny, and the instinctive impulse to possess for the preservation of material wealth. With respect to this type of means, Islamic law intervenes only for the sake of regulating and maintaining order.

4. There are still other types of means which Islamic law not only orders and regulates, but actively encourages as well.

5. Availing oneself of some means may involve a tolerable degree of hardship.

6. Both al-ʿIzz and al-Shāṭibī have valuable things to say on the related themes of (a) that which involves consideration for human desires and inclinations, and (b) that which entails hardship.

§ *Third:* Universal *maqāṣid* and rules:

Reference was made earlier to the attempts made by al-Raysuni and al-Hasani to derive rules pertaining to the *maqāṣid* from the writings of al-Shāṭibī and Ibn Ashur respectively.

(a) The success of these two attempts prompts us to affirm the distinction between rules (*qawāʿid*) and intents (*maqāṣid*) lest the two concepts be confused.

1. Whether we define a rule as a universal principle which applies to all [relevant] particulars (al-Jurjānī), or as a universal ruling which applies to all relevant particulars and on the basis of which subsidiary judgments may be derived (al-Taftazānī), and whether we view it as applying to all cases or just the majority of cases, all such definitions have to do with rulings themselves, and not with their bases (*ʿilal*), or with the wise purpose or intention which underlies them.

2. As for *maqāṣid al-sharīʿah*, be they general or specific, they are, according to the definition offered by Allal al-Fasi, "the end which it [the Law] is

intended to achieve, as well as the secrets which the Lawgiver has deposited in each of its rulings." Ibn Ashur defines general *maqāṣid* as "the meanings and wise purposes on the part of the Lawgiver which can be discerned in most or all of the situations to which the Law applies," while he defines specific *maqāṣid* as the ways in which the Lawgiver intends [for the general *maqāṣid* to be fulfilled], which includes every wise purpose for which provision has been made in the Law.

3. What al-Raysuni and al-Hasani have arrived at is a type of composite in the sense that they treat *maqāṣid* as rulings, and formulate universal rules which apply to their particulars.

There are, in fact, rules which are intimately connected with *maqāṣid*, such as: "Hardship brings ease," "Harm is to be eliminated," "The prevention of harm should receive higher priority than the achievement of benefit," and "Lesser harm may be permitted in order to prevent greater harm."

Whoever examines the *maqāṣid*-related rules formulated by al-Raysuni and al-Hasani will find that we are dealing with a type of rule that has to do with *uṣūl al-fiqh*, or the fundamentals of jurisprudence. And this is only natural, since the *maqāṣid* have always been part of *uṣūl al-fiqh*. We previously drew a distinction between four types of rules, categorized based on the subject with which they deal, namely: (1) rules governing *uṣūl al-fiqh* (*al-qawāʿid al-uṣūliyyah*) (and of which *maqāṣid*-related rules are a part), (2) theological-philosophical rules (*al-qawāʿid al-kalāmiyyah*), (3) linguistic rules (*al-qawāʿid al-lughawiyyah*), and (4) juristic rules (*al-qawāʿid al-fiqhiyyah*).[107]

§*Fourth:* Universal *maqāṣid* and positive law

At this level of research – that is, at the level of the universal *maqāṣid* – our concern with the activation of these *maqāṣid* leads us to inquire into how they are related to legal systems.

(a) Legal studies have exhibited only limited interest in *maqāṣid* and goals. Moreover, when such interest is apparent – in the context of the philosophy of law or introductions to the study of law – such studies tend to focus on the function of law in ordering society with discussions of the individualist, collective and social schools and the advantages and disadvantages of each of them on the level of theory and application from the age of the European

Renaissance up to the present time. Of particular interest in such studies is the degree of state intervention – by means of legislative mechanisms – in individuals' freedoms and rights and in the ordering and regulation of society.

(b) At the same time, such studies are largely absent within the framework of Islamic law. Hence, in an initial attempt to identify the principle guidelines in this area, I have written a number of studies entitled:

1. *Al-Sharīʿah wa Ḥarakah al-Tārīkh li al-Ishārah ilā Ghā'iyyah al-Sharīʿah* ("Islamic Law and the Movement of History as Evidence of the Purpose-fulness of Islamic Law"),
2. *Madā Tadakhkhul al-Sharīʿah fī Nashāṭ al-Insān* ("The Extent to Which Islamic Law May Interfere in Human Activity"), and
3. *Al-Sulūk al-Khārijī wa al-Niyyah* ("Outward Behavior and Intention").

When detailing the universal *maqāṣid* in Chapter Two, Theme 3, we will see the importance of treating these topics in order for the study of *maqāṣid al-sharīʿah* to complete its course toward practical application in the order of society.

[*Subtheme* 4]: *Specific Maqāṣid (al-Maqāṣid al-Khāṣṣah)*

We use the term 'specific *maqāṣid*' to refer to *maqāṣid* that pertain specifically to a particular division, or homogeneous divisions, of Islamic law, or to a homogeneous set of its legal rulings; this category also includes *maqāṣid* that have to do specifically with the human, social and cosmic sciences and which serve to regulate them by the standards of Islamic law.

Early attempts were made by scholars of Islamic law – and by scholars of *uṣūl al-fiqh* in particular – to proceed in this direction:

(a) Hence, we find that al-Ḥakīm al-Tirmidhī (of the 3rd Century AH) wrote on the subject of prayer and its *maqāṣid* and about the major pilgrimage, or *ḥajj*, and its secrets.[108]

(b) Although the books written by al-Ghazālī on *uṣūl al-fiqh* do not deal with the *maqāṣid* of each of the sciences of Islamic law, his encyclopedia *Iḥyā' ʿUlūm al-Dīn* is filled with expositions of the secrets of the Law, both in its sections devoted to Islamic forms of worship, and in those that treat customs and daily transactions.

(c) Al-ʿIzz ibn ʿAbd al-Salām sought to show that the purpose behind all Islamic forms of worship is to teach human beings to hold God in awe, to magnify and revere Him, to rely upon Him entirely, and to entrust all things to Him.[109] In another related attempt, he sought to clarify the intent (*maqṣid*) behind the appointment of the supreme imam, administrators and rulers who watch over Muslims' interests, judges, fathers and mothers, and legal trusts in general.[110] He also made an attempt of this nature in relation to daily transactions.[111]

(d) Ibn Taymiyyah made an attempt to clarify the *maqāṣid* of the various types of legal guardianship.[112]

(e) Ibn Farḥūn noted that the purpose behind acts of worship in general is to break the ego.[113]

(f) Ibn Ashur concerned himself with expounding the *maqāṣid* of rulings relating to the family, as well as the *maqāṣid* of financial dealings and transactions relating to physical labor, of rulings relating to financial contributions, rulings on the judiciary and testimony, and punishments.[114]

(g) In Chapter Two, Theme 3 of this study, I have formulated a number of *maqāṣid* within the framework of the family. [As for the *maqāṣid* which relate specifically to the human, social and natural sciences, I will discuss them in Chapter Three, Theme 4].

[*Subtheme* 5]*: Particular Maqāṣid (al-Maqāṣid al-Juz'iyyah)*

(a) The 'particular *maqāṣid*' may be defined as what the Lawgiver intends through each particular legal ruling. They are referred to by scholars of jurisprudence as wise purposes (*ḥikam,* singular, *ḥikmah*), and in place of which they use the *ʿillah*, or 'basis' when engaging in analogical reasoning (*qiyās*) given that the term *ʿillah* is considered more precise.[115]

Some scholars have sought to elucidate the secrets, bases and wise purposes of Islamic law, the most well-known writings on this theme being: (1) *Iḥyā' ʿUlūm al-Dīn* by Abū Ḥāmid al-Ghazālī; (2) *Ḥujjah Allāh al-Bālighah* by Walī Allāh al-Dahlawī (d. 1176 AH/1762 AC); (3) pp. 134–230 of the book, *Naẓariyyah al-Maqāṣid ʿInd al-Imām Muḥammad al-Ṭāhir ibn ʿĀshur* by Ismail al-Hasani (contemporary); and (4) from among the books of the Shiite

Jaʿfarites, *ʿIlal al-Sharāʾiʿ* by Shaykh Ṣadūq ibn Bābawayh al-Qummī (d. 381 AH/991 AC).

(b) Al-Ghazālī draws a clear distinction between analogical reasoning (*al-qiyās*) and the process of being guided by unrestricted interests which are based on the achievement of an intent which is known to be based on the Qur'an, the Sunnah and the consensus of the Muslim community. Moreover, the identification of a given intent of the Law is based not on a single piece of evidence but, rather, on numerous and varied pieces of evidence from the Qur'an, the Sunnah, circumstantial or factual evidence, and varied indications. Al-Ghazālī concludes that there is no basis for disagreement over whether such interests are to be heeded; on the contrary, he states, they should be declared definitively to have an authoritative claim over us (which may be the origin of the idea put forward by al-Shāṭibī three centuries later that the fundamentals of jurisprudence are definitive in nature).[116]

[*Subtheme* 6]: *Human Intents* (*Maqāṣid al-Mukallafīn*)

Al-Ghazālī wrote,

> As for the term 'interest' (*al-maṣlaḥah*), it originally referred to the achievement of benefit and the prevention of harm. However, this is not what we mean by the term. For although the achievement of benefit and the prevention of harm are human intents whose fulfillment is necessary for human well-being and integrity, what we mean by the term 'interest' is the safeguarding of the intent of the Law. The intent of the Law with respect to human beings may be summed up in the following five: the preservation of their religion....[117]

This idea may have helped lead to al-Shāṭibī's interest in human intents. However, whereas al-Ghazālī devoted a mere three lines to the subject, al-Shāṭibī expatiated on the topic for a full ninety pages, all of which revolve around the idea that what is required of those accountable before the Law is to bring their own intents into conformity with those of the Lawgiver, including a discussion of matters relating to intention, legal artifices, etc.[118]

[THEME 3]

From the Five Universals to the Four Realms[119]

What follows is an extension and application of Theme 1 of this chapter, where we discussed the matter of whether the essential interests or *maqāṣid* ought to be limited to five, or expanded to include others as well.

In what follows, we will present an expanded enumeration of the essential *maqāṣid*. This expansion brings the number of essential *maqāṣid* from a mere five to a total of twenty-four, which are divided among four realms. Each of the four subthemes below will be devoted to one of these realms, which are: (1) the realm of the individual, (2) the realm of the family, (3) the realm of the Ummah, and (4) the realm of wider humanity.

These discussions will be preceded by an explanation of the method I have adopted in treating the subject at hand, as well as a clarification of the terms *nasab* (family lineage) and *nasl* (progeny), and related issues.

§*First:* What I have done in the following pages is to propose my own conceptualization of the fundamentals around which the intents of the Law (*maqāṣid al-sharīᶜah*) revolve by distributing them over four realms of human existence. I have further divided my discussion of each *maqṣid* into three sections. In the first section, I explain the concept of the *maqṣid* under discussion. In the second section, I present evidence in its support in the form of texts from the Qur'an and the Sunnah, and in the form of an inductive reading of subsidiary legal rulings which have been issued toward the achievement of said intent, or *maqṣid*. In these two sections, I have striven for the brevity appropriate to the context, leaving it to others to provide whatever expansion, detail and explanation might be called for. As for the third section, it is devoted to an exposition of the ranks of essentials, exigencies and enhancements as they pertain to the means by which the *maqṣid* of relevance may be achieved. In this section in particular, I offer only those observations which I have at the present time, postponing the detailing of these ranks to another occasion based on the considerations which I clarified in Chapter One, Theme 4.

It bears noting here that some applications are relative in nature in the sense that they might be valid at one time and not at another, in one country but not another, or for some people but not others, a point which I likewise clarify in Chapter One, Theme 4. It will be noted in addition that I deal with the question of the arrangement of the *maqāṣid* in Chapter One, Theme 3; consequently, the arrangement followed here may be considered to be a temporary one.

§*Second: Nasl, nasab* and related terms:

(a) The terms employed to refer to one of the universals of the Law have differed from one scholar to another and evolved over time: from *al-biḍᶜ*, to *al-nasl*, to *al-nasab* and *al-ᶜirḍ*.

1. In his book *Shifā' al-Ghalīl*, al-Ghazālī refers to it as *al-biḍᶜ*, after which he settles in *al-Mustaṣfā* on the use of the term *al-nasl*.

2. In his book, *al-Maḥṣūl*, al-Rāzī uses the term *al nasab* and its plural, *al-ansāb*, though he also uses the term *al-nasl* in some places as well.

3. Al-Āmidī (d. 631 AH/1233 AC) later returns to the use of al-Ghazālī's term, *al-nasl*.

4. Al-Bayḍāwī and al-Isnawī both follow al-Rāzī in the use of the term *al-nasab*.

5. As for al-Shāṭibī, he uses the term *al-nasl*, with passing and independent references to the term *al-ᶜirḍ*.[120] In addition, he considers *al-nasl* to be a primary intent, while viewing *al-nasab* and *al-ᶜirḍ* as subsidiary intents in service and support of *al-nasl*.

6. al-Qarrāfī added *al-aᶜrāḍ* (plural of *ᶜirḍ*).[121] Al-Qarrāfī was then followed in this addition by al-Ṭūfī (d. 716 AH/1316 AC), al-Subkī and al-Shawkānī, who thus came to adopt six, rather than five, as the total number of the essential *maqāṣid*. This addition brings us beyond the question regarding the degree to which the terms *al-biḍᶜ*, *al-nasl* and *al-nasab* are synonymous to the question of what distinguishes these terms from one another.

7. After a detailed treatment of this topic, Shaykh Ibn Ashur[122] concludes that the preservation of *al-nasl* should be classed among the essentials,

whereas the preservation of *al-nasab*[123] and *al-ʿirḍ* should be classed among the exigencies.

8. Shaykh Abd al-Wahhab Khallaf considers the preservation of *al-nasl* to be part of the preservation of human life.

9. As for Ahmad al-Raysuni,[124] he holds that the term *al-ʿirḍ* lacks precision, and that together with the term *al-nasab*, it should be viewed as subordinate to, and in the service of, the preservation of *al-nasl.*

(b) In our presentation of the *maqāṣid* pertaining to the four realms of human life, we use one or more of these terms, each in keeping with what we believe will best serve to resolve this difficulty:

1. In the realm of the individual, we use the term *al-ʿirḍ* (honor); however, we use it in a sense which goes beyond the merely sexual.

2. In the realm of the family, we use the terms *al-nasl* (progeny) and *al-nasab* (family lineage) as two distinct intents.

[*Subtheme* 1]*: The Maqāṣid as They Pertain to the Individual*

Here we find the five universals which *uṣūl* scholars have enumerated, with differences relating to three points: (1) the definition of the content of 'religion', with consequent differences among scholars with respect to where they rank religion in relation to the other universals, (2) the choice of the word 'honor' (*ʿirḍ*) for the fourth universal [rather than either 'progeny' (*nasl*) or 'family lineage' (*nasab*)], and (3) revisions relating to the secondary *maqāṣid* for each of the five universals. All of these points will become clear through a more detailed presentation of the topic.

The First Intent: Preservation of Human Life

(a) The term 'preservation of human life' refers to preventing life from being destroyed entirely in the form of death, as well as to the protection of certain parts of the body from harm or damage due to the fact that damage to them would lead to the near inability to benefit from the life one has, and whose accidental destruction [by someone else] would entail the obligation to pay blood money [as though he had committed manslaughter].[125] Hence, this intent is equivalent to what is referred to in the law as the right to life, or the sanctity of the body.

(b) The preservation of human life is achieved through:

1. The provision of security in order to prevent attacks on people's lives, prohibitions against murder, assault, and suicide, enforcement of the law of retribution against those who commit deliberate aggression against others, and requiring that anyone who commits unintentional assault pay blood money as a means of deterring him and others from committing such a crime in the future.

2. Provision of what the body needs by way of food and drink (while allowing those in dire need to avail themselves of the allowances provided for in the Law), clothing and shelter; protection against infectious diseases and mortal dangers such as fire, drowning, poisoning, car accidents, machines, electricity and various sorts of radiation, as well as the provision of treatment for those afflicted by illness or accidents. All of these are means without which the preservation of life is not possible, as a result of which they take on the status of essential *maqāṣid.*

(c) Among the things that complete the fulfillment of this intent – i.e., that of preserving human life – are personal freedom and dignity, in recognition of the honor which God has bestowed specially upon human beings in distinction from the animals.[126] The fact is that both animals and humans need food and drink in order to survive, however humans also have psychological and spiritual needs. Hence, the preservation of human life is not possible apart from the preservation of all these aspects together, which thereby take on the status of essentials. In keeping with this principle, al-Shāṭibī considers the preservation of honor to be part of the preservation of human life.[127] And rather than viewing freedom and dignity as complements to the essential intent [of preserving human life], freedom can be said to belong to the level of exigencies with respect to the preservation of human life, and dignity to the level of enhancements.[128]

The Second Intent: Consideration for the Mind[129]

(a) It will be observed that the mind is an activity rather than a member of the body.[130] The member of the body relating to the mind is the brain, along with the senses which supply it with information (the organs of perception) including hearing, sight, taste, smell and touch, as well as the nervous system which performs the function of maintaining communication between these organs and the brain. The intent of giving consideration to the mind, as we see it, is composed of three main elements, namely: (1) the development of the mind, (2) the preservation of the mind, and (3) the utilization of the mind. Hence, although scholars have traditionally referred to this intent as the preservation of the mind, or human reason, we prefer to call it consideration for the mind in order to ensure that it encompasses all of these elements at once.

(b) To develop the mind means to ensure that it is in the best possible condition, whether with respect to its capacity for scientific thought, training the rational faculty, or nourishing the mind with knowledge, skills and anything else which will render it more capable of performing its functions.[131] As for the means of developing the mind, they are found in the following areas:[132] (1) producing a scientific mindset, (2) demonstrating concern for the academic curriculum, and (3) instruction at its various stages.

(c) The second element, that is, the preservation of the mind, means to safeguard the well-being of the senses, the nervous system and the brain and to maintain the mind's ability to function properly. As for the means of preserving the mind, they will be found in the following areas:[133]

1. Avoiding anything which would do damage to the mind's systems (that is, biological breakdown due to taking in intoxicants or drugs), and treating whatever sort of imbalance or malfunction they happen to suffer, such as psychological, nervous or mental disorder.

2. Eschewing behaviors that would impede the mind's functions or create mental confusion (psychological breakdown), such as surrendering unthinkingly to one's whims and desires, groundless speculation, blind imitation of one's forebears, arrogance, superstitions and false doctrines, argumentativeness, obstinacy, self-importance and hypocrisy.

3. Avoiding media and cultural outlets which engage in brainwashing operations, attempts to restrict people's thinking, and the dissemination of corrupt ways of thinking based on the sacralization of power, the justification of error, and unthinking bigotry.

(d) The third element is the utilization of the mind, that is, its activation and use. The chief means of activating the mind are those activities which might be termed 'intellectual acts of worship,'[134] which can be performed either individually or collectively, and which lead unbelievers to faith and strengthen the faith of those who already believe. Some of them can be engaged in by both scholars and lay people, such as reflection, contemplation, meditation and consideration, while others are primarily the province of the elite who have attained the rank of 'those endowed with insight', such as devotion to the acquisition of knowledge and constant remembrance of God and truth.[135]

The Third Intent: The Preservation of Personal Piety

(a) The concern here is with the preservation of personal piety and not the preservation of the religion itself.[136] In light of this distinction, it makes most sense to assign the preservation of personal piety lower priority than to the preservation of human life and the mind. After all, it is necessary first to preserve human life, which is the basis for all human action, then the mind, which is the basis for our being held accountable before God's law, and only then personal piety [which is only possible given the soundness of the first two]. I will allow this degree of detail to suffice here, since the arrangement of the *maqāṣid* was dealt with earlier in Chapter One, Theme 2.[137]

(b) As for the ways in which personal piety is preserved, they include:

1. Establishing and strengthening sound doctrine and avoiding anything which would undermine it.[138] The establishment of sound doctrine takes place through investigation, contemplation and consideration, and through a comprehension of the basic elements of doctrine from the Qur'an and the authentic Sunnah. It also takes place through the shunning of the major sins relating to doctrine, such as *shirk*, or association of partners with God, hypocrisy, showing off, unfounded religious innovations, etc.

2. Performance of the obligatory rites of worship.[139]

3. Allowing one's character to be shaped by the fundamental morals of Islam, including truthfulness, sincerity, integrity, and a commitment to righteous action.[140]

4. Performance of obligatory acts of obedience.

(c) There is also the level of exigencies, which include the elimination of hardship and adherence to emphatically enjoined practices in emulation of the prophetic Sunnah, and the level of enhancements, which includes voluntary acts of worship, charity, and self-purification.

The Fourth Intent: Preservation of Honor

(a) "Honor is that aspect of a person [on the basis of] which he seeks to protect his life and [to prevent his] noble descent or reputation from being disparaged or defamed. This applies equally whether the degradation or defamation are directed against the person himself, one of his forebears or someone for whom he is responsible; whether it is directed against his praiseworthy and blameworthy traits, or against the noble descent and good repute in which he takes pride. Moreover, the focal point of one's honor might be one's parents, grandparents, other ancestors, or one's own exemplary character."[141] Defined in this way, honor is not limited simply to the sexual aspect of one's being; rather, it includes anything related to human dignity (having been previously classed among the complements to preservation of human life, although the present classification is more fitting), reputation, and the sanctity of one's private life.[142]

(b) Protecting honor from attack means to prevent people from causing someone harm by the easiest of means, that is, through words. There are explicit texts [in the Qur'an and the Sunnah] prohibiting attacks on others' honor by means of false accusations, slander, etc. Moreover, a serious penalty is prescribed in Islamic law against those who do assault another's honor by accusing him or her falsely of sexual misconduct (*al-qadhf*), while discretionary punishments are prescribed for slander of other types.

(c) Al-Qarrāfī, al-Ṭūfī, al-Subkī and al-Shawkānī (d. 1250 AH/1834 AC) all class the preservation of honor among the essentials alongside the preservation of progeny (or family lineage in some views).[143] However, given his insistence that there is no necessary link between something's being classed among the essentials and there being a prescribed punishment for its violation, Shaykh Ibn Ashur[144] classes the preservation of honor among the exigencies despite the prescribed punishment in Islamic law for assaulting someone's honor through the crime of *al-qadhf*. I agree with Shaykh Ibn Ashur in his classification of the preservation of honor among the exigencies [rather than among the essentials] on the level of the individual[145] as it relates to the sexual dimension; as for the violation of other aspects of human dignity, I consider them to belong on the level of enhancements.

The Fifth Intent: The Preservation of Material Wealth

(a) The term 'material wealth' is being employed in this context to refer to the wealth of the individual; as for that of the family and the Ummah, the matter of its preservation will be discussed in turn. The Islamic perspective on wealth arises from the conviction that all wealth belongs to God and that human beings are God's deputies on earth, as it were, and are therefore responsible to God for how they put wealth to use.[146] In their capacity as God's deputies, human beings are likewise called upon to populate and develop the earth. What follows from the first premise [i.e., that all wealth belongs to God] is that ownership, rather than being an absolute right, has a social function, while the second premise [i.e., concerning humans' role as God's deputies on earth] leads to the conclusion that work is a duty not only in order to earn one's living but, in addition, in order to populate and develop the earth. Moreover, each of these two realms is governed by certain criteria.[147]

(b) Islam has instituted legal rulings for the purpose of providing material wealth; such rulings pertain to work, contracts which transfer ownership, inheritance, the acquisition of permissible goods, reviving uncultivated land, etc., as well as to the criteria that govern permissible material gain, the various forms of monetary expenditure, giving God His due, avoiding excessive accumulation of wealth, failure to give others their due and/or taking what is others' without right, harming others, wastefulness, conceit, and allowing the quest for wealth to distract one from the remembrance of God and gratitude to Him. In addition, there are legal rulings whose intent is the preservation of material wealth; such rulings pertain to moderation in one's spending, the avoidance of irresponsibility, extravagance and wastefulness, as well as the protection of property rights such as the legally prescribed punishment for theft and discretionary punishments for violating the other rulings listed here.

[*Subtheme 2*]*: The Maqāṣid as They Pertain to the Family*

The family is the nucleus of society and has been among the most important links in human organization throughout history. Indeed, it is unequaled in importance by any other modern social unit, including political parties, unions, societies and the like.

Islamic law has laid down numerous detailed rulings for the purpose of managing familial affairs, and in his book, *Iḥyā' ᶜUlūm al-Dīn*, al-Ghazālī discusses the intents (*maqāṣid*) of marriage in general. Ibn Ashur, by contrast, concerns himself with the intents of Islamic law in all its divisions, in the context of which he explicates two differences which distinguish the rulings relating to marriage in Islam from the situation which prevailed in pre-Islamic times. The first of these differences is the contrast between the way in which [Islamic] marriage is contracted and the ways in which a man married a woman [in pre-Islamic times], while the second is that of marriage being viewed as a permanent arrangement rather than as a temporary one. In regard to the contrast referred to above, Ibn Ashur points to the practice of the woman's legal guardian giving her in marriage, as well as to the twin conditions of a public declaration of the marriage bond and the payment of a dowry. These examples should suffice to illustrate the way in which the marriage bond is consolidated. He discusses the ways in which the bonds of common family lineage, blood relations, and relationships by marriage are secured and solidified, followed by ways of dissolving these three types of bonds.

What Ibn Ashur has done is, in essence, to clarify the *maqāṣid* of subsidiary, particular rulings within the framework of family relations – to which he refers as 'the three bonds' (*al-awāṣir al-thalāthah*) – rather than to explicate the general *maqāṣid* of Islamic law. And in fact, this makes sense given the context in which his analysis is conducted, namely, the presentation of the *maqāṣid* in one particular division of the Law.

Those who have written on the subject of *maqāṣid al-sharīᶜah* have tended to view the preservation of progeny (or the species) as the primary intent of marriage, though it may also have other, secondary, intents.[148] As for my own treatment of this subject, it differs from the traditional approach, since it examines family-related rulings in the context of viewing the family as one of the spheres for which we are searching for general *maqāṣid al-sharīᶜah*. As will become clearer below, it is this which explains the disparity in points of view.[149]

The First Intent: Ordering Relations Between the Sexes

(a) Neither Islamic law, other divinely revealed laws, nor positive laws – notwithstanding the libertine ideas which have infiltrated them at times – have been content to leave relations between the sexes to natural impulses alone as is the case with dumb beasts and animals. Rather, such laws have been keen to confine relations between the sexes within a single, organized framework, namely, that of marriage, and have established detailed rulings relating thereto, elucidating the rights and responsibilities of all parties to this relationship.

(b) In order to achieve the intent of regulating and confining relations between the sexes to the framework of marriage, a number of legal rulings have been instituted, including those which encourage marriage, sanction polygamy and divorce (with their associated conditions), enjoin the avoidance of relations outside marriage, whether in the form of adultery or sexual perversion, close off the paths to temptation by means of chastity and the wearing of *ḥijāb*, prohibit a man and a woman to be alone together,[150] etc.

(c) If marriage is classed among the essentials, and if closing off the paths to temptation is classed among its complements, then polygamy and divorce (with their associated conditions) will be classed among the exigencies,[151] their purpose being to alleviate the hardship that may exist in the situations for the sake of which they were sanctioned.

The Second Intent: Preservation of Progeny (or the species)

(a) If complete relations between the sexes lead to procreation, thereby helping to fulfill the intent of preserving progeny, then Islamic law affirms this intent by declaring the legitimate form of such relations to be one that exists between two individuals of opposite genders, since this alone will lead to procreation. As for deviant relations – even if they provide a kind of sexual pleasure – they do not lead to procreation, which reflects God's ways with all His creatures, be they humans, animals or plants.

(b) Hence, in order to achieve this intent:

1. Islamic law prohibits both homosexual and lesbian relationships.

2. It seeks to encourage marriage, prohibits the burying alive of female infants and abortion, and treats procreation as one of the requirements of the marriage contract; hence, it is not permissible for the man to engage in *coitus interruptus* without his wife's consent.

3. Ibn Ashur notes that "the males in the Ummah must be protected from emasculation, for example, and not refrain from relationships with women by remaining single, etc. Similarly, females must be protected from undergoing hysterectomies since they involve the removal of the organ by means of which they give birth, and from the spread of the phenomenon of preventing pregnancy at the time of conception."[152]

(c) Although procreation is classed among the essentials overall for the preservation of the species, the achievement of this intent in individual cases may still nevertheless be classed among the exigencies. After all, some husbands and wives may not be distressed to fall within the category of those referred to in the Qur'an when it states that God, "causes to be barren whomever He wills..." (42:50). And for those who do find this to be a source of hardship, Islamic law provides the option of divorce and remarriage or polygamy in order to meet this need.

The Third Intent: Achieving Harmony, Affection and Compassion

(a) Lest the relation between the sexes be confined to a mere physical connection, Islamic law alerts us to the fact that among the *maqāṣid* of this relationship is for each of the partners to find repose in the other, and for there to be affection and compassion between them.

(b) In order to achieve this intent, Islamic law has issued rulings concerning living together as a couple in kindness and harmony, rules of etiquette governing sexual intercourse, as well as other rulings which provide the possibility of a family atmosphere filled with warmth, tenderness and refined human sentiment.

(c) Some of the rulings referred to here represent the bare essentials, such as a sense of harmony or repose, as the term *sakan* is defined in *al-Qāmūs al-Muḥīṭ*, while others, such as those having to do with an atmosphere of affection (*al-mawaddah*),[153] fall into the class of exigencies (after all, are all marriages based on love?), or, as in the case of compassion (*al-raḥmah*), in the category of enhancements.[154]

The Fourth Intent: The Preservation of Family Lineage

(a) Preserving the ability to trace people's family lineage is an intent of Islamic law separate from and independent of the intent to preserve progeny. *Uṣūl* scholars have sometimes chosen to use only one of these two terms, and at others times they have combined them in the manner discussed in the prefatory discussion of this issue. However, our approach of examining the *maqāṣid* within the framework of the four realms of the individual, the family, the Ummah and wider humanity leads naturally to the decision to list each of these intents separately among the *maqāṣid al-sharīʿah* pertaining to the realm of the family.

(b) It is for the sake of achieving the intent of maintaining people's family lineage that Islamic law prohibits both adultery and adoption; it is likewise the basis for legal rulings pertaining to the *ʿiddah*, or the waiting period imposed on a married or divorced woman before being allowed to remarry, concealing the fact that one is pregnant, confirmation and disavowal of family lineage, as well as other rulings enumerated by Ibn Ashur.[155] There is no need to repeat Ibn Ashur's listing here; rather, it will suffice to quote the following statement of his:

> There is no doubt in my mind that preservation of family lineage through the truthful attribution of offspring to their origins will serve to lead people's offspring to conduct themselves with kindness and gratitude toward their parents and forebears, just as it will lead parents to treat their offspring with compassion and tenderness in response to an innate disposition [to care for one's own flesh and blood] and not based on some illusion. Hence, Islamic law's concern to preserve family lineage and to eliminate uncertainty in this regard is based on the awareness of a highly significant spiritual and psychological phenomenon which belongs among the mysteries of the divine act of creation. In addition, we have the outward manifestations of this concern, such as recognition of the order of the family and the prevention of disputes which may arise, either from the jealousies to which human beings are prone, or from doubts that may assail parents or children concerning their blood ties to one another.

It has become common in permissive contemporary societies for both parents and children to doubt whether the children actually belong to the parents, as a result of which relations between them grow tepid while the family as a whole is weakened and fragmented. May God protect us from such a fate.

(c) Traditionally, *uṣūl* scholars who viewed the preservation of family lineage as belonging to the universals of Islamic law classed it among the essentials. However, in his detailed discussion of this topic, Shaykh Ibn Ashur concludes that it should be classed among the exigencies despite his appreciation of the opposing point of view. He states:

> If what is meant by the preservation of human lineage is the maintenance of the ability to ascribe offspring to their parents – for the sake of which regulations concerning marriage have been instituted and adultery has been prohibited with a legally prescribed punishment for those who engage therein – someone might say: It is not clear that it should be classed among the essentials, since the Ummah has no need to know that Zayd is ʿAmr's son, for example. Rather, all it needs is for the members of the species to exist and for their affairs to be in order.
>
> However, in this case great harm is being done, since uncertainty concerning whether offspring can be attributed to their parents robs the latter of their natural predisposition to defend and care for their offspring in such a way as to ensure their survival and complete well-being by providing them with the proper upbringing and financial support until such time as they are old enough to do without such care. At the same time, and even though children may be deprived of a sense of devotion, connection and the desire to be of assistance and support in the parents' old age, such harm still falls short of the level of outright necessity, since mothers' care for children is sufficient to achieve the desired intent of preserving progeny. Hence, preservation of family lineage in this sense, in view of what occurs when it is undermined, should be classified among the exigencies.
>
> However, given the numerous and serious consequences of a failure to preserve family lineage in these respects, a failure which disturbs the order of the Ummah and erodes the foundations of the family, Muslim scholars have viewed the preservation of family lineage as belonging to the category of essentials given the stiff penalty imposed by Islamic law for adultery, as well as

> the harsh words reserved by some scholars for the practices of secret marriage, marriage without the participation of the woman's legal guardian, and marriage without witnesses....
>
> [In sum, we hold that] the preservation of family lineage in the sense of the ability to attribute children to their parents is to be considered among the exigencies for both the children and parents: for the children, given what this ensures for them by way of the meeting of their needs and a beneficial, wholesome upbringing, and for the parents, given what this ensures for them by way of the pride which the tribe can take in its members and the preservation of the family.[156]

Within the framework of the discussion of universals in general, Ibn Ashur's view is sound. However, within the framework which we have proposed – namely, the distribution of the *maqāṣid* among the four realms of the individual, the family, the Ummah, and wider humanity – and specifically, when viewed in light of the intents of the family, we hold that the preservation of family lineage should be classed among the essentials rather than among the exigencies.[157]

The Fifth Intent: Preservation of Personal Piety Within the Family

(a) It was the custom of the prophets to invite those closest to them – that is, their wives and their children – [to embrace faith in God], and to ask God to guide them aright. We see this clearly in the cases of Abraham and Jacob. Some of the prophets were unsuccessful in this endeavor, among them Noah and Lot. However, their efforts in and of themselves bear witness to the importance of personal piety in the family, striving to pass down such piety from one generation to the next, and the responsibility born by the head of the family to provide this kind of nurture. As for the success or failure of his efforts, this depends on the responses of his wife and children, who are personally responsible for their own choices.

(b) Islamic legal rulings impose this responsibility on the head of the family from its very inception by requiring him to choose a mate with religious sensibilities and to instruct his wife and children in matters of doctrine, worship and morals. As such, a generous reward is promised to those who fulfill this obligation: "And bid thy people [family] to pray, and persevere therein" (20:132).

(c) Given the results to which the loss of personal piety in the family can lead by way of corruption, fragmentation and poor upbringings for the generations that will bear responsibility for the future, we hold that the preservation of personal piety in the family should be classed among the essentials.

The Sixth Intent: Ordering the Institutional Aspect of the Family

(a) What we mean here by the institutional aspect of the family is the consideration of the family as an institution which is viewed as permanent rather than temporary, and relations among whose members are ordered by rights and responsibilities. The family is led by its head, who is assigned guardianship (*qiwāmah*)[158] and who consults with his wife concerning the family's affairs. In this context, the spouses follow an approach laid out by Islamic law for arbitration in the event of a dispute between them and for severing the marital bond if the dispute becomes insoluble. This organization is not restricted to the nuclear family, consisting only of the parents and their children, but applies equally to what has come to be termed the extended family which includes relatives and in-laws. Hence, Islamic law has established arrangements for relations among all these various parties.

(b) Islamic law contains detailed rulings pertaining to emotional and social relationships, including the husband's rights over his wife, the wife's rights over her husband, parents' rights over their children and children's rights over their parents, as well as relatives' rights over one another. Such rulings also cover areas such as prohibitions,[159] both permanent and temporary, rulings pertaining to the waiting period for a divorced woman or widow before she may remarry, guardianship over oneself, the allowance in accordance with which one has the right to be fed at one's relative's house even if one arrives without an invitation or asking for permission, as well as many others.

The Seventh Intent: Ordering the Financial Aspect of the Family

Not limiting itself to ordering the family's social and emotional affairs, Islamic law goes beyond these to encompass the most explicit, detailed financial aspects as well, a feature by virtue of which Islamic law surpasses all other systems, both those which preceded it and those which have emerged since the advent of Islam. Hence, we have, for example, the dowry which the groom commits himself to provide for the bride and the amount of which is written into the marriage contract, followed by expenses of various types which are to be provided for wives, children, divorced wives, nannies, wet nurses, and relatives; the manner in which an inheritance is to be distributed, wills made out on behalf of next-of-kin, family endowments, the requirement that the male relatives of someone who has committed involuntary manslaughter pay the blood money on his or her behalf, rulings pertaining to guardianship over money, etc.

[*Subtheme* 3]: *The Maqāṣid as They Pertain to the Ummah*

Shaykh Ibn Ashur is the first scholar to have stated expressly that the five universals [that is, the five essential *maqāṣid* of Islamic law] allow for the preservation of the interests of the Ummah alongside the interests of its individual members. Moreover, not content to illustrate this fact with reference to the essentials, Ibn Ashur makes it clear as it relates to the exigencies and enhancements as well.[160]

In keeping with our method of examining the *maqāṣid* in the realm of the Ummah independently of the manner in which they apply to other realms – while acknowledging the interconnections and commonalities among these various areas – we will discuss them as follows:

The First Intent: Institutional Organization of the Ummah

(a) The institutional organization of the Ummah consists in viewing the Ummah as a distinctive entity with its own particular characteristics, components and organizations.[161] Islamic law has developed this perspective in its objective aspects yet without overemphasizing formalistic and procedural features. This feature of Islamic law has allowed the concept of the Ummah to survive over the ages despite the political changes which have occurred in the structure of the state, including loss of autonomy and subjection to foreign powers during certain periods and, during others, the fragmentation of the Ummah into states and mini-states.

It also bears noting that Islamic law has not adopted the notion of the legal personality (*shakhṣiyyah maʿnawiyyah*) in an absolute way. Rather, it has contented itself with the notion of autonomous financial responsibility in particular cases, such as the public treasury (*bayt al-māl*), the mosque, and the religious endowment, or *waqf*. It is a known fact, of course, that the idea of the legal personality or body corporate – apart from the fact that it is a juristic fiction – is responsible for the distention of the concept of the modern state, which has become like a ferocious monster that rides roughshod over not only the rights of individuals, but the institutions of civil society as well.

(b) Islamic law focuses on specific aspects, such as:

1. Support for the unity of the Ummah as embodied in unity of doctrine, law and language. The unity of the Ummah, however, does not preclude pluralism within the framework of this unity. Unity of doctrine, for example, does not preclude the existence of varied factions representing diverse points of view on questions of doctrine. Similarly, unity of law does not preclude the existence of multiple juristic schools or the existence of various political parties with contrasting programs within the framework of the same general Islamic principles. Nor does unity of language rule out the possibility of the use of a variety of languages and/or dialects, including the use of national and local languages alongside the language of the Holy Qur'an. The modern application of these types of pluralism may take the form of parties, societies and other organizations which fall under the general heading of civil society institutions. The acceptance of pluralism requires the establishment of relevant criteria lest such pluralistic expressions deviate from the agreed-upon norm, the features of which need to be defined in the form of a 'cultural project' around which the entire Ummah – including all of its factions, schools and parties – can rally.

2. Support for the concept of vicegerency (*khilāfah*)[162] as it pertains specifically to the Islamic Ummah – though within the framework of the broader vicegerency which applies to all human beings. Such vicegerency is conditional on the Ummah's fulfillment of the obligations entailed by this role, such as enjoining the doing of what is right and prohibiting the doing of what is wrong and faith in God, all of which result in the Ummah's being characterized as a community of righteousness and blessing and the fulfillment of God's promise to grant them power on earth and firmly establish their religion[163] just as He did for nations that came before them: "If He so wills, He may put an end to you and thereafter cause whom He wills to succeed you – even as He has brought you into being out of other people's seed" (6:133); "and thereupon We made you their successors on earth, so

that We might behold how you act" (10:14); "my Sustainer may cause another people to take your place" (11:57); and, "Moses replied: 'It may well be that your Sustainer will destroy your foe and make you inherit the earth: and thereupon He will behold how you act'" (7:129).

3. A byproduct of this support is the principle of Islamic law's precedence over all other systems, laws, rulers and ruled, situations and customs such that it abrogates anything that conflicts with it.

4. The necessity of collective organization, from the simplest of levels ([as expressed in the words of the Prophet], "If there are three of you, appoint one of the three of you to be your leader"), to the appointment of an imam to lead others in communal prayer (for which the reward is more than twenty times greater than that for individual prayer), to the caliphate, which is considered to be a collective obligation such that if the Ummah does not institute it, it is guilty of an offense before God.

5. The recognition of consultation (*shūrā*) as one of the distinguishing marks of the Ummah and the foundation of its approach to managing its affairs; since the Islamic Ummah is described in the Holy Qur'an as those "whose rule [in all matters of common concern] is consultation among themselves" (42:38).

6. The recognition of enjoining the doing of what is right and prohibiting the doing of what is wrong as a collective obligation for the purpose of safeguarding the higher values which distinguish the Ummah from other nations.

The Second Intent: Maintenance of Security

(a) Security, which includes both internal and external security, is among the blessings which God bestowed upon Quraysh ("...and made them safe from danger..." [106:4]). Security is a primary component of the Ummah and one of the intents of Islamic law for its organization.

(b) 1. Maintenance of internal security is the intent of legal rulings which provide for the protection of human life, honor and material wealth and legally prescribed penalties for their violation, whether for the protection of individuals, as in the case of the law of retribution and the legally prescribed penalties for theft and false accusations of sexual misconduct, or for the protection of the community as a whole, as in the case of legally prescribed penalties for armed revolt and apostasy.

2. As for external security, its maintenance is ensured by the preparation of forces to deter others from contemplating aggression [against the Ummah], as well as by the sanctioning of jihad for the sake of defense in cases when aggression actually occurs. To this same end, self-sufficiency has been legally sanctioned in Islam as a collective obligation lest the Ummah be dependent on others, particularly for food supplies and weapons production. Islamic law also stipulates arrangements for establishing security in the event that some group within the Ummah commits aggression against another.[164] It goes without saying, of course, that the Ummah which adheres to the aforementioned principles and practices will be free among the nations and able to make its own decisions without being subject to any outside force or allowing any power to violate its sovereignty.

The Third Intent: The Establishment of Justice

There are numerous areas in which justice applies, including the individual's justice towards his Lord, himself, and his family (his wife and children), as well as justice in his relationships with others, and justice on the levels of the judiciary and government. What concerns us here is justice as it pertains to the Ummah as a whole, that is, on the level of the judiciary and government.[165]

The Qur'an considers justice to be a primary intent of the Law, declaring:

- "Indeed, [even aforetime] did We send forth Our apostles with all evidence of [this] truth; and through them We bestowed revelation from on high, and [thus gave you] a balance [wherewith to weigh right and wrong], so that men might behave with equity" (57:25).
- "Say, 'My sustainer has [but] enjoined the doing of what is right" (7:29).
- "Behold, God enjoins justice, and the doing of good, and generosity toward one's fellow men" (16:90).
- "Behold, God bids you to deliver all that you have been entrusted with unto those who are entitled thereto, and whenever you judge between people, to judge with justice" (4:58).

- "I am bidden to bring about equity in your mutual views" (42:15).

Similarly, the Qur'an lays special stress upon justice in those cases in which there is reason to believe that it may be overlooked:

- "O you who have attained to faith! Be ever steadfast in upholding equity, bearing witness to the truth for the sake of God, even though it be against your own selves or your parents and kinsfolk. Whether the person concerned be rich or poor, God's claim takes precedence over [the claims of] either of them. Do not, then, follow your own desires, lest you swerve from justice" (4:135).
- "...and when you voice an opinion, be just, even though it be [against] one near of kin" (6:152).
- "As for such [of the unbelievers] as do not fight against you on account of [your] faith, and neither drive you forth from your homelands, God does not forbid you to show them kindness and to behave towards them with full equity: for, verily, God loves those who act equitably" (60:8).
- "O you who have attained to faith! Be ever steadfast in your devotion to God, bearing witness to the truth in all equity; and never let hatred of anyone lead you into the sin of deviating from justice. Be just: this is closest to being God-conscious" (5:8).

Ibn Taymiyyah viewed justice as the foundation for a nation's survival, saying, "God establishes the just state even if it is unbelieving, and He does not establish the unjust state even if it is Muslim. The affairs of this world can be managed with justice and unbelief, but not with injustice and Islam."[166] Ibn al-Qayyim also stressed the importance of justice, saying:

> The Law is pure justice....Hence, anything which embodies injustice rather than justice...does not originate from the Law, even if it happens to have been interpolated therein by means of interpretation. Hence, Islamic law is God's justice among His servants....If the signs of justice are manifest...and if its dawn breaks in any manner whatsoever, then there is God's Law, God's religion...Rather, He has made clear by means of the paths He has laid down that His intention (*maqṣūduhu*) is for justice to be established, and for people to uphold equity.[167]

Al-Qaradawi divides justice into three basic categories, namely: (1) legal or judicial justice, (2) social justice, and (3) international justice.[168]

The Fourth Intent: Preservation of Religion and Morals

(a) Unlike secular systems, which admittedly have a limited conception of general morality based on commonly agreed upon ethical standards which are not to be violated, Islamic law does not acknowledge a separation between religion and morals and the order of society in the sense that morals and religion are to be viewed as something which concerns the individual alone and in which society has no say. Islamic law views the preservation of the religion of the Ummah as a whole – that is to say, the prevention of anything which might undermine the definitive principles of the religion (to borrow a phrase from Ibn Ashur) – as one of its primary intents. In this connection, Umarah points out that God has pledged Himself to preserve the religion, and that what is required of believers is to carry out the religion's teachings, and not merely to preserve its outward forms.[169]

(b) In order to achieve this communal intent, Islamic law has imposed the obligation of communal prayer, the Friday prayer, the communal prayers performed on *ᶜĪd al-Fiṭr* and *ᶜĪd al-Aḍḥā*, and the rites associated with the pilgrimage to Makkah, in order that all Muslims might sense the doctrinal and devotional bond that unites them. Islamic law declares the enjoining of the doing what is right and the forbidding of doing what is wrong to be collective obligations in order that there might continue to be defenders of society's fundamental values. To the same end, it declares the pursuit of knowledge pertinent to doctrine and worship to be an individual obligation given the fact that such knowledge is a means of better performing the rites of the religion. As for the pivotal importance of morals in Islamic law, it may be seen clearly in the words of the noble Messenger, "I have been sent to perfect noble traits of character," in Islamic legal rulings relating to personal or practical morals, in rulings pertaining to daily transactions in which we are exhorted to preserve morals and not to spread corruption and, lastly, in the penalties which are intended as deterrents against the commission of major sins.

(c) Writings by scholars who have concerned themselves with *maqāṣid* have tended to view noble morals as belonging on the level of enhancements. However, this classification cannot be accepted unconditionally; after all, there are some moral values which are necessary for the survival of the Ummah, such as truthfulness and integrity, whereas some others, such as certain practical rules of etiquette, might be classified as enhancements. Ibn Ashur declares,

> Interests classified on the level of enhancements are, as I see it, those things which serve to perfect the order of the Ummah with the result that it is able to live in safety and tranquility and enjoy the respect of other nations. Such enhancements likewise make it possible for the Islamic Ummah to be a nation which people have the desire to be a part of or, at the least, form close ties with. Praiseworthy habits have a role to play in this, be they universal customs such as basic dress styles, or things specific to particular nations such as certain types of innate dispositions and the practice of growing one's beard out. In short, they [enhancements in the realm of morals] are those in relation to which consideration is given to refined human sensibilities.[170]

The Fifth Intent: Cooperation, Solidarity and Shared Responsibility

(a) In addition to the interconnections among them, the values of cooperation, solidarity and shared responsibility have both a general and a particular aspect. In their general aspect, they encompass all areas of culture, society and the economy, and in their specific economic expressions, can exert a profound influence on the structure of the Ummah. However, such values cannot be imposed by force of law or coercion by higher powers. Rather, they derive from the wellsprings of faith as does human brotherhood ("All of you are descended from Adam...") and the brotherhood born of faith ("All believers are but brethren" [49:10]). [As the Prophet declared,] "One believer is related to another as one brick is to another in a mighty edifice: each one reinforces and upholds the other," and, "The believers in their mutual love, compassion and sympathy may be likened to a single body: if one of its members suffers, all its other members rally around it with wakefulness and fever."

(b) The texts and rulings of Islamic law serve to confirm and fulfill this intent: from the inclusive command to cooperate in furthering virtue and God-consciousness rather than evil and enmity,[171] to its practical manifestations such as the requirement to pay zakah and spend of one's substance in charitable ways in general, and the possibility of levying a tax on the wealthy whose proceeds go to help the poor; add to this various other expressions of charity and benevolence, such as provisions in Islamic law which allow someone to set aside up to one-third of his bequest for charitable purposes, as well as endowments set aside for charity and public interests, which have been instrumental in funding many services which fall under the heading of what has come to be termed civil society. Among the most significant expressions of solidarity among those who live in a single neighborhood or who practice a single profession or craft is the system of *qasāmah*,[172] or compurgation by oath, and the system which requires the male relatives of someone accused of manslaughter to pay the blood money on his behalf.

The Sixth Intent: Dissemination of Knowledge and Preservation of Reason in the Ummah

Ibn Ashur states that imbalance or malfunction in the minds of entire communities and in the Ummah as a whole is of graver concern than imbalance or malfunction in the mind or reason of the individual. Therefore, he concludes, the Ummah must undertake to prevent the spread of drunkenness among its members, as well as the spread of intoxicants and drugs such as marijuana, hashish, opium, morphine, cocaine, heroine and other substances whose use has become widespread.[173]

In my view, concern should not be limited to protecting the Ummah from such intoxicants; rather, it should go beyond this to protecting it from the influence of the mass media, which engages in collective brainwashing operations and besieges people's minds, giving them nothing but the news and the analyses they want and encouraging them to waste time on things which not only are devoid of benefit, but which actually bring harm. Such media train people's minds in corrupt ways of thinking based on the sacralization of power, the justification of error, and mindless bigotry. As a certain pharaoh declared of old, "I but want to make you see what I see myself; and I would never make you follow any path but that of rectitude!" (40:29).[174]

Nor does Islam's approach stop at the mere preservation of the mind. Rather, it calls emphatically for a program of scientific thinking which steers clear of superstitions and blind imitation, and for the development of people's minds by nurturing them with beneficial knowledge whether it pertains to this world or the next. The acquisition of some types of knowledge might be an individual obligation, while the acquisition of other types might be a collective obligation in order for the Ummah to achieve self-sufficiency in all areas of life and on the levels of essentials, exigencies and enhancements. Moreover, given this religious incentive, human potentials can be released into the proper channels; for while some people's intellectual capabilities are more limited, others' potentials make it possible for them to advance along the path of knowledge and creative interpretation in a variety of areas.

In order to achieve this intent, Islamic law:

1. Includes rulings which protect people's minds from biological deterioration, such as the prohibition against intoxicants and [mind-altering] drugs, as well as against spiritual or psychological damage resulting from exposure to the media.

2. Calls emphatically for [clear] thinking, prudence and reflection, and prohibits groundless imitation of predecessors and leaders; instead, Muslims are urged to demand evidence [for others' claims] and to reject superstitions.

3. Requires the pursuit of knowledge, erudition and enlightenment, urging Muslims to learn to read and write as a foundation for other skills and the acquisition of other types of knowledge. Moreover, in addition to making clear which of the various religious and secular sciences are to be classed as individual obligations and which are to be classed as collective obligations, Islamic law outlines rules of etiquette to be adhered to by both scholars and students.[175]

At all these stages, of course, some things are classed among the essentials, while others are classified as exigencies or enhancements.

The Seventh Intent: Populating and Developing the Earth and Preserving the Ummah's Wealth

This intent grows out of one of the *maqāṣid al-sharīʿah* for all of humanity, namely, the population and development of the earth. In this context, it is embodied in the population and development of that portion of Planet Earth that falls under the Ummah's sovereignty. As for the preservation of the Ummah's wealth, this intent arises from the notion that all wealth belongs to God and that human beings are God's deputies on earth, as a result of which ownership has a public function and is not an unqualified right. We find, for example, in God's exhortation: "And do not entrust to those who are weak of judgment the possessions which God has placed in your charge for [their] support..." (4:5) a reflection of the fact that although funds may belong to particular individuals (in this case, 'those who are weak of judgment'), such monies nevertheless belong to the Ummah as well.

These two intents intersect with what has come to be termed 'development.' The first area in which these intents are to be realized is that of the Ummah's cultural project to which we made reference in our discussion of the unity of the Ummah.[176]

Ibn Ashur speaks of the intent to preserve wealth as that of protecting the Ummah's material wealth from harm in the dual sense of: (1) physical damage, and (2) the full control of others over the Ummah's resources without any benefit for the Ummah.[177] This formulation, however, is more restrictive than the conception we are seeking to convey, which focuses on the principle of the possession of wealth in and of itself (and the outcomes to which it leads) as well as the extent to which society should intervene in economic activity (and the outcomes to which this leads).

In order to achieve the intent of development – with its twin aspects of: (1) populating and developing the earth, and (2) preservation of the Ummah's material wealth – a number of legal rulings have been instituted by Islamic law:

1. Based on the principle of the possession of wealth, we have Islam's legal rulings pertaining to the payment of zakah (God's right to material wealth). In addition to God's right as embodied in zakah (which is an obligatory right), there is the voluntary expenditure of one's excess wealth on behalf of others in various forms, including charitable contributions (*al-ṣadaqāt*) which are considered a temporary or immediate form of giving, and more permanent forms such as writing a will in which one sets aside part (up to one-third) of one's bequest for charitable uses, and institutional (charitable endowments).

We have explicit texts dealing with this theme, among them:

- "Believe in God and His Apostle, and spend on others out of that of which He has made you trustees. For those of you who have attained to faith and who spend freely [in God's cause] shall have a great reward" (57:7).

- "And do not entrust to those who are weak of judgment the possessions which God has placed in your charge for [their] support..." (4:5).
- "...and give them [their share] of the wealth of God which He has given you" (24:33).

2. Concerning the degree to which society should intervene in economic activity, the obligation to provide public facilities is not restricted to the ruler alone (as seen in the Prophetic hadith according to which "even if a mule were to stumble...").[178] Rather, Islamic civil society as embodied in the endowments system has underwritten a significant number of schools, research and translation centers ("houses of wisdom"), universities, observatories, hospitals of all sorts, hostels and travelers' inns, drinking water facilities, as well as other initiatives which fill the pages of endowments registers.

3. As for the inclusiveness of such services, access to them is not restricted to Muslims alone. On the contrary, they are available to all residents of the areas in which they are located (as seen in the hadith that includes the phrase, "we would have wronged him").[179] In fact, they exist not only to serve human beings, but animals as well (as evidenced by the Prophetic hadiths about kindness to cats and dogs), and plants and inanimate objects (as seen in the Islamic prohibition against the cutting down of trees and the destruction of dwellings during war time).

4. In addition we have the fact that this development is sustainable until the Day of Judgment (as evidenced by the Prophetic hadith according to which, if one of us has a palm seedling to plant, he should plant it even if the Day of Judgment is imminent).

Moreover, as was noted in connection with earlier intents, all of the aforementioned areas include some things which are classed as essentials, others which are classed as exigencies, and still others which belong among the enhancements (a noteworthy example of which can be seen in the Islamic architectural arts).

[*Subtheme* 4]: *The Maqāṣid as They Pertain to all of Humanity*

Some scholars choose to replace the more traditional term *dār al-kufr* ('the abode of unbelief') with the phrase *ummah al-daʿwah* ('the nation to be called'), while replacing the traditional *dār al-islām* ('the abode of Islam')[180] with the alternative *ummah al-ijābah* ('the nation that responds'). The term *ummah al-daʿwah* conveys the sense that the central characteristic of this nation – from the point of view of Islamic law – is that it is addressed by the call to embrace Islam.

In so saying, we must bear in mind the long-time dispute among scholars over whether non-Muslims are addressed by the subsidiary rulings of Islamic law or whether they are simply being called to faith in God. My own position on this is that universal legal rulings – as opposed to Islamic law's subsidiary rulings – are not limited to calling non-Muslims to faith in God. When the Qur'anic discourse employs the address, "O mankind!" (2:21 and elsewhere) or, "O man!" (82:6 and elsewhere), this is not limited to the call to faith, although this is its primary focus. Rather, such discourse is advocating universal principles, one's response to which does not depend on prior faith but, rather, on reason and logic. As we hope to show more clearly in what follows, people are being addressed on the basis of their innate, God-given understanding and perception, and are being called upon to embrace universal human interests which no one would dispute.

However, given the fact that such principles cannot be translated into particular, practical rulings which address all human beings as creatures accountable to the Lord of the Worlds, the burden of striving to apply them then falls upon believers. The implementation of such principles, therefore, represents the goal of Muslims' foreign policy in their dealings with other nations. Given the foregoing, *maqāṣid al-sharīʿah* as they apply to humanity as a whole may be identified as the following:

The First Intent: Mutual Understanding, Cooperation and Integration

"O men! Behold, We have created you all out of a male and a female, and have made you into nations and tribes, so that you might come to know one another. Verily, the noblest of you in the sight of God is the one who is most deeply conscious of Him. Behold, God is all-Knowing, all-Aware" (49:13). In these words addressed to all humankind, the Qur'an declares that despite the diversity of their peoples and tribes, people have a common origin ("We have created you all out of a male and a female"), and that the purpose behind this variety is that people should come to know one another. At the same time, it declares that in the sight of God, no distinction is to be accorded to any people or tribe based on any kind of innate superiority but that, rather, distinction and honor are to be based on a spiritual criterion which has nothing to do with ethnic origin, namely, consciousness of God.[181] These principles are affirmed by Prophetic hadiths ("All of you belong to Adam..." and "No Arab shall be deemed superior to a non-Arab [based on anything but consciousness of God]").

The intent of cooperation arises as a complement to the intent of mutual understanding. Similarly, the intent of integration serves to support the twin intents of mutual understanding and cooperation, since God's ways with His servants and the created universe are manifested not only in the variety among people, but in the uneven distribution of natural resources by virtue of which each people needs what other peoples have, and as a result of which we have exchanges of commodities and services in fulfillment of the intent of integration. Herein also lies the origin of [academic and professional] specialization and the distribution of labor, principles which form the basis of [modern] economic life and to which Muslim philosophers have been alluding for centuries.

Given the fact that this is a divinely established law of nature which can be perceived by the mind and sound intuition, the Qur'an contents itself with the simple mention of this intent without going into detail concerning the ways in which it is to be fulfilled. And in so doing, it provides the flexibility needed for relating to the international scene with its far-flung geographical expanses and historical depth. At the same time, however, it affirms an important standard which believers need to meet in order to be models of moral refinement and purity: "O you who have attained to faith! Be ever steadfast in your devotion to God, bearing witness to the truth in all equity; and never let hatred of anyone lead you into the sin of deviating from justice. Be just: this is closest to being God-conscious" (5:8). Thus, as if it assumes the necessity of dealings among those between whom some degree of hostility exists, the Qur'an enjoins justice and fairness between them.

The Second Intent: Realizing Human Vicegerency on Earth

- "Behold, I am about to establish upon earth one who shall inherit it (*khalīfah*)" (2:30).
- "Verily, We did offer the trust [of reason and volition] to the heavens, and the earth, and the mountains: but they refused to bear it because they

were afraid of it. Yet man took it up – for, verily, he has always been prone to be most wicked, most foolish" (33:72).

In these two verses,[182] the Qur'an proclaims that human beings have a status which is distinct from that of other creatures (that of being God's 'caliph' or vicegerent on earth), and that they have been assigned a trust which requires that they be given sufficient freedom of will to be able to pass this test with its attendant accounting, reward and/or chastisement.

This conceptualization of human beings' mission, responsibility and freedom may differ in certain details and aspects from one religion or earthly philosophy to another. Nevertheless, it remains the only conceptualization which is capable of explaining the reality of the universe, humanity and life. Such a conceptualization does not devalue human beings; on the contrary, it grants them an honor and a dignity which set them apart from other created beings. Moreover, consistent with this conceptualization is the affirmation of human beings' capacity to choose either a path of righteousness or a path of corruption. As the Qur'an declares, the human soul "is imbued with moral failings as well as with consciousness of God" (91:8); and, God "has shown him [man] the two highways [of good and evil]" (90:10). Similarly, it is consistent with the affirmation that human beings' innate understanding leads them to distinguish good from bad.

As we have mentioned, this conceptualization of human beings' place and purpose on earth is not the subject of unanimous agreement. Hence, "God has promised those of you who have attained to faith and do righteous deeds that, of a certainty, He will cause them to accede to power on earth" (24:55) given conditions which He has specified. This is the vicegerency particular to the Muslim community which we discussed above in the context of the *maqāṣid* of the Ummah.

This leads us to the concept of the vicegerency which is inclusive of all humanity and which Islam proposes as a source of common ground which – despite differing doctrines, races, and languages, and as an alternative and corrective to the notion of God's chosen people – can serve as a basis for fruitful cooperation between Muslims and all others. Were it not for the caprices and exploitative aspirations of the superpowers, it would not be difficult to imagine all governments and peoples being able to reach agreement on common goals which are achieved through international projects and enterprises, both governmental and non-governmental in nature. After all, as has been noted by numerous scholars, people's genuine interests are agreed upon by most laws.[183] Hence, the studies which have been done in the field of *maqāṣid al-sharīʿah* promise to be a rich source of guidance in drawing up the foreign policies of Islamic states, as well as those of Islamic organizations, both governmental and non-governmental.

Among the areas in which human cooperation (the first intent) can help to achieve human vicegerency (the second intent) is that of populating and developing the earth ("He brought you into being out of the earth, and made you thrive thereon" 11:61), whether in relation to environmental protection, fighting crime, agricultural, industrial and service-related development, or other areas, not to mention cooperative scientific research in the aforementioned realms.

Contrary to the materialist conception of human beings' relationship with the universe, the earth and the rest of the non-human realm are not enemies to be conquered. Rather, God has created everything for human beings' sake and has placed the heavens and the earth in subjection to them. Therefore, human beings simply need to understand the laws which govern the created realm and to populate and develop the earth for the good of all.

The Third Intent: Achieving World Peace Based on Justice

A good number of traditional juristic writings convey the sense that the fundamental relationship between Muslims and non-Muslims is one of enmity and warfare, a notion for which they cite a number of Qur'anic verses which are taken out of context. One such verse, to which they refer as 'the sword verse,'[184] they consider to have abrogated no fewer than 200 other verses in the Qur'an, including the one which reads, "There shall be no coercion in matters of faith" (2:256).

Given this perspective, the justification for waging war on non-Muslims is not aggression they have committed against Muslims, but their mere denial of Islam. However, the context of this verse makes clear that the justification for resorting to armed conflict is self-defense against aggression. As for mere unbelief, it is addressed in verses such as the following:

- "And so, [O Prophet,] exhort them; thy task is only to exhort: thou canst not compel them [to believe]" (88:21–22).

- "And [thus it is:] had thy Sustainer so willed, all those who live on earth would surely have attained to faith, all of them: dost thou, then, think that thou couldst compel people to believe?" (10:99).
- "There shall be no coercion in matters of faith" (2:256), and others.[185]

Legitimate defense against aggression is a right acknowledged by domestic penal laws, as well as by contemporary international law, which in the year 1928 prohibited resorting to war while sanctioning legitimate defense. Prior to that time, however, war had not been outlawed, as a result of which there had been no need to declare defense legitimate, since war had been considered legitimate for any reason. Moreover, a fact which is disregarded by many is that Islam was the first law to prohibit war and to establish criteria and regulations relating thereto.[186]

This brings us back to the principle that the fundamental relationship between Muslims and non-Muslims is one of peace: "But if they incline to peace, incline thou to it as well..." (8:61), and that resorting to war is only allowed in Islam when there is a need to repel aggression.[187] One means of preserving peace would be the creation of an international organization which would ensure collective security, organizing cooperation in a variety of areas arranging treaties among states and overseeing their implementation.

The peace sought is one which is based on justice; after all, peace and justice are inseparable. Moreover, the justice being spoken of here is not limited to Islamic society; on the contrary, it has been a fundamental intent in human relations throughout history:[188] "Indeed, [even aforetime] did We send forth Our apostles with all evidence of [this] truth; and through them We bestowed revelation from on high, and [thus gave you] a balance [wherewith to weigh right and wrong], so that men might behave with equity" (57:25). Indeed, the Prophet spoke in praise of 'the *Fuḍūl* Alliance'[189] in which he took part before he was called as a prophet, saying, "If I had been invited to take part in it as a Muslim, I would have done so." And in like manner, the Qur'an urges believers to adhere faithfully to covenants and contracts. In so doing, it confirms Islam's respect for international treaties, which are the primary source of law among sovereign states.

The Fourth Intent: International Protection for Human Rights

The liberation of human beings from enslavement to other human beings is a fundamental outcome of the doctrine of the oneness of God, a rejection of *shirk* in all its forms.[190] Accordingly, extending assistance to the oppressed everywhere and protection of freedoms and rights, particularly the freedom of thought and religious belief, have been among Islam's major concerns, lest tyrannical regimes prevent the Islamic message from reaching all people. Islam views such regimes as violators of human rights, a fact which it sees as justifying legitimate collective defense in order to bring such regimes down and liberate those under their rule. This view, moreover, forms the basis for most of the Islamic conquests throughout history. The international community has recently become aware of the importance of this issue, thereby sanctioning international intervention for the protection of human rights anywhere. The actual implementation of this notion has entailed disregard for the concept of national sovereignty and the unacceptability of external intervention in a sovereign state's internal affairs; similarly, it has been driven by double standards for the sake of achieving superpowers' interests; even so, however, the basic notion [i.e., the importance of protecting people's rights and freedoms through the use of force] has at least been recognized.

The Fifth Intent: Dissemination of the Islamic Message

We have delayed discussion of this intent in order to clarify the context in which efforts are made to achieve it. In view of Islam's being a universal message addressed to all people, communication of this message is the most significant of all intents of Islamic law within the general human milieu, and the burden of fulfilling it rests with Muslims.[191] The essence of the message to be communicated is the existence and oneness of God and human beings' obligation to worship Him through obedience to His commands and avoidance of what He has prohibited. The Qur'an is replete with verses which make reference to all of these elements of the Islamic message. As for its approach, Islam calls for its message to be presented through wisdom, gentle exhortation, and reasoned dialogue, but not through coercion of others to embrace Islamic doctrine.

In view of the fact that the divinely revealed message is common among all God's messengers, Islam grants a special status to Christians and Jews ('the people of the Book'). For although some messages may have been eroded by forgetfulness or distortion, there nevertheless remains a single essence embodied in faith in God and the Last Day and righteous action: "Verily, those who have attained to faith [in this divine writ], as well as those who follow the Jewish faith, and the Christians, and the Sabians – all who believe in God and the Last Day and do righteous deeds – shall have their reward with their Sustainer; and no fear need they have, and neither shall they grieve" (2:62). Herein lies the basis of Islam's call for recognition of those tenets which they hold in common with Jews and Christians;[192] moreover, it is incumbent upon Muslims to bear this call in mind and to make it part of their global policy.

The intent to disseminate the message of Islam revolves around the realization of the meaning of the verses which declare:

- "I have not created the invisible beings and men to any end other than that they may [know and] worship Me" (51:56).
- "Now [as for thee, O Muhammad,] We have not sent thee otherwise than to mankind at large, to be a herald of glad tidings and a warner" (34:28).
- "Say [O Muhammad]: 'O mankind! Verily, I am an Apostle of God to all of you, [sent by Him] unto whom the dominion of the heavens and the earth belongs" (7:158).
- "O mankind! Worship your Sustainer, Who has created you and those who lived before you, so that you might remain conscious of Him" (2:21).

Whereas in the past, the realization of this intent required bearers of the Islamic message to travel and to be in direct contact with the people they were seeking to reach, modern methods of communication have added new dimensions through audio-visual media and the Internet. Despite the availability of such means of communication, however, personal contact retains its importance, as does the living of an exemplary life on the part of Muslims (which, alas, is sorely lacking in Muslim societies and individuals). It also bears noting the lamentable fact that during the present phase of history, many Western states provide more intellectual and religious freedom than do Islamic countries. Be that as it may, however, the fulfillment of this intent requires that those bearing the message of Islam to others be given special preparation, including the training required for them to master the languages of the peoples to whom they are being sent, the study of such people's mentalities and problems, acquaintance with the proper points of entry into their minds and hearts, and the ability to present Islamic solutions to the problems they face but which differ from the problems of Muslims in their own countries.

Chapter Three

Realization of the *Maqāṣid*

Our purpose in writing this book has been twofold, namely, (1) to reconsider certain concepts relating to *maqāṣid*, and (2) to open the way for the realization of these *maqāṣid*.

In relation to the first purpose, we have dealt with numerous issues, the most important of which are:

1. The distinction between the *maqāṣid* of creation and the *maqāṣid* of Islamic law and the implications of this distinction.

2. An attempt to formulate the higher *maqāṣid* of the Law and to draw a distinction between them and foundational concepts.

3. The fact that the *maqāṣid* are comprised of the three levels of essentials, exigencies and enhancements, and that these levels are related to the means by which the *maqāṣid* are achieved rather than to the *maqāṣid* themselves.

4. The fact that legal studies dealing with positive law lack discussions of *maqāṣid*, and that Islamic legal studies lack discussions of the function of positive law in the organization of society and the extent to which the state should intervene in individual freedoms.

5. An attempt to advance writing on those *maqāṣid* which pertain specifically to the subdivisions of Islamic law and to the modern sciences.

6. An attempt to define the role of human reason and experience in the identification of *maqāṣid*.

7. Development of the notion of restricting the universals, or *maqāṣid*, of Islamic law to only five, and the addition of *maqāṣid* relating to social concerns and other areas of life.

8. A discussion of how the *maqāṣid* should be arranged in relation to each other and related difficulties.

9. An attempt to identify the criteria on the basis of which a given ruling or means may be classified as belonging among the essentials, the exigencies or the enhancements, and practical observations.

10. Proposal of the addition of the categories of 'that which falls short of the essential' (*mā dūna al-ḍarūrī*) and 'that which goes beyond mere enhancements' (*mā warā' al-taḥsīnī*), thereby increasing the number of categories or levels of *maqāṣid* from three to five.

11. The relative nature of the specification and categorization of means depending on considerations of time, place, persons and circumstances, and practical examples of this relativity.

12. Eliminating the ambiguity associated with the terms progeny (*nasl*), family lineage (*nasab*) and honor (*ʿirḍ*) and placing each in the proper perspective.

13. Defining the *maqāṣid* within the framework of four realms, that is, based upon how the five universals of Islamic law[1] apply to the individual, the family, the Ummah, and wider humanity.

As for the second purpose mentioned above, namely, the realization of the *maqāṣid*, we have treated this subject under the following five headings:

Theme 1: The current uses of *maqāṣid*
Theme 2: *Maqāṣid*-based ijtihad*
Theme 3: Juristic theorization
Theme 4:The use of *maqāṣid* in the Islamization of the human, social and cosmic sciences
Theme 5: The *maqāṣid*-informed mindset on the individual and communal levels
Theme 6: The future of *maqāṣid*: An independent science, an intermediate discipline, or an advance in the field of *uṣūl al-fiqh*?

[THEME 1]

The Current Uses of Maqāṣid

In this discussion, we seek to present a current picture of the uses of *maqāṣid al-sharīʿah* through a compilation of ancient and modern writings which adhere to traditional approaches relating to the fundamentals of jurisprudence (*uṣūl al-fiqh*). As for what might be considered innovations in these approaches, whether or not we happen to agree with them, we have postponed their discussion to another section of this book.

We will begin with a quote from Walī Allāh al-Dahlawī's work entitled, *Ḥujjah Allāh al-Bālighah*,[2] in which he enumerates the benefits of writing on the subject of *ʿilal al-aḥkām*, that is, the particular intents or bases of Islamic legal rulings. The statement below identifies five such benefits:

> There was significant disagreement among *fiqh* scholars based on their differences concerning *ʿilal al-aḥkām*. These differences led to their discussing such *ʿilal* with respect to the way in which they help to achieve human interests recognized by Islamic law. There [then] emerged in many religious discussions an insistence on what could be grasped through human reason, [as a result of which] doubts were cast upon a number of doctrinal and practical fundamentals. This situation led to the practice of citing rational evidence related to the written texts being discussed and the application of statements and accounts passed down on the authority of the Prophet (pbuh) and his companions in accordance with what could be comprehended by human reason. This development may be viewed as a solid triumph for the religion and a laudable quest to bring Muslims together, as well as being among the most significant means of drawing near to God and demonstrating obedience to Him.[3]

Hence, among the benefits of writing on this theme we have the following:

§*First:* It reveals the perfection of Islamic law.

The Apostle received from God the most consummate of all laws, one that offers benefits which human beings alone would not be able to realize. In one way or another, the people of his time recognized the nobility of what he had brought with the result that its truths began to find their way into their daily conversations and orations. When their era drew to a close, however, there arose a need in the Ummah for those who could clarify the various aspects of this type of inimitability, as well as the utterances of the Prophet and his companions which provide evidence that his Law was the most perfect and complete of all laws. People likewise needed to be reminded that the fact that someone like him (pbuh) had brought something on this order of perfection was itself a miracle of such grandeur and renown as not to require further mention.

§*Second:* It provides assurance of one's faith.

Another benefit of writing about the particular intents of Islamic legal rulings is that it can increase one's confidence in faith. As Abraham, God's beloved friend, upon him be peace, protested, "Yea, but [let me see it] so that my heart may be set fully at rest" (2:260).[4] The reason for this is that the presentation and review of the available evidence and the multitudinous paths by which one can attain knowledge gladden the heart and deliver it from turmoil and confusion.

§*Third:* It enables the believer to be certain of the legitimacy of his/her actions.

This may be seen in the fact that if those who seek virtue engage diligently in acts of obedience while being aware of the basis for their legitimacy, and if they commit themselves to preserving the divine Spirit and Light which are generated through such acts, they will receive benefit even from their most modest efforts, and will be the least likely of all people to act out of confusion or lack of insight. It is for this reason that in his 'Books of Conduct', Imam al-Ghazālī concerned himself with identifying the secrets concealed within acts of worship in Islam.

This truth may likewise be seen in the fact that scholars of jurisprudence have differed among themselves on many subsidiary juristic questions based on their disagreements concerning what they deem to be the particular intents behind legal rulings (*ʿilal*, or *al-maqāṣid al-juz'iyyah li al-aḥkām*).

However, such disputes can only be resolved by means of an independent inquiry into human interests.[5]

§*Fourth:* It serves to deter those who seek to cast doubt [on Islamic beliefs].

One way in which this is manifested is that religious innovators began to cast doubt on many Islamic teachings, saying they were inconsistent with reason and that whatever is inconsistent with reason must either be rejected or given an allegorical interpretation. They held, for example, that the torment of those in their graves is belied by the senses and human reason. They said similar things concerning the Day of Reckoning, the bridge of Hell (*al-ṣirāṭ*), and the balance [on which people's good and bad deeds are weighed on Judgment Day]. Consequently, they began putting forward far-fetched allegorical interpretations, and one particular sect[6] tempted Muslims to doubt basic tenets of Islam by saying, among other things: Why is it obligatory to fast the last day of Ramadan but forbidden to fast the first day of Shawwal?

Another like-minded group derided Qur'anic phrases which urge believers to do good and inspire the fear of doing wrong, saying that such passages are meant merely to encourage people to engage in certain types of conduct and that they have no concrete basis. Then the most despicable of individuals[7] fabricated a Prophetic hadith according to which an, "Eggplant will have whatever effect its eater intends it to have," thereby implying that even the most harmful of things is indistinguishable by Muslims from that which is beneficial.

The only way in which such corruption can be combated is for us to make clear those things which represent genuine human interests and to establish principles relating thereto as has been done in disputes with Jews, Christians, atheists and others.

§*Fifth:* It makes clear that sound Prophetic hadiths are consistent with legitimate human interests.

The truth of this statement may be seen in the fact that a group of *fiqh* scholars once claimed that it is permissible to reject a Prophetic hadith which conflicts with the results of analogical reasoning (*qiyās*) in every respect. As a result, doubts were raised concerning a large number of sound hadiths, such as the *ḥadīth al-muṣarrāh*[8] and *ḥadīth al-qullatayn*.[9] In the face of such claims, the transmitters and preservers of Prophetic hadiths had no means of obliging such groups to acknowledge the authoritative claim of sound hadiths except to demonstrate that they were consistent with the human interests recognized by Islamic law and by pointing out their innumerable other benefits.

§*Sixth:* It serves as an aid in determining which of two analogies to give greater weight.

1. Al-Āmidī, who introduced the consideration of legally recognized human interests into decisions concerning which of two analogies should be given greater weight, presents four possible situations in which such a decision needs to be made:

(a) A situation in which the intent underlying one of the two *ʿilal*[10] is classified among the essentials, while the intent underlying the other *ʿillah* is not.
(b) A situation in which the intent underlying one of the two *ʿilal* is classified among the exigencies, while the intent underlying the other is classified among the enhancements or embellishments.
(c) A situation in which the intent underlying one of the two *ʿilal* is a complement to an essential interest while the intent of the other is classified among the fundamental exigencies.
(d) A situation in which the intent underlying one of the two *ʿilal* is the preservation of the essence of the religion, while the intent underlying the other is the preservation of some other essential interest.[11]

2. Modern researchers have gone a step further in the application of *maqāṣid* to decisions of this nature by applying *maqāṣid*-based principles to juristic research as a whole, or at least, to research into specific juristic topics. An example of such an application may be seen in the work of Abd al-Qadir ibn Hirz Allah in his dissertation entitled, "*Maqāṣid*-based *Taʿlīl* of Legal Rulings Pertaining to Corruption and Falsehood in [Otherwise] Legitimate Modes of Conduct, and Their Juristic Effect,"[12] which compares and contrasts the views of various *uṣūl* scholars as they pertain to the validation of this or that *uṣūl*-related rule in accordance with *maqāṣid*-based principles. In so doing, he achieves a balance among the three aspects of legitimate conduct, namely,

(i) its *uṣūl*-related foundation, (ii) its juristic ruling, and (iii) its *maqāṣid*-related dimension.

§*Seventh:* It serves to prevent the use of legal artifices.

Al-Shāṭibī defines legal artifices (*ḥiyal*, sing., *ḥīlah*) as "the use of artful means to transmute legally legitimate, established rulings into other rulings through an action which is valid in outward appearance but invalid in essence. The rulings in relation to which such artifices are employed may be either *aḥkām taklīfiyyah*, i.e., rulings which serve to define legal obligations, or *aḥkām waḍʿiyyah*, that is, those which specify causes, conditions and/or constraints on such obligations."[13] He then declares the illegitimacy of such artifices by connecting them, in terms of both human experience and legal rulings, with the intents of Islamic law. He states:

> Since it has been established that Islamic legal rulings have been legislated in order to serve human interests, it follows that human actions are to be judged on this basis, since this is the intent of the Lawgiver with respect to them....Now, if an action is legitimate in both appearance and essence, no difficulty arises. However, if an action is consistent [with the Law] in appearance yet contrary to human interests, it is therefore invalid and illegitimate, since legitimate actions are not intended for their own sake, but rather, for the sake of other things which are referred to as their 'meanings', that is, the human interests for whose sake they were sanctioned. Hence, anyone who acts contrary to this principle is not engaged in a legitimate pursuit.[14]

Pursuing the same line of thought, Ibn Ashur presents a detailed listing of five types of legal artifices for which he cites examples[15] (some of which we do not agree with), such as the distinction between an irrevocably divorced woman's concealment, upon entering into a second marriage, of her intention to return to her previous husband (Type 2) and the intention of a man who marries an irrevocably divorced woman to render it permissible for her to remarry the man who had irrevocably divorced her (Type 5), since both such situations are contrary to the Lawgiver's intention as it pertains to remarriage by an irrevocably divorced woman.

§*Eighth:* It plays a positive role in the opening and closing of paths (*fatḥ al-dharāʾiʿ wa sadduhā*).

Al-Qarrāfī is precise in his application of the principle pertaining to *maqāṣid* and *wasā'il* (ends and means), the basis of which is the precedence given to ends over means such that the latter are evaluated in light of the former and take their legal status therefrom. According to al-Qarrāfī, the process of *sadd al-dharā'iʿ** is the act of identifying and obstructing means (or paths) which lead to corruption in order to prevent corruption from manifesting itself. Hence, when an action which is itself devoid of corruption becomes a means which leads to corruption, we are prohibited from engaging in it. However, just as it is necessary to obstruct paths which could lead to corruption, it is likewise necessary to open up [those paths which could lead to benefit].[16]

§*Ninth:*[17] Texts and legal rulings are to be understood in light of their intents.

Al-Raysuni makes clear that this is the majority opinion among Muslim scholars – in contrast to that of the Zahirites,* who differ in the degree to which they adhere to the principle that *maqāṣid* must be taken into account when confirming legal rulings and investigating the meanings of authoritative texts. He then proceeds to cite examples of this principle relating to zakah and the matter of whether a Muslim woman is allowed to travel without being accompanied by an unmarriageable male relative.

§*Tenth:* It serves to integrate general universals and particular evidence.

What is meant by general universals here is whatever is stated explicitly [in authoritative religious texts], as well as overall principles that have been arrived at through an inductive reading of a variety of particular texts and legal rulings. Al-Raysuni summarizes al-Shāṭibī's explanation of the necessity of giving consideration to particulars alongside one's consideration of universals, and vice-versa.[18] Similarly, he makes reference to a statement by al-Ḥāfiẓ ibn ʿAbd al-Barr to the effect that Imam Abū Ḥanīfah rejected numerous solitary hadiths (*akhbār al-āḥād**) passed down on the authority of reliable sources after comparing them with other agreed-upon hadiths and meanings of the Qur'an and that whatever failed to conform to these, he rejected and referred to as 'irregular' (*shādhdh*).[19]

Al-Raysuni then cites two examples, the first of which relates to modifying one's way of disposing of established rights if it is contrary to *maqāṣid al-sharīʿah* and the general principles of Islamic law (including the prohibition against the arbitrary disposal of others' rights). As for the second example cited in this context, it has to do with intervening in a legal contract if it involves some clear injustice to one of the parties thereto, either by nullifying it or by amending it in a way which ensures justice for all parties concerned. (This practice is reflected, for example, in the principles governing the payment of compensation for damaged crops, and the theory of unanticipated circumstances).

§*Eleventh:* It confirms the importance of considering future consequences.

1. That is to say, the scholar engaging in ijtihad must seek to assess the long-term consequences of the actions concerning which he is issuing a ruling or legal decision. In this connection al-Raysuni cites examples of ways in which the Apostle conducted himself in particular situations, including his decision not to have hypocrites put to death and not to rebuild the Kaʿbah, as well as his manner of dealing with the desert Arab who urinated in the mosque.

2. He then discusses the process of defining the basis (*manāṭ*) for legal rulings if it is general and inclusive in nature, such as specifying the definition of 'poor' in the sense of meriting a share of others' zakah funds, the definition of an adulterer who may be described as 'protected from adultery' (*al-zānī al-muḥṣan*),[20] and the meaning of moral integrity (*al-ʿadālah*) as it applies to the reliability of testimonies given or accounts related by this or that individual.

3. Such a basis might also pertain to a specific individual and be necessary to determine what is appropriate for him or her.

4. Closely related to this is the assertion that the person who engages in ijtihad must look anew at each case which emerges, however similar it may be to previous cases on which he has issued rulings. This is because, however much a situation resembles previous cases, it nevertheless has its own peculiarities and distinctive features.[21]

§*Twelfth:* It allows for expansion and innovation in the treatment of legal questions.

Al-Raysuni states,

> Among the ways in which *maqāṣid* and *maqāṣid*-based thinking can serve the Islamic call and those engaged therein is by giving them greater flexibility and innovativeness in relation to the means and approaches which they employ. Things which can be classified purely as methods and means, including those which are mentioned explicitly [in authoritative Islamic texts], admit of change, modification and adjustment. Moreover, even though Islam's intents (*maqāṣid*) represent the elements of stability and constancy in the religion, they also allow for flexibility, change and innovation in means and methods. Indeed, the Prophet employed specific means and approaches in communicating his call to Islam, empowering his message, organizing his community, building up his Ummah, and directing them to carry the message of Islam and right guidance all over the world; however, such means and approaches were not on the order of revelation or the fundamentals of the Law in the sense that they were not subject to amendment or adjustment. Nor should our own approaches be limited to the past or to what was adopted and applied by the Prophet himself. In fact, the Prophet's life and example lead to the very opposite conclusion, as he marshaled and made use of all available means and approaches to achieve his ends and to realize his intents.[22]

He then cites a practical, explanatory example, namely, the issue of democracy and the democratic approaches and systems which are being proposed and discussed by Islamic movements both on the level of the state and society and on the level of internal organization.

§*Thirteenth:* It makes it possible to bridge gaps and resolve differences among the various Islamic schools of thought.

The differences among the various Islamic schools of thought over juristic *istidlāl** arise from differences over *uṣūl*-related principles. However, these principles themselves are speculative rather than definitive in nature and cannot, therefore, be appealed to for the resolution of disputes. Consequently, the quest to establish definitive principles based on *maqāṣid al-sharīʿah* offers a way to eliminate disputes among scholars of Islamic jurisprudence.[23]

[THEME 2]

*Maqāṣid-Based Ijtihad**

The use of the term *maqāṣid*-based ijtihad (that is, intents-based independent reasoning) began only recently. This trend is referred to by al-Raysuni in his book entitled *Imam al-Shāṭibī's Theory of the Higher Objectives & Intents of Islamic Law*, while Nur al-Din ibn Mukhtar al-Khadimi has taken it as the title for a book in two parts which was published in the *Kitāb al-Ummah* Series.[24]

What, then, is meant by the term *maqāṣid*-based ijtihad? Is there some new concept which requires a designation, or are we dealing with the use of a new term to refer to an old entity, mechanism or type of evidence? In answer to this question, it may be observed first of all that al-Khadimi's book makes no reference to any sort of new mechanism. In fact, he stresses that in their role as evidence, the *maqāṣid* are not independent from other types of evidence derived from Islamic law. Hence, he offers no justification for applying this new designation, and fails to make clear what it adds to already recognized Islamic legal evidence. As for al-Raysuni,[25] he is clearer in this respect. He states that he is simply attempting to identify the most important approaches to *maqāṣid*-based ijtihad by striving gradually to define the areas in which such ijtihad is applicable and by establishing guidelines appropriate thereto. He declares, "This is a task of manifest difficulty and solemnity; even so, however, we have no choice but to rise to the challenge and overcome the obstacles which we are bound to encounter, if only in the early stages."

He then proceeds to outline four principles of *maqāṣid*-based ijtihad, namely: 1) The inseparability of texts and rulings from their intents, 2) Combining universal principles with evidence applicable to particular cases, 3) Achieving benefit and preventing harm, and 4) Consideration of outcomes. We dealt with principles 1, 2 and 4 in the previous section; hence, we now turn to principle 3, namely, achieving benefit and preventing harm. After presenting an overview of what al-Raysuni has to say concerning this point, we will offer some of our own observations.

Commenting on the principle of achieving benefit and preventing harm, al-Raysuni states that whenever a given human interest is identified, efforts must be made to realize this interest. This principle applies even if the interest in question is not explicitly mentioned by any specific text of Islamic law; rather, we are to content ourselves with those generally applicable texts which urge believers to seek integrity, reform, goodness and benefit. This, he says, is the realm of unrestricted interests, in support of which he cites statements by Imam al-Ghazālī and al-Shāṭibī while objecting to Muhammad Said al-Buti's stipulation that such a human interest must not conflict with the outcome of analogical deduction (*qiyās*). In addition, he introduces terms such as universal *qiyās*, interest-based *qiyās*, and unrestricted *qiyās*, in addition to terms proposed by Hasan al-Turabi such as 'broad *qiyās*', 'comprehensive *qiyās*' and 'the *qiyās* of unrestricted interests.' He concludes by saying that we are brought back to the original and most prevalent designation, namely, unrestricted interests, examples of which cited by Hasan al-Turabi include the processes of *al-istidlāl al-mursal** and *al-istiḥsān.**

This principle of *maqāṣid*-based ijtihad – namely, the achievement of benefit and the prevention of harm – involves three elements, namely: (1) an expansion of *qiyās* under different names, (2) achievement of benefit and prevention of harm relying exclusively upon texts with a general, inclusive meaning, and (3) unrestricted interests.

The first of these elements, that is, an expansion of *qiyās*, is the most narrow of the three since it keeps us within the framework of particular legal rulings even if we attempt to broaden [our conceptualization of] the relationship between cases which serve as legal precedents and cases whose rulings are derived from such precedents based on analogical deduction. As for reliance upon texts with a general, inclusive application, such as those enjoining justice, virtue, compassion, integrity, charity, reform, benefiting others and the like, these are broad expressions which require some mechanism to regulate and guide their application to specific cases. However, al-Raysuni does not provide such a mechanism; rather, the idea remains incomplete in and of itself. We have made a previous attempt to create such a mechanism by: (a) classifying such texts in terms of the higher intents of the law (*al-maqāṣid al-ʿāliyah*), and (b) by considering them within the framework of universal intents (*al-maqāṣid al-kulliyyah*) in all of their details and practical applications.[26]

With regard to the notion of unrestricted interests, it needs to be asked: Does it achieve what we are hoping to achieve? Lest we get bogged down in the details of the Zahirite-related disputes over this question among scholars of *uṣūl al-fiqh*,[27] let us begin by considering al-Ghazālī's view on *al-istidlāl al-mursal*, that is, reasoning or argumentation based on unrestricted interests, bearing in mind that human interests which are acceptable in his view are those which are recognized explicitly by Islamic law. In addition to analogical deduction, such interests may be identified in two other ways as well:

1. Based on the preservation of a legitimate aim which is known to be the intent of the Qur'an, the Sunnah and the consensus of the Muslim community, and which is not outside the purview of these fundamental sources. However, the preservation of such interests is known to be intended in Islam, not on the basis of a single piece of evidence but, rather, on the basis of numerous, indeed, innumerable pieces of evidence taken from the Qur'an, the Sunnah, circumstances, and various other indications, as a result of which they are referred to as unrestricted interests. Moreover, al-Ghazālī continues, "There is no basis for disagreement over whether they [such interests] are to be observed; on the contrary, they must be stated unequivocally to have an authoritative claim over us." Given the foregoing, al-Ghazālī does not view unrestricted interests as a fifth fundamental source to be added to the Qur'an, the Sunnah, the consensus of the Muslim community and human reason. Rather, they are a means of engaging in the search for evidence of what the Law intends on the basis of these four fundamental sources. In fact, reliance on the notion of unrestricted interests is more powerful than *qiyās*, and possesses definitive authority.[28]

2. Based on consistency with the Lawgiver's intentions or with some fundamental principle which, though it is not specified in the Law, does not conflict with the Law in any way, and which is not overridden by a definitive principle derived from the Qur'an, the Sunnah or the consensus of the Muslim community. Such interests are appropriate to the ruling concerned and are found to recur in a consistent, regular manner in other legal rulings such that they are supported by the Law as a whole. However, divisions are not precisely defined, regulated or enumerated.[29]

Based on the foregoing, it may be concluded that in al-Ghazālī's view, human interests attested to by Islamic law may be divided into three levels: (1) a lower level consisting of human interests which are determined on the basis of analogical deduction, (2) a higher level consisting of human interests which are known to be intended by God based on numerous pieces of evidence taken together, and (3) an intermediate level consisting of human interests which are consistent with the Lawgiver's intentions or with some fundamental principle which is not specified in the Law but which is consistent with the Law, and which is not overridden by some prior, definitive principle. The intermediate and higher levels of human interests are those by means of which it is possible to translate *maqāṣid al-sharīʿah* into practical rulings.

Ibn Ashur explains how *al-istidlāl al-mursal* can be applied on these two levels, saying:

> There may be a situation which lends itself to the process of *taʿlīl*, yet [the understanding of which] does not rest on a particular foundational source[30] of Islamic law but, rather, on the public interest as perceived by human reason. Now, in analogical deduction as engaged in traditionally by scholars of *al-fiqh* and *uṣūl al-fiqh*, the scholar assesses one particular ruling in light of another legally established ruling given the similarity of the two cases with respect to their perceived *ʿillah*, or basis such as, for example, a particular speculative human interest. However, when relying on unrestricted interests, the scholar assesses a particular case whose legal ruling is not yet known in light of a universal principle which has been formulated on the basis of an inductive reading of the evidence found throughout Islamic law. This process, moreover, is valid whether the inductive reading performed is definitive (in the sense of yielding conclusive certainty) or speculative (in the sense of yielding certainty which is reasonable, though not conclusive). It is apparent from the nature of this latter process that it yields more authoritative conclusions than the former (traditional analogical deduction, or *qiyās*). The reason for this is that this latter process (i.e., reliance on unrestricted interests) entails the assessment of a particular in light of a universal, or the application of a universal to a particular, whereas what is involved in traditional *qiyās* is the assessment of one particular in light of another particular, or the application of one particular to another particular which resembles it with respect to its underlying *ʿillah*, which has been identified through induction and which is generally speculative in nature.[31]

Al-Hasani, Ibn Ashur's commentator, expounds [on] this methodology saying,[32]

> This type of ground laying has the potential of bringing about a slight modification in the method of analogy-based reasoning which characterizes the science of *uṣūl*. Hence, rather than seeking evidence in "the utterances of Islamic law and what these utterances convey by way of the Lawgiver's actions and/or the Lawgiver's silence, and the unanimous agreement that such utterances may serve as the basis for universal rulings just as they may serve as the basis for particular rulings, which is most often the case" – I say, rather than relying on this method, new cases can be assessed in light of the principles intended by Islamic law, that is to say, its intents (*maqāṣid al-sharīʿah*). When this situation prevails, "it is sufficient for the scholar of jurisprudence to undertake an extended search for the meaning [i.e., intent] in its various higher forms. Then, through a process of comparison and precise definition, the person engaged in ijtihad is able to determine the intent which underlies the parallel case the ruling on which has not yet been determined. On this basis, he assesses the proposed ruling in light of its immediate universals, then in light of its higher universals, at which point it will not be difficult for him to make this determination, and the three levels will be manifested to him with the greatest clarity."[33]

From this passage it becomes clear how *maqāṣid*-based thinking contributes to the expansion of the process of assessment in *qiyās*, or analogical deduction. For instead of assessing new cases or situations in light of principles which have been stated explicitly in the form of the particular bases of particular rulings, they may also be assessed in light of principles which are not explicitly stated, namely, immediate and higher intents.

In order to provide the clearest picture possible, the following examples may be cited:

1. The principle of preserving the faculty of reason by prohibiting the drinking of wine may, through the process of regular analogical deduction, be applied to all other types of intoxicants as well on a single common basis or *ʿillah*, namely, the power to inebriate, which characterizes both the entity which serves as the basis for the analogy, namely, wine, and the entity to which the analogy is being extended, that is, other intoxicants.

2. By engaging in the process of broad *qiyās* – regardless of which of its various designations we happen to apply to it, including those which al-Raysuni

borrows from al-Hasan al-Turabi – we can abandon the shared *ʿillah* embodied in the common ability to inebriate and move a level higher, namely, to the principle of preserving the faculty of reason. In so doing, we apply the legal prohibition to everything which negatively influences one's reasoning capacity even if it does not inebriate as drugs do. Indeed, we can expand it still further by applying the same prohibition to everything which harms the mind, including superstitions, magic arts, brainwashing operations, baseless imitation of one's forebears, and the like.

3. By employing general texts which prohibit any and all kinds of harm, we can formulate a ruling according to which all such harmful practices and entities are prohibited without relying on the explicitly stated prohibition against wine as our point of departure. In so doing, we go beyond the path of analogical deduction in both its regular and broad forms.

4. By employing the mechanism of unrestricted interests and avoiding that of analogical deduction in both its regular and broad forms, it becomes possible for us to take as our point of departure intents of the Law which have been identified on the basis of innumerable pieces of evidence, or which are in keeping with some principle which, though it is not specified in the Law, does not conflict with the Law in letter or in spirit (such as the intent embodied in cultivating a scientific mindset seeking evidence on the basis of human reason, the pursuit of knowledge, contemplation, investigation, etc.).

Shaykh Muhammad Mahdi Shams al-Din affirms the adequacy of the Qur'an and the Sunnah as two fundamental sources for the derivation of legal rulings, since they include texts which are ready-made for application to all types of situations. However, this affirmation is inaccurate, since the texts found in the Qur'an and the Sunnah are most definitely inadequate in this sense. However, we might understand the adequacy of the texts of the Qur'an and the Sunnah based on the possibility of assessing all actual and potential situations in light of the universal principles embodied in Islamic legislation, in which case we will find no inadequacy whatsoever in its sources.

Shaykh Shams al-Din holds that the primary manner in which to resolve the difficulty presented by the finite nature of the texts [of the Qur'an and the Sunnah] and the infinitude of actual and/or potential situations faced by human beings is to return to two types of principles within Islamic law which call for further investigation and refinement. The first is juristic principles, a set of which is to be found in every division of Islamic jurisprudence. As for the second type, it is what Shaykh Shams al-Din refers to as 'higher evidences' (*al-adillah al-ᶜulyā*) which occupy a higher rank than that of juristic principles. The reason for this is that such 'higher evidences' are not restricted to this or that specific division of Islamic jurisprudence; rather, in Shaykh Shams al-Din's view, they encompass all realms of human activity with the exception of acts of worship. Such 'higher evidences' are the general intents of the Law (*maqāṣid al-sharīᶜah al-ᶜāmmah*), such as those reflected in the words of God Almighty, "Behold, God enjoins justice, and the doing of good" (16:90).

As we have seen, Shaykh Shams al-Din has proposed that the difficulty presented by the inability of legislative texts to account for all life situations in a literal manner may be resolved by granting a more prominent role to *maqāṣid*-based ijtihad. According to one researcher, this approach to resolving the difficulty has direct, logical implications for the mechanism by which legal rulings are derived within the realm of what has been termed 'the legislative vacuum,' an area in which Shaykh Shams al-Din has sought to formulate foundations and principles for the derivation of legal rulings.

This same researcher[34] sets out to explain Shaykh Shams al-Din's methodology. However, the only new concept of note to be gleaned from his efforts is that of procedural rulings (*al-aḥkām al-tadbīriyyah*), which depend upon the distinction between what is stated in accounts which serve as an explicit basis for legislation, and situations involving guardianship or authority which call for discretionary decisions to be made within a particular framework. As such, it is a notion which parallels that of the legislative and non-legislative Sunnah in Sunnah-related writings.

Concerning investigation of new developments, al-Raysuni states:

> One area of ijtihad in which the investigator's assessment depends on a knowledge of and experience with *maqāṣid al-sharīᶜah* is that of interest-based ijtihad. By interest-based ijtihad I mean independent reasoning pertaining to situations and legal questions concerning which there is no explicit legal text to which reference or comparison can be made. In such situations, the investigator has nothing to rely on but human interests and interest-related assessment; therefore, he or she needs a comprehensive awareness of the

> intents of the Law and those intents which the Law recognizes. Similarly, such an investigator needs to be knowledgeable of the various categories of *maqāṣid* and how they are arranged by order of priority, as well as the ways in which sound decisions may be made concerning which *maqāṣid* are to be given greater weight when they are in competition or conflict.[35]

In so doing, al-Raysuni affirms an undisputed principle. The question that remains, however, is how it is to be applied.

* * *

Based on the foregoing it may be concluded that the process to which we have been referring with the term '*maqāṣid*-based ijtihad', or intents-based independent reasoning, should not, in fact, be referred to by this designation. The reason for this is that in reality, the process we have been describing is nothing other than *istiṣlāḥ*,* that is, reasoning based on unrestricted interests. As such, it is a type of legal evidence which was first treated long ago by early scholars of *uṣūl al-fiqh*, whereas all that we have done is to develop and build on what they wrote. This being the case, it would seem most fitting – given that our theme is that of 'interests' – not to allow *maqāṣid* to be treated or viewed separately from *uṣūl al-fiqh* but, rather, to preserve them as an advanced branch of Islamic jurisprudence which serves to support and assist it in developing its remaining branches. This is an issue to which we will return in our discussion of the future of *maqāṣid*.

[THEME 3]

Juristic Theorization

[*Subtheme* 1]: *Harbingers*

Yahya Muhammad[36] has observed insightfully that the theory of *maqāṣid* was originally formulated not to provide a foundation or structure for Islamic legal rulings but, rather, in order to justify existing rulings by lending them an appearance of purposefulness and wisdom. In other words, it was formulated in order to justify an already existing state of affairs, not in order to bring into being what ought to exist. However, although this may have been true in the beginning, the subsequent development of the theory of *maqāṣid* demonstrated a keen awareness of the need to surpass the atomistic approach to understanding Islamic legal rulings and to deal with the problems which face Muslims based on a comprehensive vision which provides legitimate solutions for complex situations and legal questions.

This trend coincided with the call to recognize the necessity of refining the methodology employed in Qur'anic interpretation by introducing what has been termed theme-based hermeneutics, the purpose of which is to identify the basic theories and principle conceptualizations that represent the Islamic perspective. Rather than being content with nothing but superstructures and detailed legislation, this approach promises to make it possible to formulate a set of concepts which constitute a universal, cohesive system.[37] And in fact, modern writings in the area of Qur'anic interpretation reflect this trend, with a moral theory formulated by Muhammad Abd Allah Darraz, a penal theory by Abd al-Qadir Awdah, a legal theory by Abd al-Razzaq al-Sanhuri, and an economic theory by Muhammad Baqir al-Sadr. There has thus been a succession of writings in this direction which reflect ongoing development which promises, in turn, to lead into a phase of theoretical systemization.

The first harbingers pointing in this methodological direction may be seen in the writings of Ismāʿīl al-Fārūqī on the Islamization of the sciences, where he focuses on the human and social sciences in the manner characteristic of the Islamization of knowledge movement. Another contribution of note is that offered by Hasan al-Turabi in his unpublished book, *Tajdīd al-Uṣūl al-Fiqhiyyah li al-Islām*. In a discussion of unrestricted interests, al-Turabi states that:

> The investigation of unrestricted meanings (that is, interests) includes two approaches. The first of these approaches is that of interest assessment, which involves an inductive reading of reality itself. Such an inductive reading of reality draws upon the natural and human sciences: comparing social systems and their associated ways of life and giving due consideration to human experience and history. In this way, we are able to identify and enumerate people's aspirations, desires and needs, divide them into their various classifications and identify their overall direction. The next step is to observe the

means by which such aspirations, desires, needs, etc. – be they material or social in nature – are realized, and to arrange such means within the framework of an overall plan. In addition, *maqāṣid* and *wasā'il* (ends and means) must be related to each other in such a way that one is able to discern how they are connected and their relative degrees of importance and urgency. Once the *fiqh* scholar has identified, enumerated and thoroughly investigated human interests and their associated causes – including benefits and the means of achieving them and sources of harm and the means of averting them – he must arrive at a precise equation of such interests' relative forces. Hence, with respect to the relative seriousness of the various *maqāṣid*, the scholar identifies that which is an urgent life necessity and that which is of less urgency by way of estimated needs, moving down the scale of priorities to those things which may be classified as virtues or 'perfections' by means of which life is completed and enhanced. As for the degree to which the various *maqāṣid* are related [to one another], the scholar is called upon to identify that which is 'universal' in the sense that it has an impact on society as a whole, that which is 'general' in the sense that it concerns a large portion of society, and lastly, that which is 'specific' in the sense that it is of concern only to particular individuals or to a limited sector or class. On the level of means and expedients, the scholar must identify that which is definitive in the sense that it is certain, or nearly certain, to achieve its intended outcome; that which is speculative in the sense that it may or may not lead to its intended outcome; and that which is remote, i.e., is not expected to lead to what is intended. The majority of these divisions are familiar to those active in the realm of Islamic jurisprudence and have gained widespread use in the field of *ʿilm al-uṣūl*, or the fundamentals of jurisprudence. However, scholars have tended to give consideration to such divisions only to the extent that they apply to the religious (spiritual) aims of life. Hence, although such scholars have identified the five well-known essentials, we now stand in need of a new approach which defines the *maqāṣid* and their associated means with a precision which is appropriate to the scientific method, and which is based on a recognition of the fact that such *maqāṣid* and *wasā'il* arise out of the development and advance of life and knowledge in their entirety. Accordingly, we must make use of science in ascertaining these *maqāṣid* and *wasā'il*, bearing in mind that they are in a constant state of flux in response to changing conditions and circumstances.

As for the second approach, it involves evaluating and/or adjusting the ends and means identified in the first approach; hence, it cannot be separated from what went before it. Human interests are only recognized, and indeed, should only arise, in a Muslim society through the inspiration of Islamic teachings concerning the meaning and purpose of life. Similarly, all measures taken to achieve such interests take their standards from the purposes of religious education. For religious education is a unit within which the values of material existence are formulated against the values of spiritual existence, and in which nature and Islamic law are assimilated by human beings who are unified with respect to belief, emotion and action, the outward and the inward.

Even so, we isolate the evaluation of human interests on the level of investigation in order to devote to it the study it requires. As for the standard by which such an evaluation is to be conducted, it is taken from Islamic law in the form of general values of justice as manifested in what is known of the Law overall, and in the form of specific injunctions relating to justice as manifested through subsidiary legal rulings. This is because the interaction between human interests and their related causes within the framework of life under Islamic law overlaps, without a doubt, with particular legal rulings which regulate particular aspects of these interests and determine the details of rulings pertaining to some means; in addition such interaction enters into the universal principles of Islamic law and what is required by Islamic doctrinal principles.

As we have stated before, interests and presumptions of continuity* do not exist in a legal vacuum; rather, they are framed by principles and evidence with universal applicability. Positive law is familiar with the process of assessing interests or benefits and evaluating them in accordance with the standards of justice or equity; however, the criteria for evaluation in Islamic law are more precise than the concepts relating to positive law, including, for example, 'natural law.' The reason for this is that Islamic standards are made up of a broad set of legal rulings and principles and an overall spirit which is nurtured by the meanings of Islamic doctrine. These meanings are reflected in Islam's system of legal rulings, the fundamentals and teachings of Islamic religious guidance, the principles of Islamic law found in the Qur'an and the Sunnah, as well as the experiences contained in the history of religious life. Islamic law presumes the continuity of every scale of justice which is consistent with its guidance, whether people have become aware of it through the Qur'anic injunction to enjoin the doing of what is good and prohibit the doing of what is wrong, or gleaned it from the experience of others.

It bears noting here that although the criterion of justice depends fundamentally on Islamic law, this does not preclude development and change in legal rulings based on this same criterion, since the life circumstances which it governs and regular, recurrent experiences of its fulfillment in reality may reveal things which were not apparent before and, in so doing, call for the modification of previous rulings in light of new awareness. Hence, the evaluation of human interests – despite the constancy of its broad principles and many of its minute details, remains subject to development by way of both expansion and modernization. Without going into a discussion of the breadth or narrowness of the range within which Islamic jurisprudence functions in society (that is, the degree to which it remains a narrow specialization or broadens to take on more public roles), it behooves us to acknowledge that every individual member of society is capable of deducing and evaluating human interests and clarifying what religious life requires on the level of legal rulings pertaining to such interests. In fact, the expansion of the various sciences and the growing need to specialize in one or another of them may mean that some Muslim sociologists will have a keener perception of the process of assessing economic, political, social or health-related interests than will the *fiqh* scholar with his specialization in the system of Islamic legal rulings. In a situation such as this, the *fiqh* scholar's function is to benefit from every kind of knowledge with which others can provide him, every expression of need, and every form of justice recognized by the citizenry as a whole. Then, having drawn on others' knowledge and perceptions in this manner, his job is to prepare and adapt this material in a manner which is appropriate to the modernization of legal rulings. Specifically, he is called upon to classify such input in a precise way, applying to it the exacting standards of justice into which he has such keen insight given his juristic upbringing and his familiarity with approaches to legal rulings and disputes and ways of settling them. Lastly, he conveys this information in the linguistic style best suited to legal rulings and with the appropriate juristic terminology so as to incorporate it into the broader system of Islamic legal rulings.

When searching for evidence on the basis of human interests and presumptions of continuity, the *fiqh* scholar is faced with the task of formulating his view on the importance of this or that benefit or the seriousness of this or that source of harm or corruption, the degree to which it is related to a recognized sector of society, the definitiveness of the causal connection among the various aspects of human conduct and their presumed outcomes, the proper ruling [thereon], as well as the question of how to settle disputes and regulate transactions in such a way as to preserve life. At the same time, he is called upon to provide an equation which averts injustice and fosters equity, brotherhood and cooperation. However, the arguments which form the basis for the jurist's rulings on these broad, discretionary matters may not be as persuasive to society as arguments based on the search for evidence through [traditional] methods of interpretation, precise, disciplined analogical deduction and the like, based on a commitment to and confidence in the belief that such methods lead to an accurate statement of what the Law requires.

As we have had occasion to note, this broad set of questions has basically to do with rulings which apply to the types of daily transactions for which Islamic law has established areas of tolerance and flexibility. Consequently, their results are liable to be met not with the acceptance and acquiescence which manifests itself in the area of religious rites, for example, but rather, with an attitude of belligerence reinforced by the quest for the things of this world. In the process of defining and regulating the breadth of these questions and overcoming the fear of differences and disputes, recourse is had to the authoritative regimes established by the community as foundations for positive (i.e., secular) legal rulings in Muslim society. For most legislation based on Islamic law and communal consensus and most executive orders issued in a Muslim society which are updated by way of either repeal or amendment are simply a confirmation of rulings pertaining to human interests and transactions guided by the principles of Islamic law. Such legislation draws upon interpretative, expository jurisprudence which systematizes the requirements of religious knowledge, be they natural or legal; in so doing, it proposes the prudent solutions which may be adopted by the community based on repeated consultation in appreciation of what is required in order to respond religiously to the trials of life which face us by God's decree. It is such trials which set the stage for religious life, defining its trends and its evolving approaches and calling for a focus upon various types of *maqāṣid*: the *maqāṣid* of obligation, including jihad (the achievement of benefits) or God-consciousness (the prevention of harm and corruption); the *maqāṣid* of knowledge as embodied in cultural renaissance; the *maqāṣid* of material

> acquisition as embodied in economic revival; or the *maqāṣid* of freedom as expressed through the encouragement of development and investment, the quest for equality and reductions in income disparities, etc., all of which is subject to the evolution of fates and divine decrees.[38]

Abd al-Majid al-Najjar devotes a chapter of his book, *Fī Fiqh al-Tadayyun Fahman wa Tanzīlan* to what he terms 'the jurisprudence of formulation' (*fiqh al-ṣiyāghah*). He states,

> The Muslim can bring all of the changing circumstances of his life into conformity with the rulings of the religion, which only stipulates the universals of actions via ongoing social effort. Such ongoing social effort resembles the act of arriving at a *fatwa*, or legal decision, based on independent reasoning; however, such a *fatwa* is arrived at in the context of general conditions, not particular, personal events. In this independent reasoning, or ijtihad, the overall legal rulings of the religion are used to formulate a system consisting of the various aspects of these rulings, the ways in which they are to be applied, and their intents, or *maqāṣid*. Such a system has the potential of managing newly arising situations in a manner that achieves human interests, which is the ultimate goal of the religion. However, arriving at such a formulation is not a simple matter; on the contrary, it is a supremely weighty task involving ongoing itjihad for the sake of bringing life onto a spiritual path, as it were, despite its changing patterns and conditions. The sounder such a formulation is, the more fully it will guarantee life's advance along the spiritual path which will realize true human interests.[39]

[*Subtheme* 2]: *Juristic Theorization*

§*First:* The definition of 'theory' and the most promising places to search for its foundations in the [Islamic] heritage.

The definition of 'theory'

In my study entitled, *Al-Tanẓīr al-Fiqhī* (*Juristic Theorization*, published in 1987), I state in the introduction,

> A juristic theory may be defined as an abstract, comprehensive conceptualization of the general principles which serve to regulate particular subsidiary

rulings. As such, it is a conceptualization which exists in the mind, whether it is arrived at by means of a sequential, rational thought process, or is derived from an inductive reading of particular subsidiary rulings. This conceptualization is abstract in nature because it attempts to free itself from concrete reality in order to go beyond it to the notion which governs this reality. Moreover, it is a comprehensive conceptualization in the sense that it attempts to account for all aspects of the topic at hand, on all of its levels and in all of its dimensions. Such a conceptualization pauses at each phenomenon or related ruling, taking note of the characteristics which are common to all of the phenomena and rulings being investigated while disregarding those features which are unique to this or that specific phenomenon or ruling, its purpose being to acquaint itself with shared overall principles.[40]

As for Baqir Barri, he defines the [juristic] theory as follows:

What is meant by a [juristic] theory is a rational formulation made up of a set of Islamic principles, foundations, visions, concepts, legal rulings, and texts which are connected one to another by the fact that they serve to convey the Islamic teaching in some specific realm pertaining to human beings, the universe and/or society. It is both a formulation and a cohesive fabric whose threads make up a single, uniform sequence which is intended to enable us to identify the overall Islamic position on this or that area of life, and particularly, social areas.

Once it has been formulated, the benefit of an Islamic theory lies in what it offers by way of a conceptual system, positions, supports, and a general framework within which to move in the area with which it deals. At the same time, it affirms parameters, controls and general criteria established by the sacred Law.

No theory of this nature can be derived without a thorough understanding of the area concerned; however, given such an understanding, theory can lead us to a rational framework for movement therein. This being the case, such a theory must contain a description, an analysis and a clarification which encompasses all dimensions of the area of objective reality on which it seeks to elucidate the Islamic perspective. Moreover, since it will declare an alternative position to the existing theories in the field, it must necessarily represent a clear contrast to these other positions and offer an objective critique thereof. After all, it will not be possible for us to recommend the

> Islamic theory to others unless we have a critical awareness of existing theories in the field, and unless we can demonstrate, upon analysis, the degree to which the Islamic theory can hold up under criticism.
>
> Hence, the construction of an Islamic theory requires juristic effort which is both intellectual and synthetic in nature. Such effort is founded upon awareness and specialized knowledge in light of which Islam's teaching is seen to be based on well-defined standards and criteria. However, no Islamic theory can mature and reveal its strengths and weaknesses unless it is put to the test. That is to say, it must be applied practically to life's reality and, specifically, within the context of an Islamic system and state. The reason for this is that the practical application of an Islamic theory and the act of allowing it to serve as a concrete guide to action in its particular domain raise it to the level of accountability and experimentation, thereby opening the minds of those engaged in ijtihad to new insights which lead, in turn, to the theory's modification and development.[41]

In his article entitled, "Manhaj Iktishāf al-Milāk wa Atharuhu fī Taghayyur al-Aḥkām,"[42] Said Rahiman draws a clear distinction among: (1) a rule, (2) a theory, and (3) a system.

A *rule* is a universal judgment or ruling which contains numerous other rulings within a division, or various divisions, of Islamic jurisprudence. More precisely, a rule is a source or foundation of rulings in the divisions of daily transactions or acts of worship, such as the rule, "No harm" (*lā ḍarar*), the rule, "No hardship" (*lā ḥaraj*), and others.

A *theory* is a set of similar and related rulings on a topic which has its own peculiar structure, its own particular intent, and a single foundation. This topic may be a division of Islamic jurisprudence, as in the case of the theory of retribution or the theory of guarantees; or, alternatively, it may be part of a division or several divisions of jurisprudence as in the case of the theory of will, the theory of legal necessity, the theory of choices, etc.

As for a juristic *system*, it is a framework made up of a set of legal rulings. Related as it is to a variety of divisions of Islamic jurisprudence, such a framework seeks to convey the universal intents or goals of Islamic law and the spirit of the juristic texts with a bearing upon this set of rulings. Examples of juristic systems include the Islamic economic system, the Islamic judicial system, and others.

Where to search for a theory's foundations in the [Islamic] heritage

It is commonly stated that Islamic law contains no general theories but, rather, is a set of subsidiary legal rulings pertaining to a variety of areas. However, an overview of the progress made by early jurists in the realm of theorization makes it clear that such a statement is not entirely true, granting, of course, that those who have made this affirmation have done so with good intentions and that such a belief on their part is understandable for the following reasons.

The search for juristic theories is more difficult than the search for subsidiary rulings on juristic questions, the reason for this being that books on Islamic jurisprudence are replete with subsidiary legal rulings, yet rarely will you find in them discussions of juristic theories, since such theories are scattered here and there among innumerable writings and are, therefore, in need of being unearthed, completed and set in order. The unearthing of such theories may be facilitated sometimes if [the search] is limited to material existence; however, on many occasions they must be extracted from the subsidiary rulings within which they are concealed. For although some theories have not been given explicit expression, careful investigation of subsidiary rulings leads to the definitive conclusion that a theory did, in fact, exist in the mind of the jurist who issued them.

The extraction of theories may be also facilitated at times if the books on jurisprudence which have come down to us contain a complete set of discussions of the particular topic of concern. However, when such discussions are incomplete, the formulation of a comprehensive theory requires that a framework for the theory be established, that numerous scattered discussions be integrated into this framework, and that an attempt be made to fill in gaps when they are found to exist.

The process of arranging juristic theories in the appropriate order is necessarily related to the process of arranging the disciplines which such theories govern. This latter process requires, in turn, an investigation of which of these disciplines are to be viewed as in the service of others, as well as an inquiry into which of them constitute individual obligations under Islamic law, and which of them constitute communal obligations.

In order to limit our discussion solely to that of juristic theorization, we must exclude certain things which may appear to belong to this category but which, in reality, are separate entities. In this connection, it may be helpful to point out that subsidiary juristic rulings, that is, those which concern themselves with a specific issue or question, are not included in the realm of juristic theory even if they happen to take the form of a rule. The reason for this is that despite the standardized, rule-like formulation of such rulings, they nevertheless remain subsidiary rules which apply only to a specific question, no matter how many different behaviors and situations fall within its purview. Similarly, the *fatwa*, or legal decision of a mufti concerning a particular behavior or situation or a judge's ruling on a dispute are not considered acts of juristic theorization, since both of them are, in essence, the application of a legal verdict or ruling to a specific situation, event or action and, therefore, fall outside the realm of juristic theory.

If we arrange juristic rules according to their degree of abstraction from their particular circumstances, we come up with the following breakdown:

1. Theoretical rules:
(a) Linguistic rules, *uṣūl*-related rules,[43] and those related to scholastic theology.
(b) Rules which are common to several subdivisions of various juristic divisions.
(c) Rules which are common to several subdivisions of a single juristic division (such as contracts, for example).
(d) General rules applicable to a single juristic subdivision (such as selling, for example).

2. Non-theoretical rules:
(a) Subsidiary rules, which are, in essence, codified formulations of recurrent individual cases.
(b) Legal decisions issued by a mufti or rulings issued by a judge.
(c) The events, situations and actions to which Islamic legal rulings apply.

Where to search for juristic theories in traditional Islamic writings

The search for juristic theories in the books which make up the Islamic literary heritage requires that we not limit ourselves to books on Islamic jurisprudence, which generally concern themselves with the subsidiary legal rulings for which they provide a forum. Rather, our search must encompass a broad range of writings, including books on the fundamentals of jurisprudence (*uṣūl al-fiqh*), scholastic theology (*ʿilm al-kalām*), philosophy, Islamic legal policy, legal rulings pertaining to kings and other rulers (*al-aḥkām al-sulṭāniyyah*), the judiciary, computation, juristic rules, universal rules, legal distinctions, similitudes and parallels, derivation of branches from roots (*takhrīj al-furūᶜ ᶜalā al-uṣūl*),[44] the intents of Islamic law (*maqāṣid al-sharīᶜah*), differences among Islamic jurists, and the like.

In a discussion of juristic rules, the late Shaykh Abu Zahrah states:

> It is necessary to distinguish between the science of the fundamentals of jurisprudence (*ᶜilm uṣūl al-fiqh*) and rules which encompass particular legal rulings, namely, those which may rightly be referred to as general theories of *fiqh*, or Islamic jurisprudence. The study of rules, which is based on the act of bringing together similar issues and questions as dealt with by juristic rulings, falls within the purview of *fiqh*, not that of *ᶜilm uṣūl al-fiqh*. Consequently, we can arrange three levels which are founded one upon another: The fundamentals of jurisprudence serve as the basis for the derivation of juristic branches so that when various juristic sets are formed, it will be possible to draw connections among their branches and to gather them together into comprehensive general rules which account for their [seemingly] scattered components. It is to these rules, then, that we refer as juristic theories.[45]

Now, while we agree with Shaykh Abu Zahrah's affirmation concerning the way in which the fundamentals of jurisprudence give rise to its branches, which in turn give rise to juristic rules, we take issue with his tendency to view juristic rules as equivalent sometimes to general theories of Islamic jurisprudence, and at other times, to juristic theories. The reason for our disagreement is that we prefer to distinguish between general theories of Islamic jurisprudence – most of which we find in the field of *uṣūl al-fiqh* – and the general theories which pertain to each separate branch of *fiqh*, the beginnings of which we find in juristic theories. Juristic theories have only come to completion and maturity in the writings of modern thinkers. This, in any case, is a matter of terminology, and terminology isn't worth arguing about, as they say.

Let us now reconsider Shaykh Abu Zahrah's statement that, "The study of rules falls within the purview of *fiqh*, not that of *ᶜilm uṣūl al-fiqh*." For as we see it rules do not fall within the realm of *fiqh*, but rather belong to a category which falls somewhere in between *furūᶜ* (branches or subsidiaries) and *uṣūl* (roots or fundamentals), that is to say, somewhere between jurisprudence (*fiqh*) and the fundamentals of jurisprudence (*uṣūl al-fiqh*).

In illustration of the foundations of the theorization process, I have stated:[46]

> In his definition of juristic theories, Mustafa Ahmad al-Zarqa states, "By basic juristic theories, we mean 'constitutions' and primary concepts, each one of which individually goes to make up an objective juristic system which exists in diffuse form, as it were, throughout the volumes of Islamic jurisprudence just as the parts of the nervous system are disseminated throughout the human body. The components of this system govern all branches of legal rulings with a bearing on its subject, such as the notion of ownership and its causes, the notion of contracts and their principles and outcomes, the notion of legal competence and its types, phases and impediments, the notion of proxyhood and its divisions, the notions of falsehood or invalidity, incorrectness and *tawaqquf*,*[47] the ideas of suspension (*al-taʿlīq*), restriction (*al-taqyīd*) and subjunction (*al-iḍāfah*) in the realm of verbal expression, the notion of guarantee and its bases and types, the notion of custom and the sway it holds over the definition of social obligations, as well as the other major theories upon which the edifice of Islamic jurisprudence rests and whose influence human beings observe in the solutions to virtually all juristic questions and cases.
>
> These theories are to be distinguished from universal rules or principles, which serve as juristic criteria and fundamentals which are observed in the process of deriving concrete legal rulings within the broader parameters set by these central theories. Hence, the rule which states that 'the significance of a contract lies in its intents and meanings,' for example, is simply a criterion which applies to a particular aspect of the realm governed by 'contract theory,' as is the case with other rules as well.[48]

In addition to the basic juristic theories of which al-Zarqa gives examples, there are other, subsidiary theories which apply to divisions and subdivisions of Islamic jurisprudence. Above these there is, in addition, a general theory of Islamic law as a whole, the outlines of which we will attempt to delineate in a separate study, God willing.

We had occasion earlier to stress the importance of the 'art of compilation' in the formation of these basic subsidiary theories. For, although the practice of this art begins as nothing more than a kind of encyclopedic compilation of the material relating to the subject under study as found within the various juristic subdivisions, this process generally leads to the derivation of rules and criteria, which serve in turn to aid in the formation of the theory in question. Similarly we have the 'art of differentiation', which helps to highlight the subtle distinctions among various issues and questions, and which is among the most important requirements of theorization.

As for the study of rules themselves, it is of undoubted significance for the theorization movement, particularly if we classify such rules according to their varying degrees of abstraction. When such a classification is completed, we are then able to use each level of rules on its corresponding level of theorization. At the same time, however, we do not restrict ourselves to the level of rules which apply within juristic subdivisions and which, according to al-Zarqa, are simply criteria which govern a particular aspect of the field to which the theory relates. We will have more to say on this topic in our discussion of development, to which we will turn shortly under the heading, "A Forward Look."

Lastly, the study of differences among scholars of jurisprudence serves to fill a significant gap in the area of theorization, since it helps in the conceptualization of the theory both on the level of a particular juristic school of thought and on the level of Islamic jurisprudence inclusive of all its juristic schools. Such a comprehensive perspective serves in its turn to enrich the theory by shedding light on the varied points of view which the theory encompasses and the solutions which it offers, thereby rendering it more truly representative of the entire corpus of Islamic jurisprudence.

§*Second:* Imam al-Sadr's Method of Theorization

Writings dealing with the method underlying Islamic legal theorization are still scarce. However, the initial signs of interest in this endeavor began with a contemporary Shiite imam, namely the martyred Muhammad Baqir al-Sadr, who published a number of studies on this method of theorization.

For Imam al-Sadr, the order in which one moves when engaging in the process of theorization is from reality to the text, rather than vice-versa.[49] Summarizing this point, Baqir Barri writes:

> In the initial phase, the person engaged in the process of theorization must seek to discern the problems which have been raised by experiments in

> human thought concerning a given practical theme, the solutions which human thought has offered, as well as the questions raised and the 'lacunae' left by practical application. The purpose of this phase is to enable the thinker to arrive at an initial starting point from which he can then proceed to study the topic he has adopted and evaluate it thoroughly from the Islamic perspective in accordance with the rulings, concepts and ideas found in the Holy Qur'an and the noble Sunnah. Then, having done this, he can formulate a comprehensive Islamic theory of relevance to the topic at hand.
>
> Moreover, given that the theme-based method [of theorization] moves in the direction of Qur'anic interpretation, Imam Baqir al-Sadr alerts us to the fact that theme-based interpretation "proposes a topic relating to the doctrinal, social or cosmic realm of life, after which it proceeds to study and assess this realm from a Qur'anic perspective in order to emerge with a Qur'anic theory relating to the realm under study." The individual engaged in theme-based interpretation "takes the Qur'anic text, not only in order to adopt the role of listener or recorder in relation thereto but, in addition, in order to address the text with a topic which is saturated with innumerable human ideas and situations, then to enter into a dialogue with the Qur'anic text in a question-answer format. In light of the conclusions he or she has drawn based on accumulated human experiences, subject as they are to error, the interpreter questions the Qur'an, and the Qur'an replies. Coming as one inquiring, seeking understanding and reflecting, he or she initiates a dialogue with the Qur'anic text about the topic of concern, his/her aim being to ascertain the position taken by the Holy Qur'an on the subject at hand and to identify the theory which he/she can derive from the text's inspiration by comparing the text with the ideas and trends which he or she has absorbed in relation to this subject. This being the case, the outcomes of topic-based interpretation are invariably tied to the current of human experience, while at the same time reflecting the features and dispositions which serve to define the Qur'anic theory relating to one of life's themes."[50]

The second point has to do with an inductive reading of the legal rulings on the issue in relation to which one is theorizing. In this connection Said Rahiman states, "According to Imam al-Sadr, the raw materials which must be gathered as the basis for the inductive process are the juristic texts, rulings, and points of view which are found scattered throughout the varied writings of jurists and other Muslim scholars."[51] Hence, the two primary steps involved in forming such a theory consist, in the initial stage, of compiling and summarizing the texts, and dealing with them both atomistically and holistically.

Texts are then divided into three groups depending on their relationship to the theory which is being formulated in the scholar's mind, namely: (1) texts which explicitly support the theory, (2) texts which explicitly conflict with the theory, and (3) texts which neither support nor conflict with the theory in any explicit way. When dealing with the last group in particular, understanding the text and unearthing its content call for exceptional interpretative competence.

In the following stage, the cases are assembled and analyzed, and a comprehensive perspective is formulated in order to derive the fundamental structure – or, to use Imam al-Sadr's term, the superstructure – through the totality of texts and rulings, after which universal rules are identified on the basis of this superstructure.

What this means is that Islam is an integral religion comprised of a variety of systems. It is likewise a religion which lends itself to the formulation of [previously unidentified] systems and which calls upon us to discover these systems by means of independent reasoning (ijtihad) and a careful investigation of Islamic jurisprudence. Moreover, given that the inductive method is based upon the calculation of probabilities, scholars' views take on purely statistical value insofar as they either support or conflict with the proposed theory. Hence, legal decisions which conflict with the theory (in the jurisprudence of rulings) are not viewed negatively within the context of the jurisprudence of theories, which covers a broader inductive range.

Based on the foregoing, the overall method for discovering theories consists in proposing a theory (after having done an inductive reading of the relevant texts and rulings), conducting a study of what supports and opposes this theory, and conducting probability calculations in order to identify the degree of certainty with which the theory can be affirmed. This method derives its persuasive power and authority from the rational search for evidence, since the scholar relies in this method upon an inductive process which necessitates a kind of painstaking, thorough research which is a far cry from the selective, 'pick-and-choose' method and other unscientific approaches.

According to Imam al-Sadr, the secret to interpretative competence in Islam and the ability of its leaders to guide and direct social life lies in the appropriate synthesis of these two elements, namely, the constant and the variable, and in the direction of common goals. Such a synthesis requires that three conditions be fulfilled: (1) an understanding of the constant element, (2) an understanding of the nature and requirements of each sector or aspect of human civilization, and (3) a clear identification of the ruler's powers and the limits within which he has the right to intervene [in society's affairs].

In Imam al-Sadr's view, the concept of what has been referred to as a 'legislative vacuum' in Islam is included within the third condition mentioned above. Hence, such a 'vacuum' is not a shortcoming or deficiency in Islamic law. On the contrary, it is one of its strengths, since such 'vacuums' are left alongside the primary, original ruling so as to allow room for [flexibility in] the powers enjoyed by the ruler, who in turn fills these vacuums with secondary laws and rulings. Hence, governments fill the space which has been left intentionally by Islamic law in anticipation of the vicissitudes of time and place.

As for the third point which Imam al-Sadr discusses, it has to do with the process of making a transition from particulars to the general rule which embodies what is common to them all. In this connection, Baqir Barri writes:

> The scholar engaged in formulating a juristic theory arrives at an understanding of an Islamic theory by transcending the detailed meanings of legal rulings and Qur'anic verses, going beyond the state of diffusion and accumulation, and studying every set of Qur'anic verses or legal rulings having to do with a single topic. Such a study must be of the comprehensive sort which coordinates and unifies their detailed meanings, thereby revealing the connections among them and allowing this set of Qur'anic verses or legal rulings to delineate the outlines of a clear theory pertaining to the subject with which they deal.[52]

Concerning this practice, which leads to an understanding of Islamic theories, Imam al-Sadr states,

> It calls for a greater awareness of the Islamic legal rulings and concepts with a bearing on a single topic and which may appear to be scattered [haphazardly here and there] but which are, at the same time, seen to be integrated and in

> complete harmony when there is a conscious, all-embracing, penetrating vision of the foundations, premises, intentions and aims [which underlie them]. Consequently, the process of ijtihad in relation to the understanding of Islamic theories calls for tremendous effort and exceptional creativity, since it is not merely a matter of locating and compiling texts relating to a particular area; rather, it is a rule-based process of independent reasoning in which the jurist and the explorer are combined into one.[53]

It bears noting here that Imam al-Sadr's method is a method of discovering juristic *rules* and not juristic *theories*, although he seems to view the two processes as synonymous. As we have explained, however, they are not entirely synonymous, a point which is also clarified by Said Rahiman in his aforementioned definitions.

As for the fourth point which merits examination with respect to Imam al-Sadr's thought it is his emphasis on the importance of preserving objectivity.[54]

1. In the context of affirming this aspect [i.e., that of objectivity] of Islamic theories, Imam al-Sadr clarifies the distinction between the *discovery* of a theory and the *formulation* of a theory.[55] The individual engaged in ijtihad does not establish a theory whose source is his own subjective vision or his own personal deductions based on what he or she has observed. Rather, the scholar reveals Islam's perspective and theories, beginning with its superstructures (that is, its detailed rulings) and moving into the depths of the Islamic edifice in order to identify the ground floor, as it were. As for someone who is formulating a theory, he moves upward from the ground floor to the second floor, since he is engaged in the process of building and formation, and the second floor only comes into existence at a later stage of the building process.[56]

2. Imam al-Sadr points out that the danger which subjectivity poses to the process of theory discovery is greater than that which it poses to the process of independent reasoning in relation to particular rulings.[57]

3. He then enumerates the most important causes behind subjectivity, namely:

   1. Justification of reality.
   2. Viewing a text only within the context of a particular situation.

3. Stripping textual evidence found in Islamic law of its associated circumstances and conditions.
4. Approaching the text with preconceived attitudes.
5. The misleading influence of reality as experienced in the context of the actual application of texts.

Nor does Imam al-Sadr fail to take into account the intents of Islamic law in the process of theory discovery, a fact which has led Said Rahiman[58] to the conclusion that delineating the general outlines of a system (or, as he terms it, a set of theories) entails the following four requirements: (1) knowledge of the general trends within Islamic law, (2) an understanding of the explicitly stated intents of established legal rulings, (3) a consideration of social values, and (4) an understanding of the aims which have been defined for the ruler and which specify the areas in which he is to exercise his authority.

It should be noted, however, that Imam al-Sadr refers to *maqāṣid al-sharīʿah* in a general way only, without defining their role in the theorization process or establishing a mechanism for the fulfillment of this role.

§*Third:* The relationship between theories and the Islamic legal sciences

We will postpone a discussion of our proposed methodology to the next section below in order for it to include both juristic theorization and the Islamization of the sciences. The following diagram presents the relationships which exist between juristic theories on one hand, and the various Islamic legal sciences on the other.

At the center of the diagram on the following page we have doctrine, since it constitutes the foundation and wellspring of all Islamic sciences. Out of it also arise moral values, followed by the general theory of Islamic law which governs all branches thereof. Moral values are followed by the common rules and theories upon which more than a single subdivision of Islamic jurisprudence draws, and this on two levels: (1) the level which encompasses several subdivisions of various juristic divisions, such as forms of worship, daily transactions, and penal codes, for example, and (2) a level which encompasses several subdivisions of a single juristic division with the result that we have a kind of general theory for each particular juristic division. Within this same

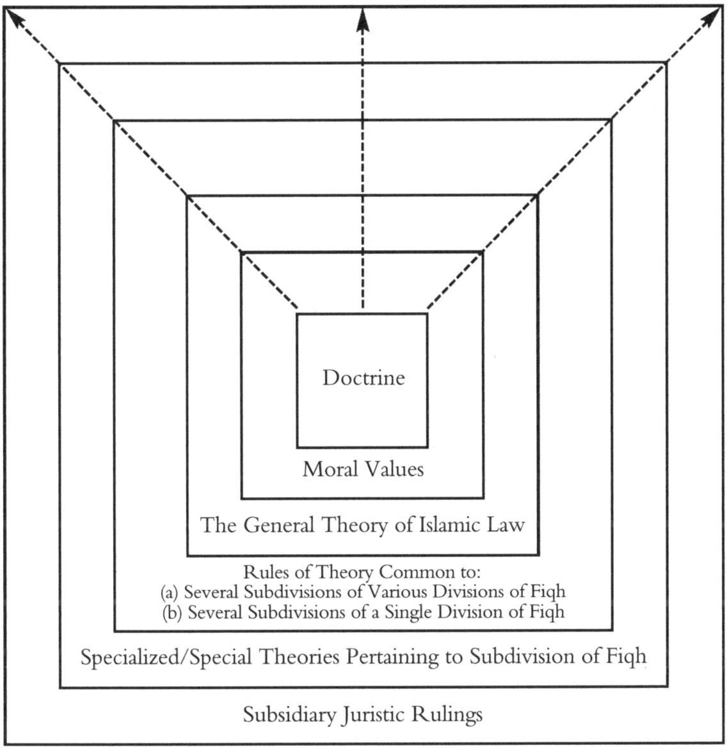

level, the various subdivisions of Islamic jurisprudence have their own independent status, as it were, such that each of them has its own general theory which governs the particulars within its specific domain.

This is the conceptualization which we believe to be the best suited to organizing and dividing *fiqh* material into parts while connecting these parts to one another in a logical manner, and while observing the priorities and functional relationships among the various rules. It is a conceptualization which, in our view, promises to be useful in identifying areas of life with respect to which there is still a need for further theorization, in drawing comparisons with positive, that is to say, secular legal systems, and in preparing the Islamic codifications for which there is a growing need.

§*Fourth:* Contemporary writings on Islamic theories

Most modern studies in this area – written in the form of doctoral dissertations – have taken a direction with clear distinguishing marks which might be summarized as: modernization, comparison, theorization, and development.

1. *Modernization:* Such studies deal with topics relating to the conditions of modern life and Muslims' current problems, and attempt to ascertain the Islamic perspective on such realities. The conclusions reached by such studies do not rise to the level of ijtihad given the writers' lack of preparation or qualification for this role. Nevertheless, by researching the Islamic literary heritage and extracting what is relevant to their topics of study from scores – nay, hundreds – of books and other writings, these writers have performed a tremendous service by helping to clarify the contents of this heritage and by making it available to other researchers. Indeed, such writers' efforts in this realm are reminiscent of the efforts made by Ibn Najīm and others in the realm of compilation.

2. *Comparison:* Such studies compare the views of Muslim scholars representative of various juristic schools as well as relevant theories, both ancient and modern, on the subject being examined. The comparative approach has enabled researchers to unearth untold treasures which would never have occurred to them had it not been for their concern and determination to do justice to such comparisons.

3. *Theorization:* These modern researchers have avoided the method which characterizes most ancient writings, namely, that of compiling subsidiary issues and identifying the theory which lies behind them. Instead, they seek to clarify definitions, distinguishing characteristics, conditions, pillars, effects, and other general matters for which subsidiary issues serve as practical examples. Most studies have succeeded so well in this task that they have become, in this respect, genuine additions to the realm of juristic theory.

4. *Development:* The process of development has received less attention than the processes of modernization, comparison and theorization. What we mean by 'development' here is the process of taking the Islamic legal sciences in the direction which they would have taken if ijtihad and intellectual creativity had not come to a standstill among Muslim thinkers over the past

several centuries. The only example which comes to mind of someone who has proceeded in the direction of development in this sense is Muhammad al-Tahir ibn Ashur in his book entitled, *Maqāṣid al-Sharīʿah*, where he attempts to take writing in the realm of *maqāṣid al-sharīʿah* a step – and, indeed, several steps – beyond the point to which al-ʿIzz ibn ʿAbd al-Salām and al-Shāṭibī once brought it.

In the area of rules, we find that contemporary writings, which are sparse to begin with, have not taken the topic much beyond the point it had reached in ancient writings. Rather, contemporary efforts have for the most part been limited to commentaries on the rules which are explicitly set forth in the legal code; two exceptions to this trend are the attempts made by Shaykh Muhammad al-Husayn al-Kashif al-Ghita and Dr. Mustafa Ahmad al-Zarqa to classify rules as either basic or subsidiary, and to add new rules as well.

As for a complete enumeration and classification of Islamic juristic rules followed by a derivation of general theories from such rules on the level of Islamic law as a whole, then on the level of each of the Law's divisions and subdivisions – and which, as we see it, is the direction in which the writings of the ancients on the subject of juristic rules had been moving – no one has yet to undertake such a task to our knowledge.[59]

§*Fifth:* A View to the Future

It will be clear from the overview above that contemporary studies are progressing rapidly toward the clarification of Islam's verdict on all aspects of modern life, and this based on theories which pertain specifically to every branch of knowledge relevant to such areas.

(a) Survey

It is likewise clear, however, that these studies are not progressing with the same speed, comprehensiveness or depth in all areas. Some areas, such as financial transactions and personal status, for example, have enjoyed significant attention, whereas some others, such as political science, the media, the arts, etc., have not received the attention they deserve. Space does not suffice here to give a detailed presentation of the areas which still need to be investigated more thoroughly, since this task itself is among a broader category of tasks which need to be commenced, and which are referred to as the 'survey phase.'

(b) Evaluation

Such deficiencies may be addressed by conducting initial studies in each area of concern. However, it will be necessary in such a case for experts to evaluate such studies in order to ensure that they have achieved what they were intended to, or to identify points in which they are lacking.

(c) Auxiliary Tasks

Among the things most deserving of attention and priority are auxiliary tasks whose function is to facilitate the studies which need to be carried out. Such auxiliary tasks include, for example, (1) editing and publishing a number of major works belonging to the Islamic literary tradition which have yet to see the light of day, (2) compilation of the encyclopedias, dictionaries and indexes needed to assist specialists in modern sciences in referencing books belonging to the Islamic heritage, and (3) the comprehensive enumeration and classification of juristic rules in such a way that they can be the starting point for the formulation of general theories both on the level of Islamic law as a whole and on the level of each of its divisions and subdivisions.

(d) Compendium

Once writing has been concluded on every branch of knowledge in general, and of Islamic jurisprudence in particular, this task will be brought to completion by the composition of a compendium for every branch. This compendium will contain the theory particular to the branch concerned and, rather than being limited to any particular school, will elucidate the view of each school of Islamic jurisprudence. At the same time, the researcher is free to express his support for a particular view with a presentation of the evidence which led him or her to this position, and with the needed comparison between the various Islamic perspectives on the topic and the views represented by non-Islamic theories, schools and trends.

(e) Codification

The final phase is that of codification, which in turn requires the completion of three sub-phases:

1. The first of these sub-phases is the study of Muslims' life circumstances throughout the world in order to identify their practical needs, customs,

habits and problems, which are bound to differ from one country to another. During this phase we are faced with a choice between two alternatives. The first alternative consists in working to pass standardized legislation which applies to all Islamic countries, while the second is simply to establish broad guidelines in conformity with which laws may differ from one country to another. Arab states have tried the first alternative – that of standardized legislation – in the area of personal status laws, as well as in civil, commercial and penal laws; however, they have yet to achieve the actual standardization of any of these laws. As for the other alternative, it has been adopted by the European Union, which has succeeded in bridging the gaps among its various laws within the parameters set by broad guidelines (known as 'directives') issued by the organization's joint bodies. This process has led to the emergence of what is termed European Law, which is not, in reality, a standardized law but, rather, a set of criteria and directives for each branch such that each European state commits itself to amending its laws in conformity with these criteria.

2. The second sub-phase consists in each Islamic country's choosing those rulings which it will adopt from among a number of legitimate alternatives within the framework of the aforementioned guidelines or criteria.

3. The final sub-phase involves the precise formulation of these rulings in the form of sets of laws which make their way toward issuance, promulgation, and application in accordance with the system prevailing in each Islamic country.[60]

[THEME 4]

The Use of Maqāṣid in the Islamization of the Human, Social and Physical Sciences

The intents of the sciences (*maqāṣid al-ʿulūm*) may be viewed as an example of the type of particular intents (*al-maqāṣid al-khāṣṣah*) which we discussed in Chapter 2 (Theme 2, Subtheme 4), where we postponed the discussion of this topic to a later part of this book. Ibn Ashur and predecessors of his to whom we have made reference have already expounded the intents of Islamic law as they pertain to specific subdivisions of Islamic jurisprudence, or even entire divisions of Islamic law, such as forms of worship, daily transactions, etc. However, we now find ourselves in the face of a new qualitative leap consisting in the introduction of the notion of *maqāṣid* into the sciences that deal with human experience, society, and the universe. Recently emerging sciences aim to study these realities, knowledge of which is constantly expanding and spawning related disciplines. Moreover, in order to regulate these disciplines by the criteria of Islamic law, we must begin by specifying the legal intent behind each of these sciences in order for it to proceed in its development and research in a manner which is consistent with the Law's guidance, that is, in a purposeful manner which builds up rather than destroys, and which offers good to humanity in an ongoing accumulation of knowledge in the service of both spiritual and material prosperity, well-being and development.

In dealing with this theme, we will begin with a discussion of its methodological aspect, then, as space permits, move to a presentation of a number of practical examples in the realm of specific disciplines.

[*Subtheme* 1]: *On Methodology*

In our discussion of Imam al-Sadr's method of juristic theorization, we arrived at the level which requires that we draw a distinction between theorization in the realm of Islamic jurisprudence with its various divisions and subdivisions, and theorization in the realm of other sciences, particularly those pertaining to human experience, society and the physical universe. Imam al-Sadr states that the person engaged in ijtihad as it pertains to juristic theorization discovers the already existing Islamic theory based on a detailed study of Islamic jurisprudence, whose rulings declare what *ought to be* (do this, don't do that), whereas in the 'reality sciences', the point of departure is the search for what is, and the space devoted to what *ought to be* is reduced in order to focus on *maqāṣid al-sharīʿah* as they apply to the topic of each scientific discipline.

This is the point of departure adopted by Ismāʿīl al-Fārūqī, pioneer of the Islamization of knowledge school. This school revolves primarily within the orbit of the reality sciences – without, of course, neglecting the need to develop the Islamic legal sciences, including Islamic jurisprudence. The Islamization of the sciences is also closely related to the process of theorization, since the goal of Islamization – namely, the establishment of a creative relationship between Islam and the various areas of knowledge – is not achieved on the level of particulars but, rather, on the level of universals and theory, that is, on the level at which Islamic thought interacts with modern sciences.

Al-Fārūqī has drawn up a work plan for the Islamization of knowledge which consists of a number of steps.[61] Of these steps, we will focus on those which have a bearing on the topic of theorization.

1. Mastery of the modern sciences and a comprehensive survey thereof (Steps 1 and 2), and identification of the most important problems faced by the Ummah and wider humanity (Steps 8 and 9). These steps parallel Imam al-Sadr's method of starting with reality and then moving to Qur'anic texts, since the modern sciences represent reality with all that it entails by way of questions and unknowns that call for dialogue.

2. Mastery and analysis of the Islamic heritage (Steps 3 and 4). Such processes parallel Imam al-Sadr's inductive reading of Islamic legal rulings since, in one respect, they are an indexing of texts (the Qur'an and the Sunnah) and the heritage (Islamic jurisprudence), and in another respect – and as a necessary requirement of the success of the indexing process – they call for the availability of word lists and glossaries which serve both to describe the Islamic system and to analyze and classify the indexed material.

3. Steps 6 (the critical evaluation of modern science), 7 (the critical evaluation of the Islamic heritage) and 10 (creative analyses and syntheses) constitute the heart of al-Fārūqī's approach to Islamization; hence, the steps which precede them are no more than preparation for this phase. It cannot be said that these steps serve as a parallel to Imam al-Sadr's transition from particulars to the universal rule, since this latter process is closer to the discovery of rules, and not of theories, as we had occasion to note earlier. However, such a transition serves as a necessary introduction to the steps outlined by al-Fārūqī, which complete the theorization process within the process of Islamization.

4. It remains to be noted that neither the importance of objectivity nor consideration for *maqāṣid al-sharīʿah* is referred to in al-Fārūqī's plan.

5. Parallel to this is the fact that al-Fārūqī's plan gives prominence to the fundamental principles of Islamic methodology,[62] namely, the unity of God, the unity of creation, the unity of truth, the unity of knowledge, the unity of life, and the unity of humanity. Al-Fārūqī's plan also stresses the view that the process of reshaping the sciences within an Islamic framework requires that we subject science's theories, methods, principles and goals to Islamic principles.

A Proposed Methodology

Despite our full appreciation of the methods proposed by al-Sadr and al-Fārūqī, we would like now to propose a method of theorization which combines the methods proposed by these two scholars, the conclusions we ourselves have reached through our study of *maqāṣid*, and our application of *maqāṣid* to theorization in the manner referred to by Hasan al-Turabi and Abd al-Majid al-Najjar. Specifically, this involves developing the *maqāṣid* in such a way as to form a complete juristic system which encompasses all branches, both present and future, without waiting for the emergence of a particular case in order to issue a legal ruling appropriate thereto. This may be done by means of the following practical steps:

1. Ascertaining the *maqāṣid* which belong to the two categories identified by al-Ghazālī, namely: (a) those which are ascertained based on numerous pieces of textual evidence and which are definitive in nature, and (b) those which are in keeping with some fundamental principle which, though it is not specified in the Law, does not conflict with, and is not overridden by a definitive principle derived from the Qur'an, the Sunnah or the consensus of the Muslim community.

2. Classifying these *maqāṣid* and building them into an intellectual edifice in which similes and parallels are brought together and divided into groups according to their subject matter, thereby revealing the features of the Islamic legal conceptualization in relation to each subject[63] according to the divisions of contemporary juristic writings.

3. Adding to each of the *maqāṣid* the means which serve to lead to its realization, drawing upon whatever modern tools and approaches do not conflict with Islamic legal principles.

4. Adding to the *maqāṣid* and *wasā'il* belonging to each group those Islamic legal rules which apply specifically thereto, as well as general Islamic legal rules of relevance. Such rules of both types may be viewed as a basic part of each group's structure, since they represent Islamic legal rulings derived from other evidence found in Islamic law.

5. Constructing an integrated theory for each group from which branches may be derived, which may be drawn upon in a way which serves to achieve the *maqāṣid*, and which harmonizes with Islamic legal principles.

6. Adding to (4) and (5) above whatever *maqāṣid* are relevant to each of the human, social and natural sciences, including: (a) divine laws of creation (*al-sunan al-ilāhiyyah*) relating to the topic of the science concerned, and (b) definitive facts which have been identified by science, to ensure that the theory applicable to each science is inclusive of all normative and objective elements relating thereto. As for the normative elements being referred to here, they include: a) the Islamic conceptualization of God, the universe, human beings and life, b) general moral values and those specifically applicable to science, c) *maqāṣid al-sharīʿah* specific to science, and d) Islamic legal principles which pertain to [human] action.

[*Subtheme 2*]: *An Example from the Realm of Education*

§*First:* The International Institute of Islamic Thought has undertaken a project which aims to provide Islamic introductions to the sciences – with each introduction to include a section clarifying the intents of Islamic law pertaining to the science under discussion. Two such introductions have been completed thus far by way of experimentation, one in the area of economics, and the other in the area of education. The study dealing with the Islamic intents underlying economics was written by Gamal Eldin Attia,[64] while the study treating the Islamic legal intents underlying education was written by Fath al-Bab Abd al-Halim.[65] In addition, a study was written by Said Ismail Ali on the aims of Islamic schools.[66]

Before attempting a comparison of the two studies dealing with the *maqāṣid* of education, we shall present a brief summary of each.

1. After an introduction to the place of goals in educational work and the sources from which the goals of Islamic education are derived, Said Ismail identifies the following goals:

- Worship and devotion.
- Liberation.
- Perfection of noble character traits and deeds.
- Instruction/Education
- Encouraging the use of reason.
- Social guidance.
- Populating and developing the earth.
- Physical fitness.
- Aesthetic and spiritual enrichment.
- Nurture and instruction of Muslim girls and boys.

2. As for Fath al-Bab Abd al-Halim, he begins with the notion that the ultimate goal of education in Islam is freedom: freedom in the sense of liberation from the shackles which impede or limit human thought, movement, action and autonomous decision making. This freedom is both an individual and collective responsibility, as well as a universal goal of education everywhere; as such, it is not restricted to Muslims alone. The author then goes on to discuss individual goals, of which he mentions the following:

- The learning of the Qur'an and wisdom.
- Self-purification and self-evaluation.
- Earning a living and practicing a profession.
- Searching for knowledge, or teaching the individual how to learn.

Based on a careful examination of these two attempts, we repeat something which we have said elsewhere,[67] namely, that the International Institute of Islamic Thought did not publish these two studies. Consequently, they have not been discussed within their intended framework, namely, Islamic points of entry to the sciences. Hence, in light of the fact that this discussion never took place, we have not yet arrived at a standardized method by which to identify the *maqāṣid* of each science, link them with the overall *maqāṣid al-sharīʿah*, and clarify the influence of these *maqāṣid* on the method, subject matter and applications of the science in question. Yet, despite their individual nature, these two efforts – together with my own attempt in relation to the *maqāṣid* of economics[68] – are necessary in order for further study to be done as a means of building upon them.

§*Second:* In a study which appeared in *al-Muslim al-Muʿāṣir* (No. 106) entitled, *"Maqṣid Iʿtibār al-ʿAql"* (Consideration for [Preservation of] the Faculty of Reason), I take this basic intent of Islamic law as my point of departure in order to establish an integrated structure for one of the most important divisions of education. My discussion covers the intellectual aspects of this *maqṣid*, as well as its instructional, research-related and rational methodology. What follows is the text of the study:

(1)

We first need to define what is meant by the terms 'reason' or 'the mind' (*al-ʿaql*) and 'preservation' (*ḥifẓ*):

1. The term 'mind' as used in this context is an action, not a member of the body. The bodily members associated with the mind are (a) the brain, (b) the five senses (organs of perception) which supply the brain with data, that is, hearing, sight, taste, smell and touch, and (c) the nervous system, whose function is to make communication possible among these organs of perception and the brain.

2. The term *ʿaql* does not once appear in the Qur'an as a noun. Rather, we have derivatives of this word in 49 verses in the form of verbs, including, for example: *ʿaqalūhu* ("they understood it", 2:75), *naʿqilu* ("used our own reason", 67:10), *yaʿqiluhā* ("those who [of us] are aware ", 29:43), *yaʿqilūn* ("who use their reason", 2:164), *taʿqilūn* ("use your reason", 2:44), etc.

3. These verses revolve around five axes: a) exhortation to make use of the mind, b) the functions and processes in which the mind engages, c) addressing those whose minds are rightly guided (*'ūlī al-albāb*), d) rebuke of those who hinder their minds' functioning, and e) Qur'anic synonyms for the term *ʿaql* (*al-lubb, al-ḥilm, al-nahī, al-ḥajar, and al-qalb*).[69]

4. The mind, or *al-ʿaql*, which is a perceptive power subject to the senses, operates in a realm which goes beyond that of the senses but which falls short of that of divine revelation. The mind performs a number of functions, including that of perceiving that which is unseen based on that which is seen, deriving universals from concrete particulars, recognizing self-evident truths, formulating theories, retrieving stored information, associating cause and effect, and others.

5. As in the case of other qualities by means of which God distinguishes individuals one from another, mental powers vary from person to person. The minimum degree of mental power is represented by what is attained by an ordinary person upon reaching maturity; as such, it is the basis for the individual's being held accountable for fulfilling the obligations set down in Islamic law. As for those who do not attain this minimum level of intelligence at maturity, or who lose it thereafter, their responsibility for their actions will be less than that borne by an ordinary person, and they may be exempted from it entirely.[70]

6. There are – in addition to innate differences in mental capacity – acquired differences which result from disparities among people with respect to the use of their minds' ability to acquire knowledge, and training and developing their mental capacities.

7. The mind is a distinguishing characteristic by which God has set human beings apart from other creatures in order for them to put it to use in the life of trial and suffering by which human beings have likewise been set apart. Hence, from this perspective as well, the mind is the basis for human accountability before the Law.

The Law's intention to grant consideration to the faculty of reason (*iʿtibār al-ʿaql*) is, as we see it, composed of three principle elements, namely: development of the mind, preservation of the mind, and use of the mind. Scholars have tended to term this intent 'preservation of the mind'; however, I prefer to refer to it as 'consideration for the mind' in order for the term to be inclusive of all three elements listed here.

According to al-Shāṭibī, the fulfillment of *maqāṣid al-sharīʿah* consists of two aspects. The first of these aspects is the establishment of their pillars and foundations, that is to say, those things which are necessary for the perpetuation and nurture of their existence. As for the second aspect, it is the prevention of imbalance or malfunction, which serves to protect them from annihilation or non-existence.[71] The *development* of the mind serves to nurture and perpetuate the mind's existence, while the *preservation* of the mind serves to protect it from annihilation. As for use of the mind, it has no place in this categorization scheme. Ibn Ashur defines preservation of the mind as preventing it from suffering any sort of imbalance or malfunction;[72] hence, his perspective is limited to the aspect of protecting the mind from annihilation.

Al-wasā'il are the means of achieving the *maqāṣid*. Hence, they are not intended for their own sake but, rather, are subordinate to the *maqāṣid*, whose fulfillment is their reason for being. In dealing with *wasā'il*, then, we have greater flexibility which enables us to employ and devise a variety of options and alternatives even as we adhere to the texts which deal explicitly with specific kinds of cases. In identifying *wasā'il*, therefore, we have greater freedom to draw upon sources other than written texts than we do when determining *maqāṣid*. In connection specifically with the *maqṣid* of giving consideration to the faculty of reason, we find that in identifying this *maqṣid*, we must rely solely on texts from the Holy Qur'an and the Sunnah, whereas in identifying relevant *wasā'il*, we need not rely solely on texts from the Qur'an and the Sunnah but can, in addition, draw upon both our wider Islamic heritage and human experience as a whole.

(2)

The first element of this *maqṣid* is the development of the mind. We do not say the *creation* of the mind, of course, since its creator is the Maker Himself, Majestic and Exalted is He. Development of the mind means causing it to be in the best possible condition, whether with respect to its capacity for scientific, academic thought, training the mental faculty, or nourishing it with information, skills and the like, all of which renders it more capable of fulfilling its function.[73]

The search for evidence of this *maqṣid* presents no difficulty; indeed, there are countless Qur'anic verses which testify to the merit of knowledge and those who possess it. We read, for example, "Say: 'Can they who know and they who do not know be deemed equal?'" (39:9). Nor does it stop at affirming the superiority of knowledge over ignorance, but declares that knowledge itself is granted in degrees -"God will exalt by [many] degrees those of you who have attained to faith and, [above all,] such as have been vouchsafed [true] knowledge" (58:11) – and encourages us to progress in our pursuit of knowledge from one degree to another: "Say: 'O my Sustainer, cause me to grow in knowledge!'" (20:114).

As for the means of developing the mind, they can be sought in the following areas: (1) formation of a scientific mindset, (2) concern for scientific method, and (3) education. Let us now take each of these means in order:

Formation of a scientific mindset:

The Holy Qur'an concerns itself with the formation of a scientific mindset in order for the Muslim's way of thinking to be based on a sound foundation. Such a mindset consists of a number of central components, including:

1. Rejection of mere speculation in lieu of certainty: "For most of them follow nothing but conjecture: [and,] behold, conjecture can never be a substitute for truth" (10:36).
2. Refusal to submit blindly to whims and emotion.
3. Rejection of blind imitation of one's ancestors and predecessors.
4. Rejection of unthinking subordination to leaders and superiors.
5. Engaging in worship and adoration together with reflection and rational inquiry (to which we have devoted a detailed discussion under the heading of 'means of using the mind').
6. Refusal to accept any claim without proof.
7. Observance of God's ways in the universe and society.[74]

In connection with the matter of conjecture vs. certainty, we find a number of juristic rules – derived originally through an inductive reading of particular legal rulings, as well as texts from the Qur'an and the Sunnah – which pertain to this topic, and which embody the features of a precise methodology. Of these rules we mention the following:

1. No weight is to be given to conjecture which is clearly in error.[75]
2. Whoever is capable of reaching certainty shall not operate on the basis of conjecture.[76]

3. The ability to reach certainty without undue hardship precludes the need to resort to independent reasoning.[77]
4. Whatever is established on the basis of proof is equivalent to that which is established through direct vision.[78]
5. Complete certainty cannot be eliminated by doubt.[79]
6. That which has been established with complete certainty can only be invalidated by means of complete certainty.[80]

There is ample room in which psychologists, educators, as well as leaders of thought, culture, the Islamic call, and the media, may develop this theme, bringing it out of the theoretical realm and into the realm of practice and application.

Concern for the scientific method:
The Holy Qur'an does not content itself with forming the scientific mindset among the general Muslim populace; rather, it goes beyond this to alert Muslim scholars to the need to adhere to the scientific method. A number of studies[81] have been written on the methods followed in the Qur'an, adherence to which has enabled Muslim scholars to establish numerous new sciences while developing a number of old ones. These studies explain such methodologies and methods of *istidlāl*, while enumerating also the Qur'anic verses in which reference is made to them. There is no need to repeat their contents here; hence, we will simply list the types of methodologies and approaches to *istidlāl*:

1. The rational search for evidence.
2. Empirical investigation or induction.
3. Historical retrieval and induction.
4. Description of social reality.
5. Description of natural reality.
6. Reasoning or argumentation based on simile and metaphor.
7. Reasoning or argumentation based on partition or division.
8. Reasoning or argumentation based on generalization followed by particularization.
9. Reasoning or argumentation based on definition.
10. Reasoning or argumentation based on comparison and contrast.
11. Reasoning or argumentation based on Qur'anic narratives.

12. Reasoning or argumentation based on debate and discussion, approaches to which include:
    (a) Probing and classification.
    (b) Challenge.
    (c) Acknowledging the strength of an opinion (*al-qawl bi al-mūjib*).
    (d) Concession.
    (e) The use of registers in which specific cases and the rulings thereon have been recorded.
    (f) Transition in the search for evidence.
    (g) Contradiction.
    (h) Granting one's opponent's position in order to reveal his error.
13. Inductive investigation in the physical sciences.
14. Inductive investigation in the realm of psychology.
15. Inductive investigation of the course of history.
16. Reflection and observation.
17. Data analysis.
18. Practical examination.
19. Consciousness of God.

Education/Instruction:
"The pursuit of knowledge is an individual duty for every Muslim (both male and female)."[82] "Whomever God wills to bless, will grow in understanding of the religion."[83] Nor is it merely an individual duty, but a social duty as well, and as such, it is among the collective obligations laid down in Islam: "...if they would but refer it unto the Apostle and unto those from among the believers who have been entrusted with authority, such of them as are engaged in obtaining intelligence[84] would indeed know [what to do with] it" (4:83). In addition, we have the hadith narrated by Muslim according to which, "Scholars are the heirs of the prophets."[85]

At this juncture we need to address two issues: (1) the type of knowledge which Muslims are required to seek, and (2) the type of obligation this entails. As for the type of knowledge to be sought, early thinkers held that it was the religious knowledge necessary for the performance of obligatory acts of worship. Some of them added to this the learning of arithmetic in order to make it possible to calculate inheritances and zakah, as well as astronomy in order to ascertain prayer and fasting times. Al-Qaradawi also adds the obligation to learn to read and write.[86] As I see it, however, and as I noted in Chapter 1, the custom of linking the types of knowledge required of Muslims [solely] to matters pertaining to worship has its roots in a narrow view of religion which limits it to the realm of the search for evidence through devotion alone. However, if we understand religion in its comprehensive sense, it will be natural for us to place it where it belongs, namely, within an integrated educational system which we will explain shortly.

As for the type of obligation entailed, that is to say, the question of whether it is an individual (*ᶜayn*) or a collective (*kifayah*) obligation, the two types need to be combined in such a way that the individual obligation is restricted to the types of knowledge acquired in mandatory general education, while the notion of collective obligation should be seen to apply to the phase of vocational and professional specialization, as will be detailed below.

The conceptualization based on these two principles may now be summed up as follows: Mandatory general education includes – alongside the study of Islamic doctrine and worship – the fundamentals of the Arabic language, mathematics (arithmetic, algebra and geometry), history, geography, physics, chemistry, the principles of the Islamic sciences (the Qur'an, the Sunnah, and the biography of the Prophet), a simplified, comprehensive overview of Islamic jurisprudence, principles of the English language, and computers.

This initial phase constitutes the level of knowledge which must be acquired by all members of society – men, women and children – in our own era as an individual duty. For children, it represents the initial, mandatory phase of their education, which lasts a minimum of six years. On the level of exigencies, this phase is supported by an integrated cultural network of school and public libraries, audio-visual, written and electronic media, specialized periodicals, general and specific references, clubs and societies. As for the level of enhancements, it encompasses the nurture and encouragement of outstanding and creative individuals who have been identified through educational activities on the levels of essentials and exigencies, and to whom the state devotes special attention.

As for specialized education, it ushers us into the realm of collective obligations in the area of knowledge as a means of achieving social development. After all, such education touches not only upon individual interests, but upon the interests of society as a whole. Hence, it entails acquisition of the knowledge and skills required for populating and developing the earth and earning a living through a variety of vocational and professional specializations. At the same time, the Ummah as a whole strives to achieve self-sufficiency in all areas of life and on all levels: essentials, exigencies and enhancements alike. Given this religious motivation, human potentials are released to fulfill collective obligations.[87] The starting point for achieving this aim in our present situation is to undertake a fundamental review of the currently prevailing system of vocational and university education, in which the situation is the reverse [of what is intended]: Graduates of vocational education are not sufficient to meet development needs, while university graduates pour forth only to suffer, for the most part, both declared and undeclared unemployment.

The first step is to define society's needs of whatever type, beginning with the most basic crafts and extending upward to the highest-level, most obscure specialties. Students may then be directed to study or training in the required areas by determining their abilities during their years of preparatory school as well as in programs for exceptional and creative students. In addition, students' test grades should constitute only one of a number of evaluative measures. As such, they should constitute only 10-20 percent of the total evaluation, and not 100 percent as is the case at present. There would, in addition, be institutes for study and vocational training of all types and on all levels, university faculties with all the specializations required to both absorb incoming students and to meet society's needs of every type and on every level, the necessary specialized libraries and laboratories, the use of advanced instructional technology, the internet, etc.

There is no particular phase or age after which learning comes to an end. Indeed, the principle of continuing education and the pursuit of advancement through ascending degrees of knowledge is affirmed explicitly in Islam: "Say: 'O my Sustainer, cause me to grow in knowledge'" (20:114).

Hence, in determining the importance of developing the mind, we have relied solely upon texts from the Holy Qur'an, while means of developing the mind may be determined through reliance upon texts from the Qur'an and the Sunnah. The means of forming the scientific mindset are supported by a number of juristic rules, while means of instruction are supported by the Islamic heritage in the form of individual and collective obligations, as well as by human experience with the educational system and its various phases.

(3)

The second element of consideration regarding the faculty of reason is preservation of the mind, which means:

1. Preserving the well-being of the physical senses, the nervous system and the brain, and avoiding anything which would lead to their organic deterioration; in this connection, the Qur'anic verses prohibiting the use of alcohol are well known.[88]

2. Avoiding behaviors which would impair or confuse mental functioning (non-organic deterioration); the Qur'anic verses which prohibit such behaviors are likewise well-known.[89]

3. Protecting the mind from the destructive effects of the various conduits of culture and the media.

Means of preserving the mind: Means of preserving the mind may be sought in the following areas:

1. Islamic law is keen to preserve the well-being of the bodily members which support the faculty of reason, including the brain, the five senses, and the nervous system; it does this, first and foremost, by forbidding the use of substances which would lead to their deterioration or destruction or hinder them from performing their proper functions (organic deterioration). Hence, it prohibits the drinking of intoxicants or the use of drugs, while imposing a penalty whose intent is to deter us from engaging in any of these prohibited acts. The Qur'anic verses which prohibit alcoholic beverages and the use of intoxicants are well known.[90]

2. Islamic law goes beyond the preservation of the organic systems which support the mind to preservation of the mind's ability to perform its functions without hindrance or confusion (non-organic deterioration). As a consequence, it prohibits unthinking surrender to desires and whims, conjecture and surmise, blind imitation of predecessors, the powerful and the influential, superstitions, false doctrines, contentiousness, obstinacy, arrogance, hypocrisy and other harmful practices and attitudes which are at odds with scientific thinking.[91]

3. In our day and age, this extends to the avoidance of communications media which engage in collective brainwashing operations and besiege people's minds, giving them nothing but the news and analyses which they want and encouraging them to waste time on things which not only are devoid of benefit, but which actually bring harm. Such media train people's minds in corrupt ways of thinking based on the sacralization of power, the justification of error, and mindless bigotry. They seem to declare, as did a certain pharaoh of old, "I but want to make you see what I see myself; and I would never make you follow any path but that of rectitude!" (40:29)

4. Any imbalance or malfunction in the organic systems associated with the brain or its functions by way of psychological or nervous disorders must be treated.

As will be clear from the foregoing, preservation of the mind and the means of achieving this intent are based not only on texts from the Qur'an and the Sunnah but, in addition, upon modern medical, psychological, sociological, media-related and educational studies which, taken together, fall under the category of general human experience.

(4)

The third element of consideration for the mind is putting the mind to use, or its activation.

1. The mind, or intelligence, is a blessing with which God has set human beings apart from His other creatures and on the basis of which they bear the trust of being God's vicegerents on earth. Hence, just as in the case of other blessings, such as length of life, health, material wealth, etc., the mind is something for which God will hold human beings accountable on the Day of Resurrection, when He will ask them whether they have used it well in carrying out the trust which they have taken on. "And never concern thyself with anything of which thou hast no knowledge: verily, [thy] hearing and sight and heart – all of them, will be called to account for it [on Judgment Day]!" (17:36).

It is on the basis of intelligence that human beings have been addressed through divine revelation, in order that they might comprehend it and carry it out in action. This concept, in turn, serves to reveal the point of comparison and contrast between a divine means of revealing the truth, namely, revelation, and a human means of doing so, namely the mind. Human beings incorporate the revelation through understanding, detailing what [God] has left ambiguous on the basis of life's vicissitudes, and striving to implement them [that is, both reason and revelation] in practical action.[92] This being the case, the Holy Qur'an draws attention to the importance of activating the mind in relation to many phenomena which are observable and perceptible to all, considering them to be 'signs for those who understand.'[93]

2. There are times when, even though human beings are in full possession of their mental faculties and are equipped with knowledge and a scientific mindset, they fail to make use of all of this; in fact, they conduct themselves as though they were ignorant or lacking in intelligence. When this occurs, it indicates the presence of a malady which the Qur'an illustrates with a number of images:

- "Will they not, then, ponder over this Qur'an? – or are there locks upon their hearts?" (47:24)
- "And most certainly have We destined for Hell many of the invisible beings and men who have hearts with which they fail to grasp the truth, and eyes with which they fail to see, and ears with which they fail to hear. They are like cattle – nay, they are even less conscious of the right way: it is they, they who are the [truly] heedless!" (7:179)
- "Or dost thou think that most of them listen [to thy message] and use their reason? Nay, they are but like cattle – nay, they are even less conscious of the right way!" (25:44)
- "Verily, the vilest of all creatures in the sight of God are those deaf, those dumb ones who do not use their reason" (8:22).

Similarly, the question, "Will you not, then, use your reason?"[94] recurs in a large number of verses.

3. The use of verbal rather than nominal derivatives of the Arabic word meaning 'mind' (*al-ʿaql*) communicates an intentional message, namely, that the mind is necessarily associated with an event, a self and a time. Hence,

rational consideration is a concrete process with dimensions and significations which are grounded in a particular reality, particular persons, and a particular time. As such, it has a practical impact on human beings themselves in determining their actions.

Thus, the dimension which is added by the Qur'an to the meanings of 'mind' or 'reason' is its connection with action. This serves to make clear that the Qur'an's concern is not with the essence of the mind but, rather, with its function. After all, the Qur'an only makes mention of *al-ʿaql* in the context of drawing attention to the need to apply it. The importance of the mind's action, or work, may be seen in the statement made by those who rejected faith while they are suffering torment in the afterlife: "Had we but listened [to those warnings], or [at least] used our own reason, we would not [now] be among those who are destined for the blazing flame!" (67:10)[95]

Means of putting the mind to use

1. Islamic law shows particular concern for what may be referred to as 'rational forms of worship', which include: consideration or observation (*al-naẓar*), seeing, having eyes to examine (*al-tabaṣṣur*), pondering (*al-tadabbur*), reflection (*al-tafakkur*), and bearing in mind, or taking to heart (*al-tadhakkur*), in support of which there are innumerable passages in the Qur'an.[96]

2. Despite their frankness, however, such Qur'anic verses only rarely receive from Muslims the attention they deserve. On the contrary, they are treated as though they were addressed to others, such as the unbelievers of the pre-Islamic era, for example, with the purpose of drawing them to faith, and as though, once they had achieved this end, they had served their purpose. However, this is a limited, mistaken understanding of them, with dangerous consequences for the cultural level of Muslim individuals and for the Ummah as a whole.

3. Rather, just as mental operations such as these can lead the unbeliever to faith, so also do they serve to establish and confirm the faith of those who already believe.[97] At the same time, they train the mind in the performance of higher functions such as rational, inductive and historical argumentation, which lead in their turn to a penetrating vision of the major issues of doctrine as well as – as we had occasion to mention in our discussion of the theme of developing the mind – to the formation of a scientific mindset.

4. These rational forms of worship are required of us both individually and collectively. As God Almighty declares, "Say: 'I counsel you one thing only: Be [ever conscious of] standing before God, whether you are in the company of others or alone; and then bethink yourselves [that] there is no madness in [this Prophet,] your fellow-man'" (34:46).

5. This provides ample room in which psychologists and educators – not to mention the Ummah's leading thinkers and proponents of Islam – can strive to delve more deeply into this theme and transfer it from the realm of theory into that of practice and application.

6. It may be stated tentatively that some of these forms of mental, or rational, worship are practiced by both the general populace and those who might be termed the intellectual elite, whereas others are practiced only by those who have attained the status of 'those endowed with insight.' As al-Nīsābūrī puts it in his discussion of such rational worship: "In the beginning it is a matter of the mind whereas in the state of perfection, it becomes a matter of the heart."

7. The first form of rational or mental worship mentioned above, namely, consideration or observation (*al-naẓar*), is based upon examination, reflection and vision. This process, which involves answering the questions, "How?" and "Why?", is mentioned in 129 places in the Qur'an. The second, namely, *al-tabaṣṣur*, which communicates the sense of seeing, or having eyes to see, is essentially a cognitive function in the sense of mental insight, and is mentioned in 148 verses of the Qur'an. The third, namely, *al-tadabbur*, which might best be translated as pondering, or seeking to understand, appears in four places in the Qur'an, in all of which it is used in relation to the Holy Qur'an itself. The fourth, or *al-tafakkur*, which conveys the sense of reflection or giving thought to, appears in sixteen places in the Qur'an which deal with the theme of reflecting on all manifestations of existence, from cosmic signs and psychological phenomena to evidence for the oneness of God, the truth of the divinely revealed messages, and the sending of God's messengers and prophets. As for the fifth form of mental worship, namely, *iʿtibār*, or contemplation,[98] it is mentioned in seven verses of the Qur'an, and includes the process of taking lessons from history and from the signs in the cosmos. Ibn Rushd sees *iʿtibār* as equivalent to analogical deduction (*al-qiyās*) in both its rational and juristic forms.

Whereas in the past, these forms of worship were practiced through direct contact between the individual and the universe, we now have intermediate ways of engaging in them such as various types of museums, satellite programs on the wonders of nature, programs and books on what is termed the scientific inimitability of the Qur'an, as well as scientific excursions and so on, all of which serve to facilitate engagement in these rational forms of worship and the use of the mind which they entail.

8. In addition to the foregoing, we also have the process referred to as *al-tafaqquh*, which involves devoting oneself to acquiring a deeper knowledge of something,[99] and which is mentioned in twenty verses of the Qur'an. *Al-tafaqquh* is a mental step which goes beyond mere thinking (*al-tafakkur* or *al-tafkīr*), since it renders human beings more aware of their surroundings and more deeply perceptive of the dimensions of their existence and their connections to the wider universe; as such, it assists people in remaining open to new insights.

As for *al-tadhakkur*, that is, the act of bearing in mind or taking to heart which is among the most sublime thought processes, it is mentioned in no fewer than 269 verses.[100]

9. On the level of specialized scholars, the use of the mind immediately raises the issue of scientific inquiry as embodied in concern for the establishment of research institutes and centers, the setting aside of sufficient budgets for such endeavors, cooperation with the private sector in this area, as well as benefiting from the system of religious endowments which sponsored this type of pursuit in the brightest eras of Islamic renewal, and investing the outputs of such research in relevant practical areas (rather than, as is the practice now, hiding them away in drawers and files) and publishing it for the benefit of specialists in relevant fields. The promotion of research requires the funding of prizes to be granted to outstanding researchers, as well as the provision of facilities for specialized libraries and laboratories and advanced educational technology, the internet, exhibitions, museums, educational missions, academic conferences, etc.

10. Likewise of the utmost importance is the need to demonstrate concern for the nurture of succeeding generations of fine scholars. After being chosen in the earliest phases of education from among outstanding students and

those with creative potentials, efforts need to be devoted to refining their mental faculties and training them in scientific methodology.

In sum, it will be clear from the foregoing that affirmation of the intent to put the mind to use and the overall means of achieving this intent are based principally upon verses from the Qur'an itself, whereas the details of the means by which it is to be achieved are derived from human experience in the areas of psychology, education and technology.

[*Subtheme* 3]*: An Example From the Field of Economics*

Given that we are attempting to arrive at a definition of the Islamic legal intents which pertain to the modern sciences and, in particular, the human and social sciences, we must bear in mind that these sciences – alongside the Islamic legal rulings related to each of these sciences and which serve as their legal and prescriptive standards – involve sets of laws and principles which govern the human and social phenomena of relevance to the fields being studied. These laws or principles serve to elucidate human and social nature, as well as the causal relationships among the phenomena under study. As a result, we must make use of the appropriate methods to ascertain the Islamic legal intent of each science in both its prescriptive and objective aspects.

This blend of objective and prescriptive aspects is reminiscent of Imam al-Shāṭibī's definition of the intent of Islamic law as being "to deliver human beings from subjection to their whims and desires in order that they might be servants of God by their own free choice just as they are, already, His servants by necessity." In other words, the intent of the Law is to create harmony between human beings' actions and voluntary behaviors as governed by prescriptive standards on one hand, and the psychological, social and natural laws and principles which govern this universe on the other.

The Islamic ideal as it pertains to science is that of seeking out knowledge which is beneficial. Indeed, the noble Prophet used to pray for divine protection against knowledge which brings no benefit. However, in order to determine whether knowledge is beneficial or not, we have no choice but to investigate its intents and goals, as well as its outcomes, effects and applications.

Research into the intents of the sciences from an Islamic legal perspective requires, of necessity, that they be linked with the overall intents of Islamic law, which virtually all scholars agree revolve around the achievement of people's best interests. Similarly, it is agreed upon that the intent of the Law overall is the preservation of five universals referred to as religion, human life, the faculty of reason, progeny, and material wealth. Hence, whatever entails the preservation of these five fundamentals is to be considered a benefit; conversely, whatever causes any of them to be lost is to be considered a source of harm. Research into the Islamic legal intents for each of the sciences in light of these overall fundamentals leads ultimately to a rational, comprehensive, detailed conceptualization of the notion of Islamic legal intents.

Research into *maqāṣid al-sharīʿah* for each of the sciences is the cornerstone of the philosophy of the science in question. Moreover, the formulation of such a philosophy helps to clarify the principal features of the Islamic sciences (legal, human and natural) inclusive of all of their branches, which are distinct from sciences founded on a materialist Western philosophy.

It is in light of the foregoing that I shall approach my discussion of the intents of Islamic economics. For the sake of maximum clarity, I distinguish among three principle discussion points: (1) Islamic legal intents for individuals within the realm of microeconomics, (2) Islamic legal intents for society within the realm of macroeconomics, and (3) the intents of Islamic economics which are inclusive of the two aforementioned realms, given that the subject of economics is the economic system.

Islamic legal intents for individuals in the economic realm[101]

A survey of texts relevant to the Islamic legal intents for individuals in the economic realm yields the following elements:

1. Islam sets forth a middle way between the life of this world and the life of the world to come. It has been related on the authority of Anas ibn Mālik that the Prophet declared, "The best among you are not those who neglect this life for the life to come, nor those who neglect the life to come for the sake of this life. Rather, each of them serves as a path leading to the other. Hence, be not a burden to others."[102] Similarly, we have on the authority of Abū Hurayrah that the Prophet used to pray, "O God, cause me to prosper in this world in which I have my earthly life, and cause me to prosper in the world to come, where I shall have my return [to You]."[103]

2. Islam delineates a framework for the individual pursuit of material wealth, stressing the soundness of both its source and the manner in which it is spent.

According to a hadith passed down on the authority of Abū Barazah al-Aslamī, the Prophet said, "On the Day of Resurrection, no human being will be released from God's presence [as Judge] until he has been asked where he obtained his material wealth and how he put it to use."[104]

3. Islam calls upon us to work to obtain material wealth and to seek legitimate means of earthly subsistence: "He it is who has made the earth easy to live upon: go about, then, in all its regions, and partake of the sustenance which He provides: but [always bear in mind that] unto Him you shall be resurrected" (67:15). In keeping with this principle, Imam Aḥmad narrates on the authority of al-Zubayr ibn al-ʿAwwām that the Prophet said, "For a man to gather firewood, bind it with a cord and come and sell it in the market – then, having become self-sufficient in this manner, to use what he has earned to support himself – is better than for him to ask of others, whether they give to him or not."[105]

4. Islam stresses in numerous texts that the source of one's material wealth must be legitimate. For example, in a hadith passed down on the authority of Abū Saʿīd al-Khudrī, the Prophet declared, "Whoever takes money which rightfully belongs to him will be blessed therein, but whoever takes money to which he has no right may be likened to someone who eats but is never satisfied."[106] In a hadith narrated on the authority of Abū Hurayrah, the Prophet stated, "God is good, and accepts nothing but that which is good. Moreover, God has given believers the same command as that which He gave to His messengers, saying: 'O you apostles! Partake of the good things of life…' (23:51) and, 'O you who have attained to faith! Partake of the good things which We have provided for you…' (2:172)." He then made mention of a certain man who, unkempt and covered with dust, would make long journeys, all the while raising his hands to God and saying, 'O Lord! O Lord!' Yet his food, his drink, his clothing and, indeed, his entire sustenance, was obtained in an illegitimate manner. How, then, he asked, can such a person expect his supplications to be heard?[107]

5. Islam views the pursuit and acquisition of material wealth as a fulfillment of human beings' mission as God's trustees on earth, so that they might put it to use in the doing of good. As God Almighty has declared, "Believe in God and His Apostle, and spend on others out of that of which He has made you

trustees…" (57:7), "and give them [their share] of the wealth of God which He has given you" (24:33).

6. Given the fact that material wealth has a social function and is not an end in itself, a number of texts forbid us to hoard wealth, thereby keeping it out of circulation:

- "But as for all who lay up treasures of gold and silver and do not spend them for the sake of God – give them the tiding of grievous suffering [in the life to come]: on the Day when that [hoarded wealth] shall be heated in the fire of hell and their foreheads and their sides and their backs branded therewith, [those sinners shall be told]: 'These are the treasures which you have laid up for yourselves! Taste, then [the evil of] your hoarded treasures" (9:34–35).
- "And they should not think – they who niggardly cling to all that God has granted them out of His bounty – that this is good for them: nay, it is bad for them. That to which they [so] niggardly cling will, on the Day of Resurrection, be hung about their necks: For unto God [alone] belongs the heritage of the heavens and the earth; and God is aware of all that you do" (3:180).

7. Within this framework in which Islam urges us to acquire material wealth but without hoarding it, material wealth is viewed as a means, or tool, of which the believer is to make use in reaching his or her goal, not an end which becomes his or her sole preoccupation. In a hadith passed down on the authority of ʿAmr ibn al-ʿĀṣ, the Prophet declared, "What a blessing wealth is in the possession of the righteous man!"[108] In a hadith passed down on the authority of ʿAbd Allāh ibn Ḥabīb on the authority of his paternal uncle, the Prophet declared, "There is nothing wrong with wealth for those who are conscious of God, Almighty and Majestic is He. However, for the God-conscious, health is better than wealth, while joyousness is [also] a blessing."[109] In a further hadith on the authority of Khālid ibn Maʿdān and Ḍamrah ibn Ḥabīb, the Prophet said, "Those who have abundant wealth have many worries, and when one has many worries, his heart is scattered among endless valleys, and God [Himself] cares not which path he treads. As for those who have one concern only,[110] God will protect them from the worries of this earthly life…"[111]

8. With regard to the spending of one's material wealth, Islam places primary importance on spending on oneself, giving this higher priority than spending on charity. It is recorded that the Prophet said, "The best charity is that which is spent out of sufficiency. Begin with those for whose material support you are responsible."[112] That is to say, the best charity or alms one can give are those which are distributed after one has done justice to oneself and one's dependents such that the person who gives the charity does not himself become dependent on others as a result of having given the charity. Hence, the term 'sufficiency' (*ghinā*) as used in this hadith refers to the availability of that which meets one's essential needs, thereby preventing one from falling into a state of impoverishment.

9. Spending on others[113] might be characterized by one of two extremes, namely, niggardliness and excess, whereas what is called for is a path of moderation which falls somewhere between these two poles. Hence, God Almighty speaks in praise of those "who, whenever they spend on others, are neither wasteful nor niggardly but [remember that] there is always a just mean between those [two extremes]" (25:67). In a similar vein He says, "And neither allow thy hand to remain shackled to thy neck, nor stretch it forth to the utmost limit [of thy capacity], lest thou find thyself blamed [by thy dependents], or even destitute" (17:29). Economy, then, is a medial degree or position. With respect to the pursuit of benefit, then, there are three degrees or positions, namely, negligence, excess, and a point equidistant between these two extremes which may be termed 'economy' (*iqtiṣād*).

- Ḥudhayfah declared, "A good deed is one which lies somewhere between two bad deeds, that is, that which goes beyond negligence while falling short of excess, and the best of all things are marked by moderation."[114] We have on the authority of Anas ibn Mālik that the Prophet said, "Inquiry is half of knowledge, moderation is half of living, those who practice moderation will not become a burden to others, excessive zeal is death's precursor, and this earthly existence is the believer's prison."[115]

10. This brings us to a discussion of human needs in Islam, which may be classified in the present context as follows:[116]

(a) Benign and harmful needs, in connection with which we read, "O mankind! Partake of what is lawful and good on earth, and follow not Satan's footsteps: for, verily, he is your open foe" (2:168).

(b) Material and spiritual needs, concerning which there are numerous Qur'anic verses. We read, for example:

- "And contain thyself in patience by the side of all who at morn and at evening invoke their Sustainer, seeking His countenance, and let not thine eyes pass beyond them in quest of the beauties of this world's life; and pay no heed to any whose heart We have rendered heedless of all remembrance of Us because he had always followed his own desires, abandoning all that is good and true" (18:28).
- "Avoid thou, therefore, those who turn away from all remembrance of Us and care for no more than the life of this world which, to them, is the only thing worth knowing. Behold, thy Sustainer is fully aware as to who has strayed from His path, and fully aware is He as to who follows His guidance" (53:29-30).
- "In the houses [of worship] which God has allowed to be raised so that His name be remembered in them, there [are such as] extol His limitless glory at morn and evening – people whom neither [worldly] commerce nor striving after gain can divert from the remembrance of God, and from constancy in prayer, and from charity: [people] who are filled with fear [at the thought] of the Day on which all hearts and eyes will be convulsed, [and who only hope] that God may reward them in accordance with the best that they ever did, and give them, out of His bounty, more [than they deserve]: for, God grants sustenance unto whom He wills, beyond all reckoning" (24:36–38).
- "And I said, 'Ask your Sustainer to forgive you your sins – for, verily, He is All-Forgiving! He will shower upon you heavenly blessings abundant, and will aid you with worldly goods and children, and will bestow upon you gardens, and bestow upon you running waters" (71:10-12).

(c) Essential needs and non-essential (or 'enhancement-related') needs. A great deal has been said on this topic by scholars of *uṣūl al-fiqh*, while proponents of Islamic economics have also discussed the application of such needs in the economic realm.[117]

(d) Current and future needs. Future needs include, for example:

- The need to prepare for one's children's future. We have on the authority of Saᶜd ibn Abī Waqqāṣ that the Prophet said to him, "To leave your heirs wealthy is better than to leave them destitute and forced to beg from others."[118] In this connection we might note that ᶜAbd Allāh ibn al-Zubayr once said that al-Zubayr's personal fortune amounted to 50 million [dirhams].[119] We are also told that the widow of ᶜAbd al-Raḥmān ibn ᶜAwf settled for a share of his estate which amounted to one-third of one-eighth, namely, 380,000 [dirhams], which means that the total value of the estate came to 9,120,000 [dirhams].[120]
- The need to prepare for old age. ᶜĀ'ishah narrated that a prayer which the Prophet used to utter almost unceasingly was, "O God, grant me Your most abundant sustenance in my later years, when my lifetime is drawing to a close and my end is near."[121]
- The need to leave a will and testament directing others to spend out of one's bequest in charity, particularly in the form of what is termed 'ongoing charity' (*ṣadaqah jāriyah*). The Prophet said, "When an individual dies, his earthly work comes to a halt with the exception of three things: ongoing charity, knowledge from which others can benefit, and righteous offspring who pray for him."[122]

(e) Individual and collective needs, the latter of which will be dealt with in our discussion of Islamic legal intents for society in the economic realm.

11. Needless to say spending on oneself or on others cannot be done on prohibited things. Al-Mughīrah ibn Shuᶜbah said, "I heard the Prophet forbid the practice of burying female infants alive, ingratitude or disobedience to one's mother, stinginess and greed, gossip, over-inquisitiveness, and wasting money."[123] A man once asked Saᶜīd ibn Jubayr what the Prophet meant by his prohibition against wasting money, to which he replied saying, "[To waste money] means for God to provide you with a legitimate source of livelihood, after which you spend your earnings on what God has forbidden to you."[124]

12. It will be clear from the foregoing that material wealth is a test and a source of temptation for human beings, both with respect to the ways in which they acquire it and the ways in which they put it to use. We have on

the authority of ᶜĀ'ishah that the Prophet used to pray, saying, "O God, I seek Your protection from the evil of the temptation posed by both wealth and poverty."[125] Similarly, it was narrated by Kaᶜb ibn ᶜIyāḍ that the Prophet declared, "Every nation has its particular trial, and my nation's trial is that of wealth."[126]

What has been stated thus far makes clear the importance of identifying the intents of Islamic law for the individual in the economic realm. These intents may be summed up as that of worshiping and revering God by giving Him His due in the realm of material wealth, and this by: (1) working and striving to make an honest living, and (2) spending material wealth moderately – falling prey neither to miserliness nor to wastefulness – on one's own legitimate needs and the needs of those whose support one is responsible for under Islamic law. Such needs include both material and non-material needs, essential and enhancement-related needs, current and future needs, and individual and collective needs. Whatever remains after one has met such needs, one is to spend on the types of charity which are commanded and/or recommended in Islamic law. Moreover, the intent behind all of this – whether in the area of earning or spending – is to carry out the trust which we have received from God to populate and develop the earth.

* * *

What has been presented here thus far has to do with *maqāṣid al-sharīᶜah* as they relate to individual activity in the realm of the economy. However, these are bound to differ from the intents of individuals themselves as they engage in their various forms of economic conduct, and which should remain within the framework of the intents of the Law which serve as their legal standard. Individual intents are the goals in the service of which people act in order to lend order to their lives, such as the transfer of ownership through selling, achieving benefit through rental agreements, and other activities which help to achieve people's private interests. Such interests differ from one individual to another and from one time to another; however, they must always be regulated by Islamic legal intents, since it is the latter which are intended to achieve individuals' genuine, as opposed to imagined, interests, just as they serve to achieve the interests of the community as a whole.[127]

Islamic legal intents for society in the economic realm:[128]
In our earlier discussion of needs, reference was made to the fact that whereas some needs constitute individual obligations, others constitute collective obligations based on the fact that they are needs which are experienced by society as a whole. Consequently, society is called upon to cooperate in meeting such needs, since otherwise all members of the society will be guilty of wrongdoing. Of the numerous examples of collective obligations cited by *fiqh* scholars, we will deal in what follows only with those that pertain to the economic realm.

1. Establishment of the caliphate in order to guarantee Muslims' unity and cooperation and the application of the principle of *shūrā*, or consultation, developments which are bound to be reflected economically in the fundamental functions of the state.

2. Jihad can constitute a collective or an individual obligation. For instance if an Islamic country is invaded, it becomes an individual obligation, a fact which is reflected in the economic realm in the form of self-sufficiency in all war industries in a way which makes it possible to make necessary preparations for combat for self-defence without reliance on non-Muslims. Jihad as an individual obligation entails mobilization of the entire Ummah in order to protect it from aggression and to ensure a just peace.

3. Commanding the doing of what is right and prohibiting the doing of what is wrong. These functions are not restricted, as they are in the writings of *fiqh* scholars, to those who occupy official positions of authority. What this means, then, is the establishment of institutions devoted to commanding the doing of what is right and prohibiting the doing of what is wrong within advanced, specialized systems. Such systems should guarantee the fulfillment of these functions without arbitrary understandings or interpretations or abusive practices, and should preserve the role of individuals in full while safeguarding and lending order to individuals' efforts to fulfill these obligations.

4. Providing needy Muslims with what they require by way of clothing and food if such needs are not being met through the distribution of zakah or the public treasury; the same applies to needy non-Muslim citizens. What this means is the setting up of systems and institutions which are capable of ensuring essential nourishment, clothing, housing, health services and education

free of charge to those who are unable to afford them, and organizing social security for all classes of citizens.

5. Earthly types of collective obligations, such as professions, trades, crafts and industries and those activities which are required for subsistence such as buying, selling, cultivating and anything else which is needed including even cupping and sweeping. The study of sciences such as medicine and mathematics have also been included by scholars among collective obligations.

6. Examples cited by early *fiqh* scholars are merely examples; as such they reflect what was suited to the needs of their own societies. As for us, we may add to the list needs which continue to arise in our own time and circumstances.

7. Achievement of self-sufficiency in all areas, beginning with essentials such as agriculture, food industries, housing, health care, and education in order to ensure economic autonomy for the Islamic Ummah; provision of such necessities free of charge for those unable to afford them, and at reasonable prices for those who are able to afford them.

8. Establishment of the educational institutions, scientific research foundations and training programs required to advance the Ummah in all spheres and the provision of the trained, qualified workers needed by such institutions.

9. Establishment of systems which will ensure the mobilization of financial savings and surpluses, investment of such resources in the aforementioned spheres, and provision of the appropriate profit and tax incentives.

10. Establishment of economic, financial and banking institutions within the framework of Islamic law and in accordance with its principles.

* * *

Given the tension between the personal incentives which fuel individual activity and the societal interests which require sacrifice on the part of the individual, personal piety emerges as a key to reconciling the public interest and personal motivation. This being the case, the establishment of public interests as collective obligations which are carried out by individuals serves to realize the meaning of personal piety whilst, at the same time, providing for the societal needs to which reference was made earlier.[129]

If we wish to define the overall intent of public expenditure in Islam, it is the meeting of public, or societal needs. In order to specify what is being referred to here as societal needs, we may say that if no individual is able to meet a particular kind of need, or if a particular individual is unable to meet a need which other individuals are able to meet, then these needs are to be considered public, or societal, needs which, according to Islamic thought, the state is duty-bound to provide on behalf of such individuals. We may thus define the concept of 'societal need' in Islamic thought as the interests of Muslims [overall] and that which cannot be done without. This type of need, the fulfillment of which yields overall benefits, may be classified among the essentials, the exigencies, or the enhancements in accordance with the limits set by Islamic law.

This overall intent, however, is made up of numerous specific intents, some of which the Islamic state shares in common with other systems. Such common intents include, for example: (1) managing relations with other sovereign states, (2) defense against any sort of external aggression, (3) internal security, and (4) justice. These are the functions of the state according to the individualist philosophy upon which liberal society rested originally. However, it later stipulated additional functions in order to achieve the welfare state and in order to avoid revolutions on the part of the poor classes. These functions, which have already been affirmed by Islam and applied in Islamic society as collective obligations, are: (5) education, (6) health care, and (7) mutual or joint responsibility and social security.

There are, in addition to the intents already listed, other intents which are likewise affirmed by the Islamic system, namely:[130] (8) the preservation of Islamic social values based on the obligation to command the doing of what is right and to prohibit the doing of what is wrong, and (9) the call to embrace Islam on a worldwide scale.

* * *

These functions, whose fulfillment meets societal needs, are categorized in Islamic thought as essentials, exigencies or enhancements. On the level of essentials we have the following functions: (1) Defense-related functions, which contribute to the preservation of religion, human life, material wealth and progeny, (2) Expenditures relating to security and the establishment of justice, which contribute to the preservation of human life and material wealth, (3) Education, which promotes the preservation and development of the faculty of reason, as well as the preservation of religion on the basis of its established fundamentals, and (4) Expenditures relating to social security, which serves to preserve human life, the faculty of reason, and progeny for those who stand in need of it.

On the level of exigencies, we have functions relating to economic development and state supervision of individual economic activity. It bears noting, however, that in some situations and at some times, a given function may belong on the level of exigencies while, in other situations and at other times, it will belong on the level of essentials, depending on its status in people's lives.

As for the level of enhancements, it expands as society progresses and as new collective needs emerge as a consequence. Functions associated with this level include, for example, the building of sports clubs, parks and recreation areas, the holding of competitions, providing various types of beneficial amusement for workers during their free time, as well as other things which encourage wholesome habits and make life more enjoyable.[131]

It is important to note here that among the societal needs which constitute collective obligations, there are some which may be fulfilled by the mother collective institution, namely, the state, just as there are others which may be fulfilled by Islamic society as embodied in other institutions. Such organizations are not necessarily subject to or funded by the mother institution; rather, they are brought into existence and managed within the framework of individuals' group initiatives, and are generally regulated by the laws which govern societies, clubs, corporations and the like.

Generally speaking, the distinction between individual activity ('microeconomics') and collective activity ('macroeconomics') is drawn for purely academic purposes. Practically speaking, however, they are interrelated and complementary. Consequently, we must not overlook the intimate connection between these dual branches of economic studies and their mutual interdependence.[132]

The intents of Islamic economics

The topic of *maqāṣid al-sharīʿah* as they pertain to both individuals and society as a whole in the economic realm leads naturally to a discussion of the intents of Islamic economics, which includes the dual spheres of microeconomics and macroeconomics. It may be said at the outset that Islamic economics aims to discover what will make it possible for individuals and society to achieve their intents in the realm of the economy. The reason for this is that individuals' and societies' achievement of their intents in the realm of the economy is an obligation [in Islam], and they will only be able to do this once this discovery has been made; moreover, anything without which a duty cannot be fulfilled is, itself, a duty.

Now, in order for economics to achieve this overall intent, it must accomplish at least three other, preliminary tasks:

§*First:* It must identify the premises upon which it bases its research.

These premises are derived from the doctrinal aspect of Islam, which serves as the basis and starting point for any discussion in the realm of the economy. Such premises include, for example, the affirmations that: (1) sovereignty and the right to be worshipped and served belong to God alone, may He be praised and exalted, (2) material wealth belongs to God and has been given to us as a trust, (3) the goal of existence on Earth is for us to populate and develop it, which in turn is related to the profitable investment of material wealth, (4) the cosmos as a whole, and the Earth in particular, have been subjected to human beings and placed at their service in order for them to fulfill their roles as God's trustees and to complete the process of populating and developing the earth, (5) God's placing of human beings in the role of trustees on Earth applies to humanity as a whole and is not a distinction conferred upon one group over another, and (6) what a human being acquires as a result of his or her labor grants him or her no distinction over others, just as the loss of what one has gained implies no deficiency in the individual concerned nor does it detract from his or her human or social rights.[133] These are just some of the premises which set Islam apart from other systems of thought and which make up the ideological dimension of the Islamic economy.

This ideological, philosophical and doctrinal dimension is the general framework for the economic dimensions which will be discussed below. Moreover, it is this ideological, philosophical and doctrinal framework which constitutes the connecting link between the economic aspects of human existence and the realms of worship, ethics, education, social relations and politics, not to mention other aspects of Islam which, taken as an integrated whole, shape the Muslim individual within the Islamic community. Hence, the Islamic economy may be described as an economy that governs a society which is ordered in accordance with Islamic teachings; the institutions of such a society operate based on true Islamic principles, while its individual members believe in Islamic values and, in their daily lives, tread the 'straight Islamic path.' As such, such a society differs fundamentally from all those societies whose constitutions profess a commitment to Islam, yet without there being any concrete indication of this commitment in the lives of their citizens.[134]

§*Second:* It must identify the divine principles and laws which govern economic relations.

(a) Some of these principles and laws are stated explicitly in the Holy Qur'an and the Prophetic Sunnah, including, for example:

- "Nay, verily, man becomes grossly overweening whenever he believes himself to be self-sufficient" (96:6–7).
- "Say: 'If you were to own all the treasure houses of my Sustainer's bounty, lo! You would still try to hold on [to them] tightly for fear of spending [too much]: for man has always been avaricious'" (17:100).
- "...you love wealth with boundless love!" (89:20).

These, of course, are only a few of the innumerable Qur'anic passages which deal with matters pertaining to material wealth and the economy. It is principles of this type which Islamic economics seeks to investigate and bring to light.

(b) Others of these principles and laws, by contrast, must be sought out and discovered by the Muslim economist through the study of the concrete reality of economic life in its past and present in an attempt to identify the forces which govern economic phenomena. Such an objective investigation of reality is indispensable for the formation of the scientific and theoretical aspect of Islamic economics.

§*Third:* There must be a thorough investigation of the Islamic legal rulings pertaining to economic matters, including both those which rely directly upon the Qur'an and Sunnah, and those which have been derived through a process of ijtihad suited to the needs of each respective time and place.

This, then, is the aspect which has to do with legal obligation; in other words, it is the prescriptive, value-related side of Islamic economics which addresses not the question of what is, but rather, of what ought to be. Of the legal rulings relevant to this prescriptive dimension, some are addressed to the individual (referred to as individual obligations, or *furūḍ ʿayn*, singular, *farḍ ʿayn*), while others are addressed to society (referred to as collective obligations, or *furūḍ kifāyah*). Without the fulfillment of these individual and collective obligations, we cannot expect to achieve the Islamically prescribed purposes of the economy, since the outcomes of the mechanisms associated with the Islamic economic system are inseparable from, and indeed, dependent upon, the action taken by both individuals and the community in fulfillment of their respective obligations.

* * *

The foregoing overview of the three tasks with which Islamic economics concerns itself should help to make clear the intent which this discipline seeks to achieve. Moreover, as we had occasion to note with respect to the distinction between individual and collective activity, the distinction among the three dimensions of economics – namely, the ideological, the theoretical, and the applied – is drawn solely for academic purposes. On the practical level, however, the ideological, theoretical and applied aspects of economics freely intermingle and interact.

It should likewise be noted that although the act of identifying the intents of a discipline lead to the specification of its subject matter and content, there nevertheless remains a distinction between the intents of economics as we have set them forth here, and the subject matter of this same discipline. As for its subject matter, authors have categorized it and dealt with its respective categories in a variety of ways.

[*Subtheme* 4]*: An Example From the Realm of Sociology*

Given that the family is the nucleus of society, it constitutes one of the most important themes dealt with by the field of sociology. Nevertheless, sociology books make no mention of the intents (*maqāṣid*) of the family as a fundamental institution within society, and they lack whatever potential discussions of the family's functions might be based thereon. In fact, social movements in the West have begun leaning toward the endorsement of diverse forms of the family by allowing both homosexuality and lesbianism. Not only this, but homosexual and lesbian marriages have been formalized in churches, and there has been a sanctioning of 'collective families' consisting of several men and several women. Indeed, even books on Islamic law rarely concern themselves with an elucidation of the intents of marriage, contenting themselves with a detailed presentation of the juristic rulings on various topics with a bearing on personal status regulations. Consequently, there is a need to elucidate the intents of marriage and to support and defend it as an institution against the sustained onslaught of Western influences being waged under the guise of globalization.

An early attempt to define the intents of the family was undertaken by Abū Ḥāmid al-Ghazālī in his book *Iḥyā' ʿUlūm al-Dīn*; a further attempt was made in modern times by Ibn Ashur in his book *Maqāṣid al-Sharīʿah*, as well as the effort I have made in this book (Chapter Two, Theme Three, Subtheme 2). What follows is a comparative study of the contributions made by al-Ghazālī, Ibn Ashur and myself on the theme of the intents of the family, beginning with a summary of each writer's thought.

Al-Ghazālī:

In the section of *Iḥyā' ʿUlūm al-Dīn* dealing with the rules of etiquette associated with marriage, al-Ghazālī outlines five benefits of marriage,[135] which are:

1. The bearing of children, which he considers to be a means of drawing near to God in four ways: (a) acting in harmony with God's love by striving to reproduce in order to ensure the survival of the human race (b) seeking the love of the Prophet by maximizing the number of those in whom he can take pride on the Day of Resurrection (c) seeking blessing through the supplications to be offered on one's behalf by one's righteous children after one

has died, and (d) seeking the intercession of which one will be the beneficiary if any of one's children dies young.

2. Fortifying oneself against the wiles of Satan by breaking the power of one's physical longings and warding off the havoc that can be wrought by one's passions, lowering one's glance [when in the presence of members of the opposite sex other than one's spouse], and chastity.

3. Reviving one's spirits and enjoying each other's companionship, looking upon one another, and bantering with each other, all of which gladdens the heart and strengthens it for worship.

4. Relieving oneself of the preoccupation with housekeeping and various other domestic tasks.

5. [The assistance provided by marriage] in the struggle to discipline and tame one's lower self (*al-nafs*) through the consideration and regard one shows toward one's wives, the care one provides for them, fulfillment of the duties entailed by one's responsibility for them, ensuring that they receive their due, patient endurance of their moral failings, offenses and insults, striving to reform them, improve them and guide them onto the path of the true religion, working hard to make an honest living for their sake, and raising one's children.

In conformity with what al Ghazālī had written, *uṣūl* scholars who succeeded him considered procreation to be the primary intent of marriage, and all other resultant benefits as secondary intents.

Ibn Ashur

Ibn Ashur presents the *maqāṣid* underlying the Islamic legal rulings pertaining to the family[136] in the following four groups:

1. Rulings relating to establishment of the marital bond: After presenting the various forms of marriage which prevailed in pre-Islamic times based on the hadith passed down on the authority of ʿĀ'ishah, Ibn Ashur explains that the intent of marriage [in Islam] has two foundations:

(a) Demonstrating the contrast between the way in which [Islamic] marriage is contracted and the ways in which a man took a wife [in pre-Islamic times].

This contrast is revealed in the following features of Islamic marriage:

- The role played by the woman's guardian in contracting the marriage.
- The necessity of a dowry to be paid by the husband.
- The stipulation that the marriage be made public, since keeping a marriage secret taints it with the appearance of illegitimacy.

(b) The stipulation that marriage not be entered into as a temporary arrangement.

2. Rulings relating to kinship bonds. In this connection, Ibn Ashur discusses attribution of fatherhood and sonship; non-marriagability based on descent (seen, for example, in the fact that a man's ascendants and descendants are non-marriageable to him) and non-marriagability based on kinship by marriage or having been breastfed by the same woman; financial support for one's children, parents, grandparents and grandchildren; kinship as a basis for inheritance rights and rulings relating to reverence for one's parents; the bond among immediate family members and other relatives; the permissibility of eating in the homes of one's relatives without an invitation and without having sought permission; and the ruling relating to displaying one's beauty and ornaments in one's relatives' presence.

3. Rulings pertaining to kinship by marriage.

4. Means of dissolving these three types of bonds.

Gamal Eldin Attia

In Theme 3 of Chapter Two of this book, we presented *maqāṣid al-sharīʿah* in relation to the family in regard to the following points:

- Regulation of relations between the sexes.
- Preservation of progeny (the species).
- The achievement of tranquility, love and tenderness [in the marital relationship].
- Preservation of family lineage.
- Preservation of personal piety in the family.
- Ordering the institutional aspect of the family.
- Ordering the financial aspect of the family.

* * *

A careful examination of, and comparison among these three conceptualizations makes clear that the reason behind the disparity in points of view lies in the difference between their starting points and methodologies. We note, for example, that:

1. Al-Ghazālī views marriage in light of general principles without concerning himself with particular legal rulings. In addition, there is a degree of inconsistency between his point concerning "relieving oneself of preoccupation with household management" and "the struggle to discipline and tame one's lower self", as it would have been more fitting to consider the point concerning the struggle against one's lower self as among the banes of marriage, not among its benefits.

2. Ibn Ashur explores particular rulings relating to marriage, seeking to extract universal themes therefrom. However, his thinking is dominated by the details of such particular rulings and the wise purposes underlying them.

3. As for my own attempt, it is characterized by a systematic vision which searches for universals within particular rulings, yet without allowing the latter to dominate its overall perspective.

[*Subtheme* 5]*: An Example From the Natural Sciences*

How is it possible to apply the notion of Islamization and, in particular, *maqāṣid al-sharīʿah*, to the natural sciences? In a Ph.D. dissertation presented at Zaytuna University in Tunisia, Musaddiq Hasan offers us an answer to this question based on a painstaking exploration of the theme of genetic engineering and *maqāṣid al-sharīʿah.*[137]

In the introduction to this study its author writes:

> This research is a partial attempt to answer the following question: Does Islamic law, given its overall *maqāṣid*, permit human intervention through the process of redesigning a living system and attempting to constitute living beings in accordance with genetic technology? That is to say, is it possible to bring about a set of genetic and physiological changes in an organism's structure and essence? Given what this question encompasses by way of social, moral and religious issues, and by virtue of the biological revolution [which the world continues to witness], this dissertation concerns itself with the

> study of the legal implications, Islamically speaking, of what genetic engineering and technology raise – through laboratory experimentation – by way of issues relating to a variety of living beings, issues which call for an Islamic legal declaration as well as keen juristic insight.[138]

The author mentions having chosen this particular topic in order to achieve the following purposes:

1. To evaluate genetic engineering in light of its Islamic legal implications given the fears aroused by this field of activity on moral and religious planes – fears which are intimately associated with concepts such as the family, marriage, paternity, maternity, identity, freedom, life, responsibility and humanity.

2. To determine the Islamic legal position with respect to experimentation on human beings, particularly as it concerns asexual reproduction, which is a topic of special significance which calls for research in the realm of Islamic law and keen insight into the subtleties of Islamic jurisprudence.

3. To provide even partial answers to the following questions: (a) Is biological experimentation degrading to human beings? (b) What is the role of *fiqh* scholars and juristic academies in genetic experimentation and its applications? (c) Does Islamic law permit the use of human organisms as 'spare parts' for other human beings? (d) Does Islamic law allow a woman to become a mother, despite the fact that she is still a virgin, by means of asexual reproduction technology? (e) Is it permissible for the gene code to immortalize prototypes of geniuses and other gifted individuals through genetic cloning?[139]

Hasan divides his research plan into two sections, the first scientific and the second pertaining to Islamic law.[140] The section pertaining to Islamic law is composed of a preface and two chapters. In the preface, he deals with the spiritual meaning of the formation of soil through a discussion of: a) divine creation and the formation of the organism, b) the honor bestowed upon human beings, and c) the miracle of life. Chapter One, entitled, "Asexual Reproduction, Fetuses and *Maqāṣid al-Sharīʿah*," discusses: 1) asexual reproduction and *maqāṣid al-sharīʿah*, 2) abortion and *maqāṣid al-sharīʿah*, and 3) fetal gender and *maqāṣid al-sharīʿah*. As for Chapter Two, entitled, "Genetic Technology and *Maqāṣid al-Sharīʿah*," it deals with: 1) genetic treatment and *maqāṣid al-sharīʿah*, 2) gene control and *maqāṣid al-sharīʿah*, and 3) animal and plant genetic technology and *maqāṣid al-sharīʿah*.

In what follows, we will take two examples from these six themes in order to see how the researcher has made use of *maqāṣid al-sharīʿah* to provide answers to the questions raised above.

Example No. 1: Fetal Gender

The question here is whether there is a conflict between technological intervention to determine the gender of a fetus and the divine will as described in the following Qur'an verse: "God's alone is the dominion over the heavens and the earth. He creates whatever He wills: He bestows the gift of female offspring on whomever He wills, and the gift of male offspring on whomever He wills; or He gives both male and female [to whomever He wills], and causes to be barren whomever He wills: for, verily, He is All-Knowing, infinite in His power" (42:49-50).

In contrast to the apparent import of this verse, and in disagreement with the views put forward by all other commentators, this researcher proposes the view that the term 'God's will' refers to the sum total of the laws which God has placed in nature and the human conscience. This divine will, he states, affirms human effort and its outcomes as a source of benefit and influence in the world. After all, God has granted human beings the capacity to be the masters of nature. By virtue of this distinction, human beings possess a will which can serve either to reveal and bring to light the divine will, or to negate and reject it. Hence, it is we human beings who manifest the divine will, and it is we who grant it impetus and force. In its most profound meanings, then, the term 'divine will' simply means the human will in its capacity as that which discloses the divine will, bringing to light its structure and manifestations in the laws of the universe, the human psyche and society, and perceiving civilization and culture as materializations of both intelligence and enigma.[141] This being the case, human interventions in these laws as a means of revealing and clarifying them are not incompatible with the divine will but, on the contrary, are expressions thereof. Therefore, there is no conflict between biomedical technology and the divine will with respect to choosing a newborn's gender. Modern biological developments are an exact expression of the laws of the supreme will as it pertains to sex chromosomes. In sum, then, there is no conflict between the content of this Qur'anic verse as it pertains to the fetus's identity, and the modern developments which have been brought about in the laboratory.[142]

In response to this discussion, the following two remarks might be made. First, the researcher makes no use of the concept of *maqāṣid al-sharīʿah* in order to resolve the difficulty raised, despite the fact that this is the theme of his research. Second, the researcher deals with this Qur'anic verse as though it were saying that God has established a law for determining the gender of a fetus, after which science undertook to discover this law and its uses. In so doing, however, he disregards the fact that this verse affirms that there are four different conditions relating to procreation and gender, and that the divine will determines for each individual the condition which it desires for him, yet without any mention of the manner in which this will is carried out such that it might be said: By means of their intervention, human beings manifest this divine will, giving it impetus and force. Such a statement assumes that human beings know what the divine will is for each individual and set about to carry it out, which is the opposite of what happens in practice.

Example No. 2: Gene Control

Given the technique of genetic synthesis, genetic control mechanisms have made it possible to envision new strains of animals and plants such as super rice, seedless tomatoes and watermelons, and many more. Hence, operations involving genetic synthesis among different organisms might take one of the following three forms:

1. Genetic synthesis among different types of plants in order to produce plant strains with new characteristics, or genetic blending of plant genes and the genes of other living things, as in the case of the 'chlorophyll man' on the level of biological aspiration.

2. Genetic synthesis among different types of animals in order to produce new varieties of animals with new characteristics on the level of both structure and substance, or genetic blending of animals and human beings.

3. Genetic control operations affecting human genes, and reshaping certain hereditary traits of human beings.

Possibilities 1 and 2 above may be assumed to fall under the rubric of divine subjugation [of nature to human beings], human sovereignty, and that which is legally permissible within Islam with the exception of genetic blending between two living beings which differ in both structure and essence, which is inconsonant with human dignity. With respect to possibility 3, the researcher touches upon the distinction between beneficial change and harmful change in the structure of the human body. He then declares the former permissible on the condition that it serves to alleviate hardship by endowing the person affected with certain aesthetically desirable bodily characteristics, or by eliminating hereditary diseases. The latter, however, which includes the use of human beings as the subjects of laboratory experimentation, he declares impermissible, since it is a source of harm given the fact that it undermines human dignity, and because it involves tampering with the order of the divine creation.

Hasan bases this distinction upon the principle of benefit and harm, and on Ibn ᶜAṭṭiyah's[143] interpretation of the verse which reads, "...and I shall command them – and they will corrupt God's creation" (4:119), as well as on the following:

- "Now, indeed, We have conferred dignity on the children of Adam" (17:70),
- "God has exalted him above you, and endowed him abundantly with knowledge and bodily perfection" (2:247),
- "...behold, the best [man] that thou couldst hire is one who is [as] strong and worthy of trust [as he]" (28:26),
- The hadith which declares that "the strong believer is better and more beloved to God than the weak believer," and
- The hadith in which the Prophet instructs us to "take in marriage those who are not your kin."

The author then concludes his discussion by identifying a number of criteria applicable to the processes of gene control, including the principle that human beings must not be used as subjects of experimentation given the sacredness of their humanity.[144]

The question which I would raise in connection with this study is: How is it possible for us to discover what is beneficial or harmful, to the end that we might avoid the latter and pursue the former, without experimentation? Isn't experimentation the means by which discoveries are made, and the means by which we acquire knowledge needed to distinguish the beneficial from the harmful? If so, then in accordance with the principles of *fatḥ al-dharā'i*ᶜ* and the subordination of means to ends, the experiments conducted become subject to the same legal ruling which applies to the scientific knowledge required.

In sum, this serious study lacks clear mechanisms for the use of *maqāṣid* in the process of ijtihad, or independent reasoning. However, it is a step in the right direction.

[THEME 5]

The Maqāṣid-Informed Mindset on the Individual and Communal Levels

The benefits of the *maqāṣid* are not limited to the process of independent reasoning concerning juristic questions; rather, they extend to other practical realms as well, the most important of which may well be the realm of thought, whether on the level of the individual or on the level of the community. Hence, we will discuss these benefits under two subthemes, namely: (1) the *maqāṣid*-informed mindset on the level of the individual, and (2) the *maqāṣid*-informed mindset on the level of the community.

[*Subtheme* 1]: *The Maqāṣid-Informed Mindset in the Intellectual Realm*

In his introduction to Ismail al-Hasani's book, *Naẓariyyah al-Maqāṣid ʿInd al-Imām Muḥammad al-Ṭāhir ibn ʿĀshūr*, Taha Jabir al-Alwani states[145] that in order for *maqāṣid*-related studies to take their methodological course and to become part of a network of methodological and epistemological determinants which enable the *maqāṣid* to perform their role in dealing with the current intellectual crisis, there must be a focus upon what are termed the 'universal *maqāṣid*' of the Islamic message and the Law which it brought with it. The reason for this is that particular, detailed *maqāṣid* will keep *maqāṣid*-related Islamic thought imprisoned within the realm of juristic codification which, however much it expands, will always remain narrow to a certain extent, and however much it is generalized, will remain applicable to the realm of *fiqh* in particular. Consequently, unless there emerges an awareness of the universal *maqāṣid*, and unless it becomes possible to deal with them as methodological determinants which regulate the Islamic intellectual and epistemological movement, the partial or particular view will retain its central position not only in Islamic jurisprudence, but in Islamic thought as a whole. If and when this takes place, the universal *maqāṣid* will be transformed into part of an Islamic system of logic which regulates not only Islamic jurisprudence, but the movement of Islamic thought as a whole, thereby protecting it from error and distortion.

In the same vein, Umar Ubayd Hasanah states in his introduction to *al-ijtihād al-Maqāṣidī* that limiting *maqāṣid*-based ijtihad to the juristic and legal realm alone – however great its importance and however profoundly it influences the various sectors and classes of human society – reflects a serious imbalance and leads to major complications. Specifically, it engenders backwardness and helplessness, giving rise to purposelessness and lack of direction in numerous different areas of life, the inability to define goals and, as a consequence, a lack of responsibility and the absence of the mentality which calls for self-examination, criticism and evaluation.

The reason for this is that the fundamental approach of the *maqāṣid*-related mindset is to discover potentials and to lay plans appropriate to their use; to establish the foundations for one's starting points; to define intermediate and strategic goals; to plan programs; to innovate means; to define responsibilities; to identify areas of inadequacy, incompetence and imbalance; to discover the reasons for the inadequacies or oversights identified; to push for review and evaluation; to exploit potentials and historic opportunities; to benefit from experience; to acquire the capacity for analysis and interpretation; to engage in inductive and analogical reasoning; to form a vision of the future in light of one's vision of the past; and to guard against frustration and the tendency to confuse potentials with wishes. In other words, nurturing a purposeful, *maqāṣid*-based mentality reflects positively on all aspects of life, both individual and collective, achieving harmony between the laws of the natural universe and God's ways with human beings, and enabling individuals to recognize the causes which lead to the results [they seek] and the possibilities of intervention and use called for by Islamic law.[146]

Expounding this same theme, al-Raysuni states,

> The benefit to be gained through the *maqāṣid* is not limited to the process of ijtihad and those who engage therein; on the contrary, it extends to everyone

who has absorbed and comprehended their meaning and importance, and even to those who have only limited access to them. In such a case, the benefit they have to offer varies according to the individual's knowledge and understanding of the intents of the Law, and according to the degree to which he or she adopts them and relies upon them in his or her thought and inquiry.

The *maqāṣid*, with their foundations and purposes, their universals and particulars, their subdivisions and levels, their paths and means, constitute a distinctive method of thought and inquiry, analysis and evaluation, inference and synthesis.

Whereas early Islamic thought – as embodied primarily in scholastic theology, the subdivisions which it engendered and the influences to which it led – neglected the *maqāṣid* in terms of both methodology and content, modern Islamic thought is called upon, both now and in the future, to benefit from the *maqāṣid* and *maqāṣid*-based methodology, particularly in light of the growing numbers of writings and studies which are preparing the way for and assisting in this endeavor.[147]

The first way in which *maqāṣid*-based methodology serves to benefit thought and thinkers is that it causes one's thinking to become purposeful or goal-oriented. As such, one identifies one's intention and evaluates the feasibility of this intention before opening up related issues and entering the battles which are sure to ensue. After all, it is the identification of one's intention and the assessment of its relative importance, its appropriateness, its feasibility and its legitimacy which determines whether or not one will proceed with a given course of action. It is likewise these processes which determine what does and does not warrant a significant focus.

This leads us to a discussion of what the *maqāṣid* and the *maqāṣid*-based culture give rise to by way of a methodical mindset which arranges and prioritizes not only sources of benefit and harm, but all of life's affairs. This ability is something which most people, and even many thinkers and theoreticians, lack. Hence, you find them, for example, defending the economy and economic development even as they destroy people and human development. Similarly, they may warn against and wage war on mad cow disease while they spread and encourage human madness. You find others defending freedoms and individual rights even as they forget or trample upon the rights of entire peoples and societies, or defending people's right to make a living while ruining people's morals. You find still others combating pollution on land and sea, yet showing no concern for the pollution of people's souls and the poisoning of their minds. Similarly, you find a growing sanctification of homeland and soil coupled with the deliberate desecration of doctrine and religion.

Moreover, just as *maqāṣid*-based thought is 'ordinal' in the sense of being orderly and methodical, it is also synthetic in nature. For just as the overall *maqāṣid al-sharīʿah* are founded upon comparison, contrast, and arrangement, they are likewise based on inference and synthesis. Thus, dealing with the *maqāṣid* and *maqāṣid* scholars gives rise to a synthetic manner of thinking which engages in an inductive reading of particulars and draws connections among them, then puts them together to arrive at universals. Induction is the most advanced of all scientific methods, and knowledge which is arrived at through inference and the formulation of universals is the most advanced, efficacious form of knowledge. The reason for this is that it combines the knowledge of particulars with the knowledge of universals. Inductive questions begin initially with a broad, thorough search on the level of particulars, after which they move to the process of connection and synthesis to arrive at last at universal rulings and facts. As such, inductive questions combine science with particulars, with universals, and with the processes of connection, coordination and synthesis; hence, they constitute the most advanced form of scientific activity and reasoning.

This *maqāṣid*-based view, moreover, is the best guarantee of balance between constants and variables, flexibility and rigidity, and lenience and austerity.

[*Subtheme* 2]*: The Maqāṣid-Informed Mindset on the Communal Level (The Realm of Islamic Legal Policy)*

§*First:* Al-Hasani affirms clearly and decisively that the realm in which there is the greatest need for the formulation of principles and the derivation of laws and criteria is that of Islamic legal policy. This realm deals with issues of supreme importance in the life of the state in modern Islamic society.[148]

Al-Ubaydi places this issue within the framework of the political reform theory introduced by al-Shāṭibī, who concludes that political authority is a necessity of the religion, and that the establishment of the state in Islam is among *maqāṣid al-sharīʿah*. That is to say, policy grows out of Islam itself, and the ruler must lead Muslims and assess their best interests in accordance with the rulings of the religion. Moreover, the Ummah which has guardianship over such a ruler is required to provide for his sustenance, to supervise him and to limit his authority if he attempts to transgress the rule of law and to govern by the dictates of his own desires.[149]

Abd al-Majid al-Saghir's book, *Al-Fikr al-Uṣūlī wa Ishkāliyyah al-Sulṭah al-ʿIlmiyyah fī al-Islām*, revolves around an elucidation of the fact that, like the interest once demonstrated by scholars in formulating principles for the science of the fundamentals of Islamic jurisprudence (*ʿilm uṣūl al-fiqh*), the current interest in *maqāṣid al-sharīʿah* grows out of a concern to regulate political authority in accordance with the standards of Islamic law, an aim whose fulfillment requires attention to *maqāṣid al-sharīʿah* as well as a focus on human interests and the critical importance of creativity.[150]

This idea is developed and clarified by Ibn Ashur in his discussion of the process of establishing the political foundations for human interests. He states that the establishment of a powerful, confident Ummah which commands respect from other nations requires that the social body as represented by the Ummah's leaders and authority figures pass laws and establish an executive organ whose responsibility it is – whether through enticements and incentives, or through threats and punishments – to ensure that people preserve the best interests of the Ummah. In so doing, the executive organ performs the state's deterrent functions, foremost among which is the establishment of justice. Justice, moreover, has a dual basis: (1) the demonstration of people's legitimate rights, and (2) establishment of Islamic law. Also necessary for the realization of justice are: regulation of the Ummah's material wealth, identification of the means by which the caliph is to delegate authority, defense of the Ummah and its possessions and, lastly, determination of the areas in which state policy needs to be formulated and enforced.[151]

Al-Hasani then proceeds in his analysis of Ibn Ashur's thought to a discussion of the need for well-informed experience with the Ummah's needs. He states:

> Ibn Ashur appears to be referring here to the necessity of respecting the principle of academic specialization, a principle which arises by necessity out of the growth and expansion of knowledge and the increasing complexity of the areas encompassed by societal organization, particularly at the present time. Matters such as these, by virtue of their varied requirements, make it necessary for those engaged in Islamic legal inquiry to comprehend the facts relating thereto, in order thereby to verify their bases (*taḥqīq al-manāṭ*).*[152]

And this, in turn, requires that the conditions for the validity of ijtihad be fulfilled and that those engaged in this process be thoroughly acquainted with the subject being researched.

As has been mentioned, realities such as these call for recognition of the need for academic specialization. In this connection, al-Hasani makes reference to the point of view expressed by al-Khamlishi, according to whom it is difficult, if not impossible, at the present time to issue any sort of legislation even in those areas which have been treated in detail by Islamic jurisprudence without drawing upon the expertise of specialists in many branches of knowledge, including legal scholars, sociologists, politicians, representatives of professional sectors and institutions, and many others, not to mention the specializations that make up the empirical sciences such as medicine, engineering, and the like. Moreover, such individuals' role is not limited to that of verifying the bases of legal rulings (*taḥqīq al-manāṭ*); rather, they also assist in the process of extracting (*takhrīj al-manāṭ*) or isolating their bases (*tanqīḥ al-manāṭ*).

§*Second:* We return now to the area of Islamic legal policy, which is characterized by greater flexibility than the area of Islamic jurisprudence given the fact that it rests upon human interests more than on texts. Writing in this area, however, has been at a standstill since the days of the great thinkers Abū Yūsuf, al-Māwardī, Ibn Salām and others, whose writings covered the needs of the eras in which they lived. Unfortunately, such thinkers' writings are still viewed by the vast majority of modern thinkers as representing the Islamic perspective on this theme for our day as well. Hence, we continue to read things written by those who include the *kharāj,** the *jizyah** and the *ʿushr** among the state's financial resources, and others who speak of the Ministry of Authorization (*wizārah al-tafwīḍ*), the Ministry of

Implementation (*wizārah al-tanfīdh*), and the Ministry of Mastery (*wizārah al-taghallub*) as administrative departments and political organs.

What I propose is that in order to advance on a *maqāṣid*-related basis, the area of Islamic legal policy must be dealt with on two levels:

1. The organizational level, which operates on the basis of the constitution, laws and regulations and which is to be treated like other divisions of Islamic jurisprudence. I have included this level within the plan for juristic reform, a step which, in effect, brings Islamic legal policy back under the umbrella of Islamic jurisprudence as it was before it became an independent discipline.[153]

2. The level of execution and application, which consists of policy-making, planning and decision-making. In relation to this level, the introduction of the notion of *maqāṣid* is a new development not only in our Arab and Islamic countries, but in the world at large.

What I have just said may appear to be inconsistent with reality, where we view the developed countries as having solid, cohesive policies and plans. In reality, however, these countries have concerned themselves with only one aspect of the planning process while neglecting other aspects. Such aspects include the universal perspective, the spiritual, ethical and social dimensions, a scale of priorities, and others.

This spirit of neglect, together with other things, has infected our Arab and Islamic nations as well. We find, for example, that there are Arab countries whose populations lack the most basic necessities, while their budgets are burdened with debts both domestic and foreign. Such countries spend tens, nay, hundreds of millions of dollars on sports, art and media festivals and millennium celebrations. However, had such funds been earmarked for areas of genuine need in accordance with a carefully studied scale of priorities for the purpose of providing for essentials and exigencies before concerning themselves with enhancements, actual living conditions in these countries – and not only their outward appearances – would have changed, and they would have taken at least a step in the right direction.[154]

However, the 'infection' referred to above continues to afflict us. After all, the 'developed world' spends hundreds of billions of dollars on weapons production while it preaches peace, and spends hundreds of billions of dollars on drugs while it sings the praises of human rights.

The point I am trying to make here is that both as individuals and as communities, we lack what might be termed 'the planning mentality.' As a consequence, our actions are haphazard and confused and we have little to show for our efforts. Both as individuals and as communities, we need desperately to define our mission in life and, in light of this mission, to set long-term and short-term goals or, stated in another way, our long-term strategy and short-term tactics. Having done this, we need to translate these goals into practical action plans as well as whatever evaluation, supervision and follow-up processes follow therefrom. Then, last but not least, we need to link all of the foregoing to *maqāṣid al-sharīᶜah*.

Indeed, it is my belief that those occupied with planning, whether on the level of private institutions or governmental departments, stand to benefit in their work from our rich heritage of *maqāṣid*-related thought and production, including the areas of higher *maqāṣid*, universal *maqāṣid*, or special *maqāṣid*, primary and secondary *maqāṣid*, the relationship between *maqāṣid* and *wasā'il*, the gradation among essentials, exigencies and enhancements, scales of priorities, and so on.

[THEME 6]

The Future of Maqāṣid: As an Independent Discipline, an Intermediate Discipline, or an Extension of Uṣūl al-Fiqh?

Contemporary interest in research relating to *maqāṣid al-sharīᶜah* has been accompanied by thought concerning the future of such research. Hence, while some call for *maqāṣid* to be considered an independent science given its newness, others call for it to continue to be viewed as a discipline which is intermediate between Islamic jurisprudence (*fiqh*) and the principles of jurisprudence (*uṣūl al-fiqh*).

The first scholar to call for the establishment of an independent science of *maqāṣid al-sharīᶜah* was Ibn Ashur; however, this call was preceded by a number of muted references to such a step in the writings of forerunners the likes of al-Qarrāfī,[155] Ibn Taymiyyah[156] and Ibn al-Qayyim,[157] who alluded simply to the importance of *maqāṣid* rather than to its establishment as a self-contained discipline. Other harbingers of Ibn Ashur's call include the work done by al-Shāṭibī in his books *al-Muwāfaqāt* and *al-I*ʿ*tiṣām*, where he strives to formulate definitive fundamentals or principles of Islamic law without stating explicitly that such principles should be viewed as independent of *ʿilm uṣūl al-fiqh*; on the contrary, he views such principles to be, themselves, the fundamentals of Islamic jurisprudence.

After discussing the desire demonstrated by al-Shāṭibī and others to view the fundamentals of jurisprudence as definitive principles, Ibn Ashur states,

> If we wish to record definitive principles for the sake of a deepening understanding of the religion, we must address the customary questions relating to *uṣūl al-fiqh*, then recast them in the crucible of written formulation, evaluating them by the standards of inquiry and criticism and stripping them of those foreign elements which have become associated with them. We must deposit within them the precious metals of the understanding of Islamic jurisprudence and inquiry, then reformulate this science and refer to it as *ʿilm maqāṣid al-sharīʿah*. In so doing, we leave the science of *uṣūl al-fiqh* as it is even as we derive from it the methods of gathering juristic evidence. We address those issues of *uṣūl al-fiqh* which do not fall within the province of this intent of ours (namely, to record *maqāṣid al-sharīʿah*), treating them rather as principles of this majestic science, the science of *maqāṣid al-sharīʿah*. Hence, we must say: *Uṣūl al-fiqh*, that is, the fundamentals of jurisprudence, must be definitive. That is to say, scholars have the right not to include in *uṣūl al-fiqh* anything but that which is definitive, either by necessity or based on convincing inquiry. Numerous attempts have been made to reach a conclusion in this connection, and the issue is still under investigation. Indeed, attempts to reach definitive conclusions in this connection have filled the studies of researchers....[158]

Modern researchers concerned with *maqāṣid al-sharīʿah* have taken this ball and run with it, as it were, the distances varying from one researcher to another. Al-Raysuni, for example, concludes his book *Imam al-Shāṭibī's Theory of the Intents of Islamic Law* with the following clearly worded query:

> Lastly, one might ask: Will expanding research on the intents of the Law lead us to achieve what has been advocated by Shaykh Muhammad al-Tahir ibn Ashur, that is, the distillation of the intents and definitive truths of the religion into a separate discipline known as "the science of the intents of the

> Law"? Or, as a number of modern scholars of *uṣūl al-fiqh* have claimed, are the intents of the Law an inseparable part of the science of *uṣūl al-fiqh* itself, that is, the fundamentals of jurisprudence? In point of fact, this question is of little importance so long as we are in agreement on the need for the major expansion being spoken of here and for the utmost care to be devoted to the intents of the Law. Once this has been agreed on, it is of little concern whether or not we refer to it as a 'science.' Moreover, we may be relieved of the need to pose this question, at least for a time, by a statement made by Shaykh Abd Allah Darraz, who holds that "the process of deriving legal rulings consists of two components. The first of these is the science of the Arabic language, while the second is the science of the hidden wisdom and intents of Islamic law."[159] It is these two sciences which go to make up the science of the fundamentals of jurisprudence. Hence, the intents of the Law are both a science and a component of a science. What matters in the final analysis, of course, is the realities with which we deal and the aims we seek to achieve, not the terms we apply to such realities or the means by which we seek to achieve such aims.[160]

As for al-Hasani, Ibn Ashur's commentator, he has taken steps toward the establishment of an independent discipline under the rubric of *maqāṣid al-sharīᶜah*. To this end, he has undertaken a detailed study of the meaning of *maqāṣid* and the components of the science of *maqāṣid al-sharīᶜah*, including its goal, its subject matter and its methodology.[161]

There is no need to go into the details of al-Hasani's discussion here, since our primary concern is the question of whether, as a matter of principle, the *maqāṣid* are to be treated as an independent discipline. Therefore, what I wish to focus on is al-Hasani's view on this question as recorded in more than one place, and which may be summed up by saying that if it is valid to speak of *maqāṣid al-sharīᶜah* as autonomous from *uṣūl al-fiqh*, then it must be spoken of as a relative autonomy required by methodological necessity, since in fact, the entire process of juristic reasoning is based on *maqāṣid al-sharīᶜah*.[162]

Al-Hasani makes his position still clearer through his explanation of the complementarity between *maqāṣid* and the various methods of deduction (*al-istinbāṭ*),* which is the substance of *uṣūl al-fiqh*. He treats *uṣūl al-fiqh* as a *maqāṣid*-based science by breathing into it the spirit of *maqāṣid al-sharīᶜah*, while at the same time drawing attention to the relative autonomy of these two disciplines on the levels of method, subject matter, and aim.[163]

There follows logically from this a notion which has been proposed by Hasan al-Turabi in his unpublished book, *Tajdīd al-Uṣūl al-Fiqhiyyah li al-Islām*, where he states,

> General juristic principles, rules and concepts are at times attributable to roots,[164] and at other times, to branches.[165] Hence, perhaps the most effective manner of approaching the situation is to map out – somewhere between the science of roots and [the science] of branches – an independent science which concerns itself with general juristic principles and concepts, especially given the fact that in our Islamic jurisprudence they are present in such abundance, so highly developed and, therefore, worthy of being dealt with in a consistent fashion.[166]

As I note in my book, *al-Tanẓīr al-Fiqhī*, the notion of intermediate sciences, including the sciences of rules and *maqāṣid*, has been neglected despite its importance and its undeniable role in the mechanisms of *istinbāṭ*.

Returning to the theme of this study, and in keeping with the view advocated by al-Hasani concerning the relationship between *maqāṣid* and *uṣūl al-fiqh,* we reiterate what we have stated elsewhere concerning the importance of the link between *maqāṣid* and *uṣūl al-fiqh*, as well as the importance of developing them within a single framework. As for the view held by Ibn Ashur in favor of establishing an independent science of *maqāṣid al-sharīʿah* while leaving the science of *uṣūl al-fiqh* as it is, my own view is that this would be harmful to both sciences, since it would, in effect, freeze *uṣūl al-fiqh* in its present state and deprive it of the spirit of *maqāṣid*; in addition, it would exclude *maqāṣid* from the practical role which they perform at present, a role which we must do our utmost to support, sustain and develop.

CONCLUSION

In conclusion, I would like to reiterate what I stated in my introduction to this study, namely, that I have not covered all areas of research of relevance to the theme of *maqāṣid*. Moreover, the possibility of my having erred is a real one; therefore, my readers are called upon to offer corrections as required. In addition, I would like to suggest a number of *maqāṣid*-related topics which call for further elaboration by researchers; these include:

1. The theory of *maqāṣid* in the writings of al-Ghazālī.
2. The theory of *maqāṣid* in the writings of Ibn Taymiyyah.
3. The theory of *maqāṣid* in the writings of Ibn al-Qayyim.
4. The theory of *maqāṣid* in the writings of al-ʿIzz ibn ʿAbd al-Salām.
5. The theory of *maqāṣid* in the writings of Walī Allāh al-Dahlawī.
6. The higher *maqāṣid* of Islamic law and foundational concepts.
7. The *maqāṣid* specific to each division of Islamic jurisprudence, as well as those specific to each of the human, social and natural sciences (several studies).
8. A detailed study of each of the four realms to which the universal *maqāṣid* apply (that is, the realms of the individual, the family, the Ummah, and wider humanity).

NOTES

Preface to the Arabic Edition

1. (SWT) – *Subḥānahu wa Taʿālā*. May He be praised and may His transcendance be affirmed. Said when referring to God.
2. (ṢAAS) – *Ṣallā Allāhu ʿalayhi wa sallam*: May the peace and blessings of God be upon him. Said whenever the name of the Prophet Muhammed is mentioned.
3. Unless otherwise specified, Qur'anic quotations will be taken from Muhammad Asad's translation (*The Message of the Qur'ān*, Gibraltar: Dār al-Andalus, 1980) [translator's note].
4. *Maqāṣid al-Sharīʿah al-Islāmiyyah*. Translated into English and published by the IIIT in 2006 under the title: *Ibn Ashur: Treatise on Maqāṣid al-Sharīʿah.*
5. Translated and published by the IIIT in 2005 under the title: *Imam al-Shāṭibī's Theory of the Higher Objectives and Intents of Islamic Law.*

Introduction to the First Edition

1. *Al-Burhān*, 2:115.

Chapter One

1. The Arabic word *maqāṣid* (singular, *maqṣid* or *maqṣūd*), which means simply, 'aims' or 'intents', will be used throughout the book to refer specifically to the aims or purposes of Islamic law [translator's note].
2. See *al-Muwāfaqāt* 313, 169, 168-391, 316-399; Ibn Ashur 20-22; Yusuf al-Alim, 112–122; Hammadi al-Ubaydi 124–129; and Ahmad al-Raysuni 241–256.
3. Ibn Ashur, 57.
4. That is, what the scholar concerned believes to be the basis (*ʿillah*) for the ruling in question, and/or the situation out of which he believes that the ruling arose [translator's note].

5. *Al-Burhān*, 2:1113.
6. Ibid., 2:1114.
7. Ibid., 2:1117.
8. *Qawāʿid al-Aḥkām*, 1:5–7.
9. Ibid., 1:10. [The Arabic phrase rendered below as "otherworldly sources of benefit and harm and their causes" (*maṣāliḥ al-ākhirah wa asbābuhā wa mafāsiduhā*) is a correction of what appears in the Arabic text, namely, *maṣāliḥ al-dārayn wa asbābuhā wa mafāsiduhā*, which would translate as, "both earthly and otherworldly sources of benefit and harm and their causes." The remainder of this note is the author's commentary on this apparent error in the Arabic text – translator's note] It appears that what is actually intended here is *maṣāliḥ al-ākhirah* (otherworldly sources of benefit), in order for there to be a [meaningful] comparison between this and what he mentions thereafter, namely, *maṣāliḥ al-dunyā* (earthly sources of benefit). This being the case, the Arabic phrase *maṣāliḥ al-dārayn* is a scribal error. On the other hand, what might be intended by the use of this phrase is those interests or benefits which combine what is good both in this world and the next, in which case the meaning is correct. However, I favor the former possibility, which is confirmed by the fact that when al-Shāṭibī quotes the same passage elsewhere in order to respond to it, he uses the phrase, *maṣāliḥ al-dār al-ākhirah* (see *al-Muwāfaqāt*, 2:48); it is likewise confirmed by the text as it appears in his book, *al-Fawā'id*, which will be mentioned below.
10. Ibid., 2:189.
11. *Al-Fawā'id fī Ikhtiṣār al-Maqāṣid* (also known as *al-Qawāʿid al-Ṣughrā*), 1st Edition, 1988, 45.
12. *Naqḍ al-Manṭiq*, 29. (The Arabic word rendered in this Qur'anic verse as 'what is wrong' (*munkar*) is derived from the verb *ankara*, which is rendered as "spurn" (*ankarat*) in Ibn Taymiyyah's discussion. By using this particular word in his description of the instinctive human reaction to evil, he draws attention, albeit indirectly, to the fact that rather than being an arbitrary judgment imposed by an external authority, the term 'evil' or 'wrong' describes a reality which is contrary, by its very nature, to all that is truly beneficial for God's creatures. At the same time, it bears noting that since, in actually daily experience, we do not, in fact, always feel an aversion toward those things which would be harmful for us, Ibn Taymiyyah is using the term *fiṭrah*, translated here as 'inborn nature', to refer to pristine, uncorrupt human nature [translator's note].)
13. *Aʿlām al-Muwaqqiʿīn*, 3:3.

14. Ibid., 4:273.
15. *Al-Muwāfaqāt*, 1:35.
16. Ibid., 1:87-91.
17. Ibid., 2:170.
18. Ibid., 2:306.
19. Ibid., 2:307.
20. That is, given the denial that it is possible through human reason to determine whether a given act is good and praiseworthy, or evil and blameworthy, even in the absence of the explicit declarations of the Law [translator's note].
21. Ibid., 2:315.
22. Ibid., 2:48.
23. Al-Hasani, 111.
24. Al-Fasi, *Maqāṣid al-Sharīʿah*, 189-201.
25. For further analysis of Ibn Ashur's thought, see al-Hasani's study, pp. 307-308.
26. For details on this topic, see pp. 51–55.
27. 'Kindness' in this context is defined as those circumstances and conditions which make it easier and more likely for human beings to obey God's commands and prohibitions rather than disobey them. According to most Muʿtazilites, belief in God's justice entails the belief in the necessity of such kindness, since in their view, its absence would be inconsistent with this divine attribute. The Ashʿarites, by contrast, deny its necessity [translator's note].
28. Al-Raysuni, 137, 216, 44–229.
29. Ibid., 229-240. The reader is also encouraged to read pp. 216-228 of the same discussion, which is of great value in understanding the topic at hand.
30. *Al-Ijtihād al-Maqāṣidī*, 1:168.
31. *Aʿlām al-Muwaqqiʿīn*, 3:3.
32. Ibid., 4:273.
33. Reliance upon a Qur'anic text which is speculative with regard to its meaning (*ẓannī al-dalālah*) or upon a text from the Sunnah which is speculative with regard to its chain of transmission (*ẓannī al-wurūd*), its meaning, or both, is treated in the same manner as other methods of *istidlāl* with respect to the conditions it must meet in order for it to be considered an independent source of evidence. These conditions will be discussed below. (For a discussion of the concept of *ẓannī*, see the Glossary of Terms at the conclusion of the book [translator's note].)
34. Ibn Ashur, *Maqāṣid al-Sharīʿah*, 51.
35. Al-ʿIzz, 1:22, 29, 36, 44, 54, 57.

36. See al-Alim, 189 and al-Raysuni, 50, quoting from al-Buti, 249-250.
37. *Al-Mustaṣfā*, 1:258.
38. Ibid., 1:256.
39. *Al-Maḥṣūl*, 2, Section 2, 220.
40. Ibid., 2, Section 2, 612.
41. *Al-Aḥkām*, the Mu'assasah al-Ḥalabī Edition, 2:252, and the Ṣabīḥ Edition, 3:71.
42. Ibid., Mu'assasah al-Ḥalabī Edition, 4:243–245 and the Ṣabīḥ Edition, 3:287-288.
43. *Sharḥ Tanqīḥ al-Fuṣūl*, The Azharite Colleges Library Edition, 391.
44. *Minhāj al-Wuṣūl ilā ʿIlm al-Uṣūl*, the Ṣabīḥ Edition, 59.
45. *Majmūʿ Fatāwā ibn Taymiyyah*, 1:343.
46. *Nihāyah al-Sūl*, Vol. 4:75, 82–84.
47. Ibid., 4:388.
48. Ibid., 4:515.
49. *Zawā'id al-Uṣūl ʿalā Minhāj al-Wuṣūl*, 422–423.
50. *Jamʿ al-Jawāmiʿ bi Ḥāshiyah al-Banānī*, 2:281.
51. *Al-Muwāfaqāt*, 1:38, 2:10, 3:10, 4:27-32.
52. Ibid., 3:47.
53. *Al-Iʿtiṣām*, 2:179 and *al-Muwāfaqāt*, 2:299.
54. *Al-Muwāfaqāt*, 2:299.
55. *Al-Baḥr al-Muḥīṭ*, 5:208-213.
56. Ibid., 6:188-189.
57. Ibn Farḥūn, 2:133–134.
58. Al-Badakhshī's commentary on *Minhāj al-Wuṣūl*, known as *Manāhij al-ʿUqūl*, the Ṣabīḥ Edition, 3:223–225.
59. Ibn Ashur, 79.
60. Al-Alim, 290-297.
61. Al-Raysuni, 49.
62. This group includes al-Rāzī in two places, and al-Bayḍāwī, al-Qarrāfī, Ibn Taymiyyah and al-Zarkashī as presented above; in fact, even al-Ghazālī himself falls within this group.
63. *Al-Mustaṣfā*, 1:265.
64. Al-Zarkashī, 6:188-189.
65. Ibid., 220.
66. Ibid., 612.

67. Ibid., 223.
68. Ibid., 222.
69. That is, free, non-Muslim subjects living in a Muslim county [translator's note].
70. That is, the legitimacy of putting to death someone who has been found guilty of murder, thereby enforcing the Islamic law of retribution (*al-qiṣāṣ*) [translator's note].
71. That is, by carrying out the law of retribution and thereby satisfying the human thirst for revenge [translator's note].
72. "Giving priority to God's right" refers to the decision to refrain from enforcing the law of retribution by not putting the murderer to death, thereby deferring the person's punishment to the afterlife and, at the same time, denying satisfaction of the thirst for revenge which, as treated in this passage, is a human right [translator's note].
73. Al-Āmidī, *al-Aḥkām*, 4:243–245.
74. *Al-Fawā'id*, 58-64, 100; al-Alim, 317-319.
75. For a discussion of whether the death penalty for apostasy has an actual basis in Islamic law, see Taha Jabir al-Alwani, *There Shall Be No Compulsion in Matters of Faith: The Islamic View of Apostasy and Apostates From the Dawn of Islam to the Present Day*, translated by Nancy Roberts (London: The International Institute of Islamic Thought, forthcoming).
76. *Al-Ibhāj*, 3:164, quoting from al-Ḥafnāwī.
77. Al-Badakhshī, 3:223–224.
78. *Al-Muwafaqat*, 2:153–154 (marginal gloss).
79. *Al-Madkhal*, 126-131.
80. The correctness of this statement cannot be taken for granted, as evidenced by the fact that the traditional example which recurs repeatedly throughout their books is that of jihad.
81. *Qaḍāyā Islāmiyyah Muʿāṣirah*, No. 8:150.
82. *Ahammiyah Maqāṣid al-Sharīʿah fī al-Ijtihād*, 16.
83. This group is represented by al-Rāzī, al-Āmidī, al-Qarrāfī, Ibn Taymiyyah, al-Isnawī, al-Shāṭibī in two places, as well as al-Zarkashī, Ibn Farḥūn and al-Badakhshī as can be seen from the presentation of their views above.
84. My comments on al-Āmidī's statements are in parentheses.
85. Ibn Ashur, 81–82.
86. Al-Āmidī, 4:245.
87. Al-Badakhshī, 3:224–225.

88. This group includes al-Rāzī, al-Bayḍāwī, al-Qarrāfī, Ibn Taymiyyah, al-Isnawī, Ibn al-Subkī and Ibn Ashur.

89. Passed down on the authority of Saʿīd Ibn Zayd and narrated by Aḥmad, Abū Dāwūd, al-Tirmidhī, al-Nasā'ī, and Ibn Ḥabbān in his *Saḥīḥ*, as well as in *Saḥīh al-Jāmiʿ al-Ṣaghīr* (6440).

90. *Al-Burhān*, 2:942.

91. *Al-Mustaṣfā*, 1:265.

92. *Al-Fawā'id*, 100.

93. *Al-Muwāfaqāt*, 2:299.

94. An agreed-upon hadith passed down on the authority of ʿAbd Allāh ibn ʿAmr (*Saḥīh al-Jāmiʿ al-Ṣaghīr*, 6444).

95. From a seminar on Islamic Legal Priorities, 13.

96. Al-Ubaydi, 190.

97. *Al-Muwāfaqāt*, 2:17.

98. Aḥmad al-Ghazālī, *Murā'āt al-Maqāṣid fī Fiqh ʿUmar Ibn al-Khaṭṭāb*, 406.

99. Seminar on Islamic Legal Priorities, 28-29.

100. This seminar was held on April 5, 2000 on the theme, "Views on *Maqāṣid al-Sharīʿah*."

101. Seminar on Islamic Legal Priorities, 44–46.

102. *Qaḍāyā Islāmiyyah Muʿāṣirah* magazine, No. 8:155.

103. Al-Raysuni, 314.

104. Ibn Ashur, 126-129.

105. Al-Shāṭibī in *al-Muwāfaqāt*, 2: 13, 16, 24, 101; al-Alim, 155, 167; al-Raysuni, 246.

106. *Al-Muwāfaqāt*, 2:364; al-Alim, 155, 163; and al-Hasani, 46. However, al-Alim mentions on p. 65 that most *uṣūl* scholars do not consider enhancements to have associated complements (*mukammilāt*), nor do they divide them into the categories of primary and secondary.

107. Al-ʿIzz Ibn ʿAbd al-Salām, *al-Qawāʿid*, 2:71.

108. *Al-Muwāfaqāt*, 2:23.

109. Al-Alim (pp. 171–172) notes this and uses the word *maṣlaḥah*.

110. *Al-Muwāfaqāt*, 3:206.

111. Al-Alim, 286-297.

112. That is, the realm of actions about which there is no clear legal ruling concerning their permissibility or impermissibility [translator's note].

113. *Al-Iʿtiṣām*, 2:178; al-Alim, 197-198.

114. *Al-Muwāfaqāt*, 2:49-52.

115. *Al-tawātur al-maʿnawī* may be defined as certainty which is based not on a single text or piece of evidence but which, rather, looks to the overall, inner spirit of the Law rather than just its outward details or particulars. It involves the marshalling of numerous texts which embody a variety of intents and which, when added one to another, yield a single conclusion upon which they all agree (see *al-Muwāfaqāt*, 2:51) [translator's note].

116. According to the author of *al-Mawāhib al-Saniyyah*, 116, the person who made this statement was al-Zarkashī.

117. According to the author of *al-Farā'id al-Bahiyyah*, al-Suyūṭī may have meant to say *ḥalāl* (permitted) rather than *ḥarām* (forbidden) here, whereas the author of *al-Mawāhib al-Saniyyah* has no difficulty with the term *ḥarām* as used here. In fact, he cites an example which confirms its correctness, namely, the use of gold and silver utensils (117).

118. Al-Suyūṭī, *al-Ashbāh wa al-Naẓā'ir*, Dār al-Fikr Edition, 61.

119. *Qawāʿid al-Aḥkām*, 2:205–210.

120. *Al-Muwāfaqāt*, 2:163.

121. Ibid., 2:167-168.

122. Ibid., 214.

123. In the course of discussing Imam al-Ghazālī's categorization of the levels [of human interests] and the examples which he cites for each category (p. 45), al-Raysuni suggests that the question of how to divide legal rulings among these various levels, and in particular, the levels of exigencies and enhancements, is interpretative and approximate at best. This statement might be taken to imply that al-Raysuni himself would have no interest in pursuing the question. However, in the context of his discussion of the horizons of *maqāṣid*-related research at the conclusion of his book (p. 314), he proposes the establishment of clear criteria for distinguishing among all the various categories or levels of human interests.

124. *Qawāʿid al-Aḥkām*, 1:8-9.

125. Ibid., 1:22–23.

126. Ibid., 1:54–56; this statement is then followed by a discussion of the benefits associated with acts classified as permissible.

127. Ibid., 2:189.

128. *Al-Fawā'id fī Ikhtiṣār al-Maqāṣid*, referred to as *al-Fawā'id al-Ṣughrā*, 1st Edition, 1988, 38-40.

129. Ibid., 41–42.

130. Just as one might refer to someone as a lion or as a donkey as figurative ways of saying that he or she is courageous or lacking in intelligence respectively, so the phrases 'of great ashes' and 'having a timid dog' are metaphorical ways of saying that someone is very hospitable. This is because the hospitable person, given all the fires he has to kindle in order to roast meat for his guests, accumulates great piles of ashes around his home, and because such a person's dog, so accustomed is he to seeing new faces all the time, has stopped barking at newcomers [translator's note].

131. *Al-Muwāfaqāt*, 3:153.

132. Examples of complements include the prohibition against looking [desirously] at someone other than one's own spouse as a complement to the prohibition against adultery, or the prohibition against drinking an amount of wine or liquor which would be insufficient to cause drunkenness as a complement to the prohibition against drinking enough to cause inebriation (from Shaykh Abd Allah Darraz's commentary on *al-Muwāfaqāt*).

133. Ibid., 3:209. In other words, a free woman's seeking to conceal her private parts is not the same as seeking to honor one's guest; similarly, forbidding usury is not the same as seeking to practice abstinence in relation to things which are not clearly forbidden; nor is seeking to adhere to recommended practices relating to ritual purity the same as adhering to practices without which the minimum required ritual purity would be forfeited. All these examples are taken from the realm of enhancements (Abd Allah Darraz's commentary).

134. In other words, if the essential interest concerned can be provided for without performance of the action being enjoined [translator's note].

135. *Al-Muwāfaqāt*, 3:209-211.

136. In other words, how can we come to know something based on an unknown? [translator's note]

137. Ibid., 2:298-300.

138. Ibid., 2:204.

139. Ibid., 2:206; see also his explanation of this principle on the same page.

140. Ibid., 2:180-185.

141. Ibn Ashur, 81–82.

142. It isn't clear how the view expressed here under (2) contrasts with the one described before it under (1) [translator's note].

143. *Al-Burhān* 2:924–925, 938-941.

144. *Al-Muwāfaqāt*, 2:11.

145. Ibid., 2:19-20, and Abd Allah Darraz's commentary on this passage.

146. The prophetic hadith which states, "God will not accept prayer which is performed without ritual purity" is narrated by all transmitters of sound hadiths with the exception of al-Bukhārī.

147. Examples of ritual purity in this sense include the performance of ritual ablutions before engaging in *dhikr* (that is, divine remembrance, or invocation of the Divine name) or going to sleep, or repeating one's ablutions before each obligatory prayer [even though nothing has occurred to invalidate one's previous ablutions].

148. Al-ʿIzz Ibn ʿAbd al-Salām, 1:101.

149. Al-Alim, 226-227.

150. Ibid., 234.

151. Ibid., 246.

152. This point is, in fact, noted explicitly by al-Alim on p. 245.

153. Ibid., 234–236.

154. Al-Hasani, 300.

155. *Al-Muwāfaqāt*, 3:209, including the examples cited in the body of the text and Darraz's commentary thereon; see also pp. 153, 255–257.

156. Ibid., 1:213.

157. Ibid., 2:299-300.

158. Ibid., 1:109-147.

159. In this connection, see Theme 3 of Chapter Two below, "From the Five Universals to the Four Realms."

160. Ibid., 2:165.

161. *Al-Muwāfaqāt*, 1:109ff.

162. Ibid., 2:119ff.

163. Ibid., 2:176ff.

164. For a summary of this topic, see al-Raysuni, pp. 147-155, and *al-Muwāfaqāt*, 1:181–187.

165. If, rather than saying, "*and not to* what is static… " he had said, "*in addition to* what is static…," this statement would be more accurate and more consistent with the rest of what he has to say.

166. If he had added the phrase, "..than at any time in the past…", he would have avoided giving the impression that he is saying that Islamic society needs to preserve these things more than it needs to preserve the five essentials originally identified by Muslim scholars.

167. Al-Hasani, 299.
168. Al-Alim, 164.
169. From a seminar entitled, "God's Ways as Manifested in the Horizons and the Human Soul" (*Sunan Allāh fī al-Āfāq wa al-Anfus*), 90, *Madkhal li Dirāsah al-Sharīʿah al-Islāmiyyah*, 74–75.
170. Al-Raysuni, 314.
171. The Soviet Union used to provide housing for its citizens on the basis of an estimated 9 square meters per person, and the various classes of housing units were graded on this basis (9, 18, 27 and 36 square meters).
172. *Fiqh al-ʿIlm*, 194.
173. In other words, some members of a community, having limited abilities or aptitudes, may not be able to excel academically or otherwise; yet in the positions they occupy in the society, they are able to perform needed functions [translator's note].
174. Other members of the same community, by contrast, having greater aptitudes, go on to obtain advanced knowledge or training in this or that discipline, by virtue of which they are enabled to fulfill certain collective responsibilities, such as the dissemination of knowledge, scientific research for the good of society, the provision of medical care, etc. [translator's note].
175. *Al-Muwāfaqāt*, 1:176-181.

Chapter Two

1. *Al-Aḥkām*, 3:252.
2. *Qawāʿid al-Aḥkām*, 1:42, 50-53, where he divides both religious obligations and Sunnah-based practices into collective and individual.
3. Ibid., 1:43.
4. Ibid., 1:53–54.
5. Ibid., 1:22, 29, 54–56.
6. Ibid., 1:153.
7. Ibid., 1:155.
8. Ibid., 1:167.
9. Ibid., 2:71.
10. Ibid., 2:77.
11. Ibid., 2:78.
12. *Majmūʿ Fatāwā Ibn Taymiyyah*, 11:343.

13. Ibid., 32:234.
14. Ibid., 11:343.
15. *Al-Muwāfaqāt*, 2:177.
16. Ibn Farḥūn, 2:133–134.
17. Al-Shāṭibī in *al-Muwāfaqāt*, 2:308. (Given the view that rulings on worship are to be taken at face value and not be traced back to a particular basis or *ᶜillah*, it is held that, as a consequence, they are not to be used as the basis for analogical deduction, or *qiyās* [translator's note].)
18. *Maqāṣid al-Sharīᶜah*, 63.
19. Ibid., 80, 81, 139.
20. *Tafsīr al-Taḥrīr wa al-Tanwīr*, 1:38.
21. *Maqāṣid al-Sharīᶜah*, 139.
22. Ibid., 96-99; al-Hasani, 274–276.
23. *Maqāṣid al-Sharīᶜah*, 130-135.
24. Ibid., 150-154.
25. *Uṣūl al-Niẓām al-Ijtimāᶜī*, 186.
26. *Maqāṣid al-Sharīᶜah*, 56, 59, 60; Sarmad al-Tai in *Qaḍāyā Islāmiyyah Muᶜāṣirah*, No. 8:242.
27. *Wujhat Naẓar*, 1:249-250, 300, 1988 Edition, and 2:126, 1998 Edition.
28. Seminar on Sunnah-based practices, January 10, 1990, p. 90; *Madkhal li Dirāsah al-Sharīᶜah,* 1990 Edition, 73–79.
29. Ibid., 57, 314.
30. Ibid., 299.
31. Seminar on Islamic Legal Priorities, 13–14.
32. Ibid., 15–16.
33. Ibid., 25.
34. *Wujhat Naẓar*, 2:126.
35. Seminar on Sunnah-based practices, 90.
36. *Madkhal li Dirāsah al-Sharīᶜah*, 62.
37. Ibid., 74–75.
38. *Kayfa Nataᶜāmalu maᶜa al-Qur'ān*, 71–76.
39. Al-Raysuni, 47-57, 314.
40. Al-Hasani, 299.
41. *Qaḍāyā Islāmiyyah Muᶜāṣirah* Magazine, No. 8:147, 151.
42. Ibn Ashur, 130-135.
43. Allal al-Fasi, 244–258.

44. *Al-Fawā'id*, 102.
45. Allal al-Fasi, 264.
46. Ibn Ashur, 95–96; al-Hasani, 274–276.
47. *Al-Muwāfaqāt*, 2:30.
48. Ibid., 3:119-122.
49. Ibid., 2:171.
50. Ibid., 2:168.
51. Ibid., 2:169-170.
52. Ibid., 2:331–332.
53. Al-ʿIzz, *Qawāʿid al-Aḥkām*, 2:68.
54. Ibn Ashur, 63–72; Allal al-Fasi, 41–52; al-Raysuni, *al-Fikr al-Maqāṣidī*, 16-21.
55. Al-Rifaiyah, *Ahammiyah Maqāṣid al-Sharīʿah fī al-Ijtihād*, 26-30.
56. Yahya Muhammad, *Qaḍāyā*, No. 8:151–155.
57. Allal al-Fasi, 69, quoting Abū al-Qāsim al-Iṣfahānī.
58. Yahya Muhammad, *Qaḍāyā*, No. 8:155–163.
59. Ibn Ashur, 56-62, Allal al-Fasi, 65–76; and al-Hasani, 382–408.
60. See also Qur'an 17:9.
61. See also Qur'an 2:129, 151 and 62:2.
62. Narrated by Aḥmad and al-Bukhārī in *al-Adab al-Mufrad* and by al-Ḥākim on the authority of Abū Hurayrah.
63. Ibn al-Athīr, *al-Kāmil*, 2:320 and Ibn Kathīr, *al-Bidāyah wa al-Nihāyah*, 7:39.
64. *Al-Mustaṣfā*, 1:257-258, 264.
65. Ahmad al-Raysuni, "Al-Manḥā al-Maqāṣidī fī Fiqh Ibn Rushd," in *Qaḍāyā Islāmiyyah Muʿāṣirah*, No. 8:207-224, particularly, p. 223.
66. Al-Rāzī, 2/Section 2:218.
67. *Al-Qawāʿid*, 1:11–12.
68. *Al-Fawā'id*, 34–35.
69. Al-ʿIzz, 1:8.
70. *Al-Muwāfaqāt*, 2:6, 8.
71. Ibid., 2:168.
72. Ibid., 2:168, marginal comment.
73. Ibn Ashur, 108.
74. Ibid., 56.
75. Ibid., 60.
76. Ibid., 130, 133–135.
77. Ibid., 96.

78. Ibid., 150.
79. Ibid., 14.
80. Ibid., 51.
81. Ibid., 63.
82. Ibid., 64.
83. Ibid., 78.
84. Ibid., 102.
85. Allal al-Fasi, 41–44.
86. Muhammad Siraj expresses the view that Ibn Ashur and Allal al-Fasi have introduced a new system for the conceptualization of the *maqāṣid* which, rather than being an addition to the one introduced by al-Shāṭibī, is parallel to it. (Seminar on Legal Priorities, 26)
87. *Qaḍāyā Islāmiyyah Muᶜāṣirah* Magazine, No. 8:147-151ff.
88. Ibn Ashur, 56-62; Allal al-Fasi, 65–76; al-Hasani, 382–408.
89. Yahya Muhammad, "Naẓariyyah al-Maqāṣid wa al-Wāqiᶜ," in *Qaḍāyā Islāmiyyah Muᶜāṣirah* Magazine, No. 8:127-174, particularly p. 160.
90. As do most of those who have written on the subject of *maqāṣid*.
91. Al-Fasi, 193.
92. The process by which this takes place will be discussed under Theme 3 of this chapter.
93. Al-Raysuni, 280-284.
94. Al-Hasani, 425–429.
95. Al-Raysuni, 280.
96. Al-Hasani, 426.
97. *Al-Muwāfaqāt*, 3:46-50.
98. Al-ᶜIzz, 1:198; al-Shāṭibī, 2:19, 101.
99. Al-Shāṭibī, 2:396.
100. Ibid., 2:399.
101. Al-Qarrāfī, *Al-Furūq*, 58; al-ᶜIzz, 1:53; *al-Muwāfaqāt*, 2:212; Ibn Ashur, 145, 148; al-Alim, 198; al-Hasani, 60.
102. *Al-Muwāfaqāt*, 2:19, including Shaykh Abd Allah Darraz's commentary on it.
103. Al-ᶜIzz, 1:124–125.
104. Ibn Ashur, 146.
105. The term 'bearing of testimonies' (*taḥammul al-shahādāt*) refers to the process of examining an event which may require that testimony be given concerning it (see al-Qalᶜajī, *taḥammul*) [translator's note].

106. Ibn Ashur, 146.
107. See our *Al-Tanẓīr al-Fiqhī*, 77ff., and *Al-Naẓariyyah al-ʿĀmmah li al-Sharīʿah al-Islāmiyyah*, 131ff.
108. Al-Raysuni, 32–34.
109. *Al-Qawāʿid*, 2:72.
110. Ibid., 2:68-69, 79-80.
111. Ibid., 2:78-79.
112. Al-Raysuni, 55–56.
113. Ibn Farḥūn, 2:133–134.
114. Ibn Ashur, 145–207; al-Hasani, 250-255.
115. Given my intention to write another study on the theme, "Naẓarāt fī Uṣūl al-Fiqh," I have postponed discussion of the terms *al-ḥikmah* and *al-ʿillah* until such time as I can deal with them in that context.
116. *Al-Mustaṣfā*, 1:264–265.
117. Ibid., 1:258.
118. Umar Sulayman al-Ashqar (contemporary) has written on the subject of human intents (specifically, the theme of 'intention in acts of worship').
119. My sister, Dr. Zaynab Attia, may God reward her richly, helped me to identify the Qur'anic verses pertaining to *maqāṣid.*
120. *Al-Muwāfaqāt*, 3:48; 4:29.
121. Commentary on al-Qarrāfī's *Tanqīḥ al-Fuṣūl*, 304.
122. *Maqāṣid al-Sharīʿah*, 81–82.
123. Despite his understanding of the reasons that have led other scholars to class *al-nasab* among the essentials.
124. *Naẓariyyah al-Maqāṣid*, 51.
125. Ibn Ashur, *Maqāṣid al-Sharīʿah*, 80.
126. Ibn Ashur, 130-135; Allal al-Fasi, 235–248.
127. *Al-Muwāfaqāt*, 3:48; the same position is taken by Abu Zahrah in *Tārīkh al-Madhāhib al-Islāmiyyah*, 308, 312, as he considers the preservation of dignity to be included within the preservation of human life; see also al-Qaradawi, *Kayfa Nataʿāmalu maʿa al-Qur'ān*, 70ff.
128. This is the view proposed by Zaynab Attia.
129. See also the sixth intent (subtheme 3) in the realm of the Ummah (the dissemination of knowledge and the preservation of reason within the Ummah).
130. See Fatimah Ismail, 63 and Yusuf al-Alim, 326-340.
131. Al-Alim, op. cit., 350-366.

132. For more detail on this topic, see Chapter Three, Theme 4, Subtheme 2 of this book.

133. Al-Alim, op. cit.

134. Ibid.

135. Ibid., 326-392; Fatimah Ismail, op. cit., 63–72, 104–153; Yusuf al-Qaradawi, *Fiqh al-ᶜIlm*, 187-198ff.

136. In the discussions of the third and fourth realms (those of the Ummah and wider humanity respectively), our concern will be with the preservation of the religion itself.

137. Reference is being made here to the views of al-Āmidī, Shaykh Abd Allah Darraz, and Ali Jumah.

138. Al-Qaradawi, *Kayfa Nataᶜāmalu maᶜa al-Qur'ān*, 65–69.

139. Ibid., 77-82.

140. Ibid., 83–85.

141. Al-Fayrūz Abādī in *al-Qāmūs al-Muḥīṭ*.

142. Al-Raysuni holds that the term 'preservation of honor' (*ḥifẓ al-ᶜirḍ*) is imprecise, while Al-Qaradawi states, "As we use it, the term 'honor' refers to one's dignity and reputation." Al-Qaradawi agrees that the preservation of honor should be added [to the listing of essential *maqāṣid*], in support of which he cites the Prophetic hadith which states, "A Muslim's honor, blood and material wealth are to be held sacred by every other Muslim," noting that in so saying, the Prophet links honor with blood (that is, human life) and grants it priority over material wealth (*Madkhal li Dirāsah al-Sharīᶜah*, 60).

143. See the Introduction to this study.

144. Ibn Ashur, 81–82.

145. See our discussion of the fourth intent in the realm of the family.

146. Al-Alim, 486-490.

147. Ibn Ashur specifies a number of *maqāṣid* in relation to material wealth, namely, circulation, clarity, preservation, stability and justice (175–183); see also al-Hasani, 174–185; and al-Alim, 495–568.

148. *Al-Muwāfaqāt*, 2:396; al-Alim, 403–414, 459-465.

149. For an earlier comparison [of this nature], see Theme 2, Subtheme 4 of this chapter.

150. That is, a man and a woman who, though not married to each other, would be eligible as potential mates [translator's note].

151. Al-Hasani, 210.

152. Ibn Ashur, 81. This appears to be a reference to methods of contraception which prevent pregnancy by hindering the process of conception [translator's note].
153. That is, love, as given in *al-Qāmūs al-Muḥīṭ*.
154. This term is defined in *al-Qāmūs al-Muḥīṭ* as "gentleness, forgiveness, and empathy." See also Al-Alim, 412–413.
155. Ibn Ashur, 162–164.
156. Ibid., 81–82.
157. See the fourth intent in the realm of the individual.
158. The noun *qiwāmah* as used here is based on the Qur'anic verse which states that "men shall take full care of women (*al-rijālun qawwāmūna ʿalā al-nisā'*) with the bounties which God has bestowed more abundantly on the former than on the latter, and with what they may spend out of their possessions" (4:34) [translator's note].
159. That is, prohibitions against relatives being marriageable to another [translator's note].
160. Ibn Ashur, 80-83, 139.
161. Al-Qaradawi, *Kayfa Nataʿāmalu maʿa al-Qur'ān*, 96-102.
162. The term *khilāfah*, translated here as 'vicegerency', is most frequently rendered as 'caliphate'; however, given the fact that the term is being employed here to refer to a function which is common to Muslims and non-Muslims alike, I consider 'vicegerency' to be the more appropriate rendering [translator's note].
163. See Qur'an 24:55.
164. "Hence, if two groups of believers fall to fighting, make peace between them; but then, if one of the two [groups] goes on acting wrongfully towards the other, fight against the one that acts wrongfully until it reverts to God's commandment; and if they revert, make peace between them with justice, and deal equitably [with them], for verily, God loves those who act equitably" (49:9).
165. Al-Fasi, 45–56, 209-213, 266-269.
166. Ibn Taymiyyah, *al-Ḥisbah*, Maṭbūʿāt al-Shaʿb, 9.
167. Ibn al-Qayyim, *Aʿlām al-Muwaqqiʿīn*, 1:3, 12–14.
168. Umarah in "Islamic Legal Priorities…", 44.
169. *Madkhal li Dirāsah al-Sharīʿah*, 78.
170. Ibn Ashur, 82–83.
171. Qur'an 5:2.
172. A *qasāmah* is an oath taken by 50 male relatives of someone who has been slain but whose murderer has not been identified through definitive evidence. If these

fifty men swear that a particular individual suspected of the murder is, in fact, guilty of the person's slaying, they are entitled to the blood money for the person's murder. If these men refrain from making such an oath based on inconclusive evidence, the accused can swear to his own innocence (some imams say that one oath is sufficient, while others hold that he must take the oath fifty times), in which case he will be absolved. However, if the accused refrains from swearing to his own innocence, the relatives of the slain are given a choice between having the accused put to death or demanding the blood money from him (al-Azharī). For variant interpretations of *qasāmah*, see *Lisān al-ʿArab*, q – s – m [translator's note].

173. Ibn Ashur, 80.

174. See also Dr. Umarah in "Islamic Legal Priorities," 44.

175. Al-Alim, 350-266 and Dr. Rifat al-Awadi in "Islamic Legal Priorities," 18-19.

176. See the discussion above under the heading of the first intent (the Ummah's institutional organization).

177. Ibn Ashur, 80; al-Hasani, 410-412.

178. This hadith states, in effect, that "even if a mule were to stumble," ʿUmar ibn al-Khaṭṭāb, in his capacity as caliph, would bear responsibility for helping the mule to right itself again [translator's note].

179. Referring to a Jew who once asked Muslims for alms, the Prophet (pbuh) stated that if his request was not granted, the Muslims would be guilty of neglecting their responsibility toward him [translator's note].

180. Attributed to al-Qaffāl al-Shāshī by al-Rāzī in his Qur'anic commentary (Taha Jabir al-Alwani, *Qaḍāyā Islāmiyyah Muʿāṣirah*, No. 8:124).

181. For more detail on the meaning of human brotherhood and equality, see Yusuf al-Qaradawi, *Kayfa Nataʿāmalu maʿa al-Qur'ān*, 105–107.

182. There are also other verses which speak of the general *khilāfah*, or vicegerency, which is common to all mankind, including: "He it is that has made you inheritors on earth: If, then, any do reject (God), their rejection (works) against themselves" (35:39, Yusuf Ali translation); see also 6:133 and 10:14.

183. Al-ʿIzz, *Qawāʿid al-Aḥkām*, 1:5–7, as well as later scholars who wrote on the subject of *maqāṣid*.

184. The relevant verse reads in full, "And so, when the sacred months are over, slay those who ascribe divinity to aught besides God wherever you may come upon them, and take them captive, and besiege them, and lie in wait for them at every conceivable place. Yet if they repent, and take to prayer, and render the purifying

dues [zakah], let them go their way: For behold, God is Much-Forgiving, a Dispenser of grace" (9:5) [translator's note].

185. For a brief clarification of this issue, see Yusuf al-Alim, 252–257.
186. Allal al-Fasi, 231–235.
187. Al-Qaradawi, *Kayfa Nataʿāmalu maʿa al-Qur'ān*, 109-111.
188. Allal al-Fasi, 269-272; Al-Qaradawi, Ibid., 107-108.
189. The '*Fuḍūl* Alliance' (*Ḥilf al-Fuḍūl*) is an alliance which was formed in pre-Islamic times through a gathering of tribal leaders which took place in the home of ʿAbd Allāh ibn Judʿān. The purpose of the alliance was to make a joint statement of determination to ensure the rights of the weak in defense against the strong who sought to exploit them and the rights of strangers in defense against residents who sought to deprive them of their due. It was named *Ḥilf al-Fuḍūl* based on the fact that those who entered into it included three men from the Jurhum tribe, all of whom bore the name al-Faḍl, namely, al-Faḍl ibn al-Ḥārith, al-Faḍl ibn Wadāʿah, and al-Faḍl ibn Faḍālah (*al-Fuḍūl* being the plural of *al-Faḍl*). (See *Liṣān al-ʿArab*, f – ḍ – l) [translator's note].
190. Al-Qaradawi, op. cit., 105.
191. Ibid., 103–104.
192. See Qur'an 3:64 [translator's note].

Chapter Three

1. That is, the preservation of religion, human life, reason, progeny, and material wealth [translator's note].
2. 1:17–18.
3. A reading of this passage does not yield a clear enumeration of the five benefits referred to by the author [translator's note].
4. In the passage which precedes this, Abraham says, "'O my Sustainer! Show me how Thou givest life unto the dead!' Said He, 'Hast thou, then, no faith?' [Abraham] answered, 'Yea, but [let me see it] so that my heart may be set fully at rest'" [translator's note].
5. See also al-Raysuni, *al-Fikr al-Maqāṣidī*, 115–122 and al-Ubaydi, 193.
6. That is, the Ismaelites, a sect of Batinites* whose origins are traced to Ismaʿil ibn Jaʿfar al-Ṣādiq. Its adherents believe that they are exempted from all requirements and obligations entailed by Islamic law and that the divine essence is devoid of attributes (see Qalaji, et. al., *Muʿjam Lughah al-Fuqahā'*, p. 48) [translator's note].

7. Ibn al-Rawandi.
8. The term *muṣarrāh* refers to a she-camel, cow or she-goat whose udders have been allowed to become gorged for several days in order to give potential buyers the impression that the animal yields copious milk and, as a consequence, ensure its sale. In a hadith recorded by Muslim we read that, "If someone has purchased [such an animal], then if, after three days, he wishes to return the animal to its original owner, he should return it together with a *ṣāʿ* of some kind of food, not [necessarily] wheat." [The negation of the necessity of returning wheat seems to be based on the fact that in earlier times, wheat was more costly than other foodstuffs that might have been given as compensation in such a situation – translator's note.]
9. That is, the hadith concerning two *qullahs*, a *qullah* being a huge jug with a capacity of 500 *ratls*, and concerning which the Prophet (pbuh) said, "If the amount of water comes to two jugs' full, it cannot be rendered ritually impure."
10. The plural of *ʿillah**, or the basis of a legal ruling [translator's note].
11. Al-Āmidī, *al-Aḥkām*, the Ṣabīḥ Edition, 3:286-288, and al-Hasani, 50.
12. Unpublished dissertation presented in partial fulfillment of the requirements for the Master's Degree in *Uṣūl al-Fiqh* (Fundamentals of Jurisprudence) from the National Institute of Higher Education for Islamic Sciences, Batinah, Algeria, 1997, p. 302.
13. *Al-Muwāfaqāt*, 2:380.
14. Ibid., 2:385; al-Hasani, 68, 391–395.
15. *Maqāṣid al-Sharīʿah*, 110-115.
16. Al-Qarrāfī, *al-Furūq*, 2:32–33; Ibn Ashur, 116-138; al-Hasani, 56, 371–373, 384–391; al-Raysuni, *al-Fikr al-Maqāṣidī*, 105–109.
17. This point and the two points subsequent to it are mentioned by Dr. al-Raysuni together with a fourth point. However, I have postponed the discussion of this fourth point to the next section of this chapter, since it falls more appropriately under the heading of *maqāṣid*-based ijtihad than do these three points, which are simply old mechanisms upon which al-Raysuni has shed new light. See al-Raysuni, *Naẓariyyah al-Maqāṣid ʿInd al-Imām al-Shāṭibī*, 294–312. As for the consideration of human intents, it falls outside the purview of this discussion. See al-Raysuni, *al-Fikr al-Maqāṣidī*, 110-114.
18. *Al-Muwāfaqāt*, 3:5–26.
19. *Al-Intiqā' fī Tārīkh al-Thalāthah al-A'immah al-Fuqahā'*, 149.
20. The term *muḥṣan*, which means literally, "protected" or "fortified," is used to

refer to someone who is married, that is, whose circumstances 'fortify' him against falling into adultery. The word *muḥṣan* is also employed as a legal term referring to someone who, if found guilty of adultery, is to be subjected to the maximum prescribed penalty for adultery. The conditions which must be fulfilled in order for someone to be classified as *muḥṣan* in this sense are that he or she must: (1) be Muslim, (2) be in full possession of his/her mental faculties, (3) be a mature adult, (4) be free (i.e., not a slave), and (5) have consummated his/her marital relationship (see al-Qalaji, et. al., *muḥṣan*) [translator's note].

21. As I see it, each of these final three topics could have been treated under its own separate heading rather than being listed under the heading of "consideration of long-term consequences."

22. Al-Raysuni, *al-Fikr al-Maqāṣidī*, 129-134.

23. Al-Hasani, 98-112; and Abd al-Jabbar Shararah in his review of al-Hasani's book in *Qaḍāyā Islāmiyyah*, No. 4:473–475.

24. Al-Ubaydi devotes a chapter of his book dealing with al-Shāṭibī and *maqāṣid al-sharīʿah* to the theme of *maqāṣid* and ijtihad (pp. 179-187); however, he fails to go beyond an affirmation of the principle to an exposition of its mechanisms.

25. Al-Raysuni, *Naẓariyyah al-Maqāṣid*, 294–312.

26. See Chapter 2, Theme 3.

27. See Husayn Hamid Hassan, 608.

28. *Al-Mustaṣfā*, 1:257-265; Hassan, 424–465; also included here is that which is essential, definitive and universal, since al-Ghazālī considers it to fall under the category of *al-istidlāl al-mursal* (*al-Mankhūl*, 370, margin).

29. *Al-Mankhūl*, 364–372.

30. The four foundational sources (*uṣūl*) are the Qur'an, the Sunnah, the consensus of the Muslim community (*ijmāʿ*) and analogical deduction (*qiyās*) [translator's note].

31. Ibn Ashur, 2:85 (explanatory footnote); al-Hasani, 301.

32. Al-Hasani, 437.

33. Ibn Ashur, 108-109.

34. Sarmad al-Tai, "*Maqāṣid al-Sharīʿah fī Āthār al-Shaykh Shams al-Dīn,*" *Qaḍāyā Islāmiyyah Muʿāṣirah*, Nos. 9-10:225–242, particularly 230-234.

35. Al-Raysuni, *al-Fikr al-Maqāṣidī*, 96.

36. Yahya Muhammad, "Naẓariyyah al-Maqāṣid wa al-Wāqiʿ", *Qaḍāyā Islāmiyyah Muʿāṣirah*, 8:150.

37. Al-Maysawi, 46-47.

38. Hasan al-Turabi, *Tajdīd al-Uṣūl al-Fiqhiyyah li al-Islām: Mudhakkirah Ghayr Manshūrah*, 98-102.
39. 2:61–62.
40. *Al-Tanẓīr al-Fiqhī*, 9-14.
41. Baqir Barri, "Fiqh al-Naẓariyyah ʿind al-Shahīd al-Ṣadr," *Qaḍāyā Islāmiyyah Muʿāṣirah*, Nos. 11–12:170.
42. *Qaḍāyā Islāmiyyah Muʿāṣirah*, Nos. 9-10:179-180.
43. That is, a rule relating to the fundamentals of jurisprudence (*uṣūl al-fiqh*) [translator's note].
44. As when one derives subsidiary rulings (*al-aḥkām al-firʿiyyah*) from fundamental principles (*al-uṣūl*) [translator's note].
45. Muhammad Abu Zahrah, *Uṣūl al-Fiqh*, 9-10.
46. *Al-Tanẓīr al-Fiqhī*, 210-212.
47. The term *tawaqquf*, or 'suspension' refers to the inability to arrive at a decision as to which of two or more views has more evidence in its favor [translator's note].
48. Al-Zarqa, *Al-Madkhal al-Fiqhī al-ʿĀmm*, 1:250-251.
49. *Al-Sunan al-Tārīkhiyyah*, 34–38.
50. *Qaḍāyā Islāmiyyah Muʿāṣirah*, Nos. 11–12:177-178.
51. Said Rahiman, "*Manhaj Iktishāf al-Milāk wa Atharuhu fī Taghayyur al-Aḥkām*," *Qaḍāyā Islāmiyyah Muʿāṣirah*, Nos. 9-10, 190-194. This step represents the process of indexing the Qur'an, the Sunnah and the Islamic written heritage. See *Dalīl al-Takshīf wa ʿAmal al-Makāniz*.
52. Barri, op. cit., 180.
53. Muhammad Baqir al-Sadr, *Iqtiṣādunā*, 358; and *al-Sunan al-Tārīkhiyyah*, 36-39.
54. *Iqtiṣādunā*, 364–384.
55. Ibid., 352–355.
56. Ibid., 354; Baqir Barri, 190.
57. *Iqtiṣādunā*, 366-390.
58. Said Rahiman, 194.
59. Gamal Attia, *al-Tanẓīr al-Fiqhī*, 185–187. This is not, of course, to deny recent beginnings of interest in research into juristic rules, as evidenced by Ali Ahmad al-Nadwi's, *al-Qawāʿid al-Fiqhiyyah* (1986); Muhammad Sidqi ibn Ahmad al-Burnu's *Al-Wajīz fī 'Īḍāḥ Qawāʿid al-Fiqh al-Kulliyyah* (1994); Muhammad al-Ruki's *Naẓariyyah al-Taqʿīd al-Fiqhī* (1994) and *Qawaʿid al-Fiqh al-Islāmī* (1998); Yaqub ibn Abd al-Wahhab al-Bahisin's *al-Qawāʿid al-Fiqhiyyah* (1998) and *Qāʿidah al-Yaqīn Lā Yazūl bi al-Shakk'* (1996); Muhammad Hisham

al-Burhani's thorough study of certain rules and the beginnings of the formation of theories therefrom, as in the area of *sadd al-dharā'i*ᶜ (1985); and Ahmad al-Raysuni's *Naẓariyyah al-Taqrīb wa al-Taghlīb* (1994).

60. Ibid., 215–217.

61. Al-Fārūqī, *Aslamat al-Ma*ᶜ*rifah*, 93–108.

62. Ibid., 62–91.

63. We have made a detailed proposal in this connection under the title, *Tajdīd al-Fikr al-Islāmī*, Dialogues for a New Century Series, Damascus: Dār al-Fikr, 2000.

64. Published in the *Faculty of Islamic Law Annals*, Qatar University, No. 11 (1993), and in *Qaḍāyā Islāmiyyah Mu*ᶜ*āṣirah*, No. 8; we will return to this point in Subtheme 3 below.

65. Published as part of the proceedings of the conference entitled, "Toward the Construction of a Modern Islamic Educational Theory," Amman, 24–27 July, 1990.

66. Presented at a conference on Educational Methods, Cairo, 29-31 July, 1990.

67. *Qaḍāyā Islāmiyyah Mu*ᶜ*āṣirah*, No. 8, 74, 83.

68. Ibid., 175–194; *Faculty of Islamic Law Annals*, Qatar University, No. 11.

69. Fatimah Ismail, *al-Qur'ān wa al-Naẓar al-*ᶜ*Aqlī*, 63–80.

70. Yusuf al-Alim, *al-Maqāṣid al-*ᶜ*Āmmah li al-Sharī*ᶜ*ah al-Islāmiyyah*, 326-340.

71. Al-Shāṭibī, *al-Muwāfaqāt*, 2:8.

72. Ibn Ashur, op. cit., 80.

73. Al-Alim, op. cit., 350-366.

74. Al-Qaradawi has devoted a significant part of one of his books to this theme; for his full discussion, see al-Qaradawi, *al-*ᶜ*Aql wa al-*ᶜ*Ilm fī al-Qur'ān al-Karīm*, Maktabah Wahbah, 1996, 247-282.

75. Stated by al-Suyūṭī (d. 911 AH/1505 AC) under No. 33.

76. Stated by Ibn al-Subkī (d. 771 AH/1370 AC)

77. Stated by al-Maqqarī (d. 758 AH/1259 AC) under No. 124.

78. Vol. 75, *al-Aḥkām al-*ᶜ*Adliyyah* magazine.

79. Together with three other rules, al-Marwazī (d. 462 AH/1069 AC) treats this as a fundamental principle of Islamic jurisprudence; so also does Ibn Najīm (d. 970 AH/1562 AC), Ibn al-Subkī and al-Suyūṭī.

80. Stated by al-Zarkashī (d. 794 AH/1391 AC)

81. See, for example: Labib al-Said, *Manāhij al-Baḥth al-Ijtimā*ᶜ*ī fī al-Qur'an* (ᶜUkāẓ, 1980); Ghazi Inayah, *Manhajiyyāt al-Baḥth al-*ᶜ*Ilmī* ᶜ*ind al-Muslimīn* (Qasanṭīnah:

Dār al-Ba'th, 1985); Fatimah Ismail, *al-Qur'ān wa al-Naẓar al-'Aqlī* (IIIT, 1993); Muhammad Ali al-Jundi, *Taṭbīq al-Manhaj al-Riyāḍī fī al-Baḥth al-'Ilmī 'ind al-'Ulamā' al-Muslimīn* (Dār al-Wafā', 1990); Muntasir Mahmud Mujahid, *'Usus al-Manhaj al-Qur'ānī fī Baḥth al-'Ulūm al-Ṭabī'iyyah* (IIIT, 1996).

82. Narrated by Ibn Mājah, 244; as for the Qur'anic verses which call for the pursuit of knowledge, they are well known, including: Surah 96, Surah 68, Surah 9:122 and 20:114.

83. An agreed-upon hadith.

84. In an explanatory note on the phrase rendered "such of them as are engaged in obtaining intelligence" (*al-ladhīna yastanbiṭūnahu minhum*), Muhammad Asad states that the literal meaning of the phrase is "those from among them who elicit [the truth]," whom he identifies as "the special organs of the state entrusted with gathering and evaluating political and military intelligence." [translator's note]

85. Muslim, 48.

86. Al-Ghazālī, *al-Mustaṣfā*, Introduction, and al-Qaradawi, *Fiqh al-'Ilm*, 355, 366.

87. The intent of preserving the faculty of reason intersects here with that of preserving material wealth in an intermediate sphere which calls for more thorough study.

88. Fatimah Ismail, op. cit., 366-392.

89. Ibid., 104–109. As for the Qur'anic verses, they are as follows: 2:170; 4:157; 5:48, 104; 6:116, 119, 148; 9:31; 28:50; 30:29; 38:26; 53:28; and 79:40.

90. Al-Alim, op. cit., 366-393, as well as the Qur'anic verses and hadiths which he cites. This, too, is an 'intermediate sphere' which lies somewhere between the intent of consideration for the mind and the intent of preserving human life, since these systems are part of the human body.

91. Fatimah Ismail, op. cit., 104–109 and the Qur'anic verses which she cites; Labib al-Sa'id, op. cit., 47, 58, 84, 94, 117-124 and the Qur'anic verses which he cites.

92. Abd al-Hamid al-Najjar, *Khilāfah al-Insān*, The International Institute of Islamic Thought (1993), 72–73.

93. See Qur'an 2:164; 13:4; 16:12, 67 and 30:24. Fatimah Ismail, op. cit., 64–66.

94. Qur'an 2:44; 3:65; 6:32; 21:66-67; 28:60, and others, with the total number of verses calling for the use of reason coming to 750.

95. Fatimah Ismail, op. cit., 78-79.

96. Ismail, op. cit., 64–72; as for verses of relevance, they include: 2:44, 219, 221; 3:7, 13, 65, 190, 191; 4:82; 6:32, 50, 65, 98, 126; 7:179-185; 8:22; 9:87;

10:3; 11:24–30; 12:111; 13:3, 19; 14:25; 16:11–17; 21:67; 23:68-85; 24:44; 25:44; 26:28; 28:60, 72; 32:27; 34:46; 38:29; 39:9, 18, 21; 45:13; 47:24; 51:21; 59:2, 21; 80:24; 86:5.

97. It will be noted here that what we have termed the rational forms of worship represent an intermediate region in which there is an overlap between the *maqṣid* of granting consideration to the mind and that of personal piety and preservation of the religion.

98. The fifth form of mental or rational worship as it appears in the author's original listing is that of *al-tadhakkur*, which might be rendered 'bearing in mind' or 'taking to heart,' and which is mentioned in Qur'an 13:7, 19 [translator's note].

99. See, for example, Qur'an 9:122 [translator's note].

100. The author refers to *al-naẓar, al-tabaṣṣur, al-tadabbur, al-tafakkur* and *al-iʿtibār* as 'the first type, and to *al-tafaqquh* and *al-tadhakkur* as 'the second type.' However, the basis for this division is not explained [translator's note].

101. Mention may be made in this connection of a number of references from the Islamic literary heritage which have treated this topic, foremost among which are:

(a) *Al-Iktisāb fī al-Rizq al-Mustaṭāb* by Imam Muḥammad Ibn al-Ḥasan al-Shaybānī (d. 234 AH/848 AC). This book deals with the subject of material gain (*al-kasb*): its definition, its benefits, its types, occupying oneself therein and its various levels. In addition, it deals with the topics of wealth and poverty, human beings' economic needs, work, renunciation, and those who receive charity and those who give it.

(b) *Iṣlāḥ al-Māl* by Abū Bakr ibn Abī al-Dunyā (d. 281 AH/894 AC), in which the author discusses the merits and beneficial use of material wealth, earning one's living by legitimate means, moderate living, good management, practicing a profession, the most meritorious and blameworthy types of commercial trade, as well as the purpose of money, food and clothing, and material abundance and poverty.

(c) *Al-Ishārah ilā Maḥāsin al-Tijārah* by Abū al-Faḍl Jaʿfar ibn ʿAlī al-Dimashqī (a scholar of the 6th Century AH). In this book, the author discusses the true nature of material wealth, the various types of wealth, and the need for it; he also discusses cash, price, value, the reasons for acquiring ownership, crafts and trades, sciences, and means of preserving material wealth.

102. Quoted by al-Suyūṭī in *al-Ḥāwī li al-Fatāwī* 2/89:110, and al-ʿAjlūnī in *Kashf al-Khafā'*, 2:238.

103. Traced back to its original sources by Muslim in his *Ṣaḥīḥ* (4:208), by al-Nasā'ī in his *Sunan* (3:73), and by Aḥmad in his *Musnad* (4:399).

104. Ibn Abī al-Dunyā, *Iṣlāḥ al-Māl*, 30. The hadith is traced back to its sources by al-Tirmidhī in his *Sunan* (4:614) with an addition; hence, the version he includes reads, "…until he has been asked how he spent his life, what he did with his knowledge, where he obtained his material wealth and how he put it to use, and how he expended his bodily energy." Moreover, al-Tirmidhī classifies this hadith as good and sound.

105. Narrated by Muslim, al-Tirmidhī and [Aḥmad ibn ʿAbd al-Raḥmān al-Bannā in] *al-Fatḥ al-Rabbānī fī Tartīb Musnad Aḥmad*, 15:2.

106. Excerpted by Muslim in his *Ṣaḥīḥ* (2:72), by al-Nasā'ī in his *Sunan* (5:60), by Ibn Mājah in his *Sunan* (3:1323) and by Aḥmad in his *Musnad* (3:7) from a longer hadith.

107. Included by Muslim in his *Ṣaḥīh* (2:703), by al-Suyūṭī in *al-Durr al-Manthūr fī al-Tafsīr al-Manthūr* (1:168, 5:10), by al-Qurṭubī in his *Tafsīr* (11:69), and by al-Mundhirī in *al-Targhīb wa al-Tarhīb* (2:545).

108. Traced back to its original sources and quoted in full by al-Bukhārī in *al-Adab al-Mufrad*, 132, excerpted by Aḥmad in his *Musnad*, 4:197, 202 from a long hadith, and by al-Haythamī in *Mawārid al-Ẓam'ān*, 268.

109. Traced back to its original sources by al-Bukhārī in *al-Adab al-Mufrad*, 134, by al-Ḥākim in *al-Mustadrak*, 2:3, where he declares it to be a sound hadith, by Ibn Mājah in his *Sunan*, 2:724, and by Aḥmad in his *Musnad*, 5:372.

110. That is to say, those whose sole concern is God [translator's note].

111. Ibn Abī al-Dunyā, *Iṣlāḥ al-Māl*, 23. Part of this hadith is included by al-Ḥākim in *al-Mustadrak*, 4:329, where it appears with the following wording: "If anyone reduces all his concerns to one, God will protect him from whatever might cause him concern both in this world and in the next. As for those who allow their concerns to lead them first in one direction, then in another, God cares not in which of this world's valleys they perish." Al-Ḥākim judges this hadith's chain of transmission to be sound, while al-Tirmidhī traces it back to its original sources in his *Sunan*, 4:642. Anas ibn Mālik reports that the Messenger of God (pbuh) once declared, "If anyone makes the life to come his sole concern, God will place his wealth in his heart and gather together whatever he has lost, and the things of this world will become his even against their will. As for those who make this world their concern, God will afflict them with poverty, causing whatever they have to be scattered, and all they will receive of this world is what has been apportioned to them."

112. *Fatḥ al-Bārī*, 3:296.

113. The Arabic text reads 'spending on oneself' (*al-infāq ʿalā al-nafs*), whereas it appears from the context that it was meant to read 'spending on others' [translator's note].

114. Al-ʿIzz ibn ʿAbd al-Salām, *Qawāʿid al-Aḥkām*, 2:205.

115. The *Musnad* of Aḥmad ibn Ḥanbal, 1:447.

116. Muhammad Abd al-Munim Afar, *al-Iqtiṣād al-Islāmī*, 3:23–34.

117 Yusuf Ibrahim Yusuf, *Istrātījiyyah wa Taktīk al-Tanmiyah fī al-Iqtiṣād al-Islāmī*.

118. Traced back to its original sources by al-Bukhārī in his *Ṣaḥīḥ*, by Ibn Ḥajar al-ʿAsqalānī in *Fatḥ al-Bārī*, 7:269, by Muslim in his *Ṣaḥīḥ*, 3:1250, al-Tirmidhī in his *Sunan*, 4:430, and by Ibn Mājah in *Sunan*, 2:904.

119. Ibn Abī al-Dunyā, *Iṣlāḥ al-Māl*, 418.

120. Ibid., 427.

121. Ibid., 151.

122. From a hadith on the authority of Abū Hurayrah which is narrated by al-Tirmidhī in his *Sunan* and which is traced back to its original sources by al-Albānī in his *Ṣaḥīḥ Sunan al-Tirmidhī*, 111–403, 2:50; it is also narrated by Ibn Mājah in his *Sunan*, 1:43, from a hadith on the authority of Ibn Qatādah which has been passed down in a different version. The hadith passed down on the authority of Abū Hurayrah reads as follows: "Among the actions and good works which follow a believer after his death are: knowledge which he disseminated, a righteous son or daughter whom he left behind, a copy of the Qur'an which he bequeathed, a mosque which he built, a shelter which he built for wayfarers, a waterway which he opened, and charity which he distributed out of his wealth during his lifetime and days of good health" (1:44).

123. Traced back to its original sources by al-Bukhārī in his *Ṣaḥīh* (*Fatḥ al-Bārī*, 3:340), and by Muslim in his *Ṣaḥīḥ*, 3:1341.

124. Ibn Abī al-Dunyā, *Iṣlāḥ al-Māl*, 115.

125. Traced back to its original sources by al-Bukhārī in his *Ṣaḥīh* (*Fatḥ al-Bārī*, 11:176, 181, 182), by Muslim in his *Ṣaḥīḥ*, 4:2078, by al-Nasā'ī in his *Sunan*, 8:262 and by Ibn Mājah in his *Sunan*, 2:1262.

126. Al-Tirmidhī in his *Sunan*, 4:569.

127. Ibn Ashur, *al-Maqāṣid*, 146-147.

128. In this connection, mention may be made of a number of references from the Islamic literary tradition which deal with this theme, foremost among which are: (a) Abū Yūsuf (d. 183 AH/799 AC), *al-Kharāj*, which deals with three themes,

namely: state financial resources, state expenditures, ethics of the financial system, and the duties incumbent upon the state treasury.

(b) Yaḥyā ibn Ādam al-Qurashī (d. 203 AH/818 AC), *al-Kharāj.*

(c) Muḥammad al-Tāwdī al-Fāsī (d. 209 AH/824 AC), *Kashf al-Ḥāl ʿan al-Wujūh Allatī Yantaẓimu minhā Bayt al-Māl,* which is still in manuscript form.

(d) Abū ʿUbayd al-Qāsim ibn Salām (d. 224 AH/383 AC), *al-Amwāl.*

(e) Ibn Zanjawayh (d. 251 AH/865 AC), *al-Amwāl.*

(f) Aḥmad ibn Naṣr al-Dāwūdī (d. 307 AH/919 AC), *al-Amwāl,* which is still in manuscript form.

(g) Imam ibn Ḥazm al-Ẓāhirī (d. 456 AH/1063 AC), the conclusion to 'Kitāb al-Zakāh' in his book *al-Muḥallā,* which deals with the problem of poverty not with respect to the duty of the wealthy to be charitable to the poor but, rather, with respect to the rights of the individual in relation to society. Ibn Ḥazm writes: "It is the obligation of the wealthy in every country to show concern for their poor, and the sultan [or whoever rules the country] obliges them to do so; thus, if such aid is not available through zakah funds [as when, for example, those with sufficient wealth to pay zakah are non-Muslims and when the conditions of Muslim citizens do not permit them to distribute sufficient zakah to meet the needs of the poor – translator's note], they are to be provided [by the state] with the essential staples, with clothing suitable for winter and summer, and with dwellings to shelter them from rain, heat, the sun, and the stares of passersby." Then, after detailing the evidence in support of his view and discussing opposing views, he states, "They say that if someone is so thirsty that he has reason to fear that he will die, it is incumbent upon him to take water from wherever he can find it and [even] to fight for it. Abū Muḥammad asks: What difference is there between the combat which they allow him for the sake of that by which he can prevent himself from dying of thirst, and the combat which they forbid to him for the sake of that by which he might prevent himself from dying of hunger or nakedness? This is in conflict with the consensus of the Muslim community, the Qur'an, the Sunnah and *qiyās*, or analogical deduction."

Abū Muḥammad also states that it is not permissible for a Muslim in dire straits to eat pork or the flesh of an animal which has died on its own [that is, without having been slaughtered according to the prescribed Islamic rite] if he finds that one of his companions, be he a Muslim, a Christian, or a Jew, has a surplus of food. The reason for this is that the person who has a surplus of food has the obligation to feed the one who is hungry. And this being the case, the hungry person is not truly obliged to eat either pork or the flesh of an animal which died on its own. And to God belongs all success.

Such a person [who finds himself in need of food] is entitled to fight for it. If he is killed in the course of such armed conflict, the person who killed him will merit retaliation, and if the person seeking to prevent him from obtaining the food sought is killed, he will die under God's curse, since he deprived another of a legitimate right and is to be considered to have acted wrongfully: "...if two groups of believers fall to fighting, make peace between them; but then, if one of the two [groups] goes on acting wrongfully towards the other, fight against the one that acts wrongfully until it reverts to God's commandment" (49:9). After all, anyone who seeks to deprive another of a legitimate right has acted wrongfully toward his brother to whom the right is due. It was on this basis that Abū Bakr the Righteous waged war on those who sought to withhold payment of zakah [to the Muslim state]. (Ibn Ḥazm, *al-Muḥallā*, Dār al-Āfāq al-Jadīdah, 6:156-159, Question 752)

(h) Ibn Rajab al-Ḥanbalī (d. 795 AH/1295 AC), *al-Kharāj*, 'Kitāb al-Istikhrāj.'

(i) Aḥmad ibn ʿAlī al-Daljī (d. 799 AH/1396 AC), *al-Filākah wa al-Maflūkīn*. What is meant here by '*al-filākah wa al-maflūkīn*' is 'poverty and the poor.' This work deals with the problem of poverty not merely as a manifestation of material deprivation but, in addition, as an impediment to the practice of worship and the achievement of fully integrated faith, and as one of the causes which underlie moral failings such as lying, deceit, hatred, bitterness, envy, flattery, obsequiousness and others. In addition, it leads the poor to seek the overthrow of the state in the hope of changing the condition [in which they find themselves]. Similarly, poverty causes the poor to pin their hopes on impossible causes such as the stars and alchemy, that is, the transformation of base metals into gold.

Al-Daljī discusses the fact that *al-tawakkul*, or complete reliance upon God, does not preclude attachment to earthly causes, and that *al-zuhd*, or renunciation of the world, does not preclude the possession of material wealth. In addition, he demonstrates the hold that poverty has on people, as well as the fact that it is more prevalent among the learned and, hence, more likely to be observed among them than among other groups of people. He devotes a large section of the book to biographical sketches of scholars who enjoyed little in the way of earthly fortune, and quotes from poetry composed by the indigent. This book is characterized by an inductive reading and skilled analysis of reality, a fact which attests to the author's wide knowledge and his mastery of the topic at hand.

(j) Abū Yaʿlā al-Ḥanbalī (d. 560 AH/1165 AC), *al-Aḥkām al-Sulṭāniyyah.*

(k) Al-Māwardī (d 450 AH/1068 AC), *al-Aḥkām al-Sulṭāniyyah.*

129. Muhammad Baqir al-Sadr, *Iqtiṣādunā*, 287.
130. Yusuf Ibrahim, *Al-Nafaqāt al-ʿĀmmah fī al-Islām*, 130, 134, 190, 386, and *Istrātijiyyah wa Taktīk al-Tanmiyah al-Iqtiṣādiyyah fī al-Islām*, 380.
131. *Al-Nafaqāt al-ʿĀmmah*, 378-381.
132. Muhammad Abd al-Munim Afar and Yusuf Kamal in *Uṣūl al-Iqtiṣād al-Islāmī*, 1:66.
133. Abd al-Hamid al-Ghazali, *Fī al-Dīn wa al-Iqtiṣād*, ed. Murad Wahbah, 14; Suad Ibrahim Salih, *Mabādi' al-Niẓām al-Iqtiṣādī al-Islāmī wa Baʿḍ Taṭbīqātihi*, 43–51.
134. Abd al-Aziz Fahmi Haykal, *Madkhal ilā al-Iqtiṣād al-Islāmī*, 16.
135. *Al-Iḥyā'*, Beirut: *Dār al-Kutub al-ʿIlmiyyah*, 2:27-40. These rules are found in the second book belonging to the 'quarter' (*rubʿ*) of *Iḥyā' ʿUlūm al-Dīn* devoted to daily transactions (*al-ʿādāt*), the others being devoted to forms of worship (*al-ʿibādāt*), entities which lead to perdition (*al-muhlikāt*) and entities which lead to deliverance (*al-munjiyāt*) respectively [translator's note].
136. *Maqāṣid al-Sharīʿah*, 155–166.
137. 1996/1997, unpublished.
138. *Al-Handasah al-Wirāthiyyah wa Maqāṣid al-Sharīʿah*, 1.
139. Ibid., 2–3.
140. Ibid., 6-7.
141. Ibid., 176.
142. Ibid., 177.
143. Abū Muḥammad ʿAbd al-Ḥaq ibn Ghālib ibn ʿAṭṭiyyah al-Andalusī, *Al-Wajīz fī Tafsīr al-Kitāb al-ʿAzīz* (The Qur'anic Exegesis) (Dār al-Kutub al-ʿIlmiyyah, Beirut, 1st edn, 1993), vol.2, p.114
144. Ibid., 192–200.
145. Al-Hasani, 6.
146. *Al-Ijtihād al-Maqāṣidī*, 1:18-19; see also 16-17.
147. From his book entitled *al-Fikr al-Maqāṣidī*, Pocketbook Series, 99-104.
148. Al-Hasani, 407.
149. Al-Ubaydi, 241–249.
150. Al-Saghir, 462, 483.
151. Al-Hasani, 296-298, 400-401.
152. Ibid., 405–406.
153. *Tajdīd al-Fiqh al-Islāmī*, Gamal Eldin Attia and Wahbah al-Zuhayli, Dialogues for a New Century Series (Damascus: Dār al-Fikr, 2000).

154. Where is the national plan to broaden the umbrella of genuine social and health guarantees to include all citizens? And where is the national plan to wipe out illiteracy in two or three years' time?

155. Al-Qarrāfī states, "The fundamentals of Islamic law may be divided into two categories, one of which is referred to as the fundamentals of Islamic jurisprudence, and the other of which is made of up of a large number of clear, highly significant, universal juristic principles which encompass the secrets and wise purposes of the Law, but which have yet to be detailed" (*Al-Furūq*, 1:2–3).

156. Based on his statement, "Realization of the attributes which influence Islamic legal rulings, in terms of both their literal content and the wise purposes and meanings contained within Islamic law, is among the most noble of sciences" (Al-Hasani, 62, quoting *al-Qiyās* by Ibn Taymiyyah).

157. Based on a reference made by Ibn al-Qayyim to the fact that the texts of Islamic law are inclusive of Islamic legal rulings in a way which may not provide a sufficient basis, in and of itself, for formation of opinions and the practice of analogical deduction (*Aʿlām al-Muwaqqiʿīn*, 1:350-355, 382).

158. Ibn Ashur, *Maqāṣid al-Sharīʿah*, 8.

159. From his introduction to *al-Muwāfaqāt*, 1:5.

160. Al-Raysuni, 315.

161. Al-Hasani, 98-112, 113–120, 128, 425.

162. Ibid., 433.

163. Ibid., 437-440.

164. That is, to the fundamental principles of Islamic jurisprudence [translator's note].

165. That is, subsidiary rulings which branch off from the fundamentals of Islamic jurisprudence [translator's note].

166. *Tajdīd al-Uṣūl al-Fiqhiyyah li al-Islām*, 26.

BIBLIOGRAPHY

BOOKS

Abu Zahrah, Muhammad, *Tārīkh al-Madhāhib al-Islāmiyyah.*

Afar, Muhammad Abd al-Munim, *Al-Iqtiṣād al-Islāmī: Al-Iqtiṣād al-Juz'ī.* 1st Edition. 3 parts (Jeddah: Dār al-Bayān al-ʿArabī, 1985).

Al-Ajlawani, Ismail ibn Muhammad, *Kashf al-Khafā' wa Muzīl al-Albās ʿamma Ishtahara min al-Aḥādīth ʿalā Alsinah al-Nās.* 3rd Edition (Beirut: Dār al-Kutub al-ʿIlmiyyah, 1988).

Al-Alim, Yusuf Hamid, *Al-Maqāṣid al-ʿĀmmah li al-Sharīʿah al-Islāmiyyah* (London: The International Institute of Islamic Thought, 1991).

Al-Āmidī, *Al-'Iḥkām fī Uṣūl al-Aḥkām*, Al-Ḥalabī Edition, 4 parts. Ṣabīḥ Edition, 3 parts (1968).

Al-Ashqar, Umar Sulayman, *Maqāṣid al-Mukallafīn.*

Attia, Gamal Eldin, Proceedings of the Seminar on 'Sunan Allāh fī al-Āfāq wa al-Anfus' (Cairo, 10 January, 1990).

———, *Al-Tanẓīr al-Fiqhī* (1987).

———, *Al-Naẓariyyah al-ʿĀmmah li al-Sharīʿah al-Islāmiyyah* (1987).

———, and Wahbah al-Zuhayli, *Tajdīd al-Fiqh al-Islāmī.* The Dialogues for a New Century Series (Damascus: Dār al-Fikr, 2000).

Al-Badakhshī, *Manāhij al-ᶜUqūl Sharḥ Minhāj al-Wuṣūl.*

Al-Bayḍāwī, *Minhāj al-Wuṣul ilā ᶜIlm al-Uṣūl.* Maḥmūd Ṣabīḥ Edition.

Al-Bukhārī, Muḥammad ibn Ismāᶜīl, *Al-Adab al-Mufrad.* 1st Edition. (Beirut: Mu'assasah al-Kutub al-Thaqāfiyyah, 1986).

Al-Dahlawī, Aḥmad Shāh Walī Allāh, *Ḥujjah Allāh al-Bālighah* (Beirut: Dār al-Kutub al-ᶜIlmiyyah, 1995).

Al-Daljī, Aḥmad ibn ᶜAlī, *Al-Filākah wa al-Maflūkīn* (Maṭbaᶜat al-Shaᶜb, 1904).

Al-Fārūqī, Ismāᶜīl, *Aslamah al-Maᶜrifah.* 1st Edition. Trans. Abd al-Warith Said (Kuwait: Dār al-Buḥūth al-ᶜIlmiyyah, 1984).

Al-Fasi, Allal, *Maqāṣid al-Sharīᶜah al-Islāmiyyah wa Makārimuhā* (Dār al-Gharb al-Islāmī, 1993).

Al-Fayrūz Ābādī, *Al-Qāmūs al-Muḥīṭ* (Beirut: Mu'assasah al-Risālah, 1986).

Al-Ghazali, Abd al-Hamid, *Fī al-Dīn wa al-Iqtiṣād.* Ed. Murad Wahbah (Cairo: Sīnā' li al-Nashr, 1990).

Al-Ghazālī, Abū Ḥāmid, *Al-Mustaṣfā.*

———, *Al-Mankhūl.*

———, *Iḥyā' ᶜUlūm al-Dīn.*

Al-Hafnawi, Muhammad, *Al-Taᶜāruḍ wa al-Tarjīḥ ᶜind al-Uṣūliyyīn.* (Al-Manṣūrah: Dār al-Wafā', 1987).

Hasan, Husayn Hamid, *Naẓariyyah al-Maṣlaḥah fī al-Fiqh al-Islāmī* (Dār al-Nahḍah al-ᶜArabiyyah, 1971).

Al-Hasani, Ismail, *Naẓariyyah al-Maqāṣid ᶜInd al-Imām Muḥammad al-Ṭāhir ibn ᶜĀshūr* (London: The International Institute of Islamic Thought, 1995).

Haykal, Abd al-Aziz Fahmi, *Madkhal ilā al-Iqtiṣād al-Islāmī* (Beirut: Dār al-Nahḍah al-ᶜArabiyyah, 1983).

Al-Haythamī, Nūr al-Dīn ᶜAlī ibn Abī Bakr, *Mawārid al-Ẓam'ān ilā Zawā'id Ibn Ḥabbān*. Ed. Muhammad Abd al-Razzaq Hamzah (Beirut: Dār al-Kutub al-ᶜIlmiyyah, 1985).

Ibn ᶜAbd al-Barr, *Al-Intiqā' fī Tārīkh al-Thalāthah al-A'immah al-Fuqahā'*.

Ibn ᶜAbd al-Salām al-Sulamī, ᶜIzz al-Dīn ᶜAbd al-ᶜAzīz, *Qawā ᶜid al-Aḥkām fī Maṣāliḥ al-Anām*. Ed. Taha Abd al-Rauf Saad. 2 parts (Beirut: Dār al-Jīl, 1980).

———, *Al-Fawā'id fī Ikhtiṣār al-Maqāṣid*, referred to as *al-Qawāᶜid al-Ṣughrā* (1988).

Ibn Abī al-Dunyā, Abū Bakr, *Iṣlāḥ al-Māl*. Ed. Mustafa Muflih al-Qudah. 1st Edition (Cairo: Dār al-Wafā', 1990).

Ibn Ashur, Muhammad al-Tahir, *Maqāṣid al-Sharīᶜah al-Islāmiyyah* (Al-Sharikah al-Tūnisiyyah, 1978).

———, *Tafsīr al-Taḥrīr wa al-Tanwīr* (Al-Dār al-Tūnisiyyah).

Ibn al-Athīr, *Al-Kāmil fī al-Tārīkh*, ed. Muhammad Munir al-Dimashqi.

Ibn Farḥūn, *Tabṣirah al-Aḥkām ᶜalā Hāmish Fatḥ al-ᶜAlī al-Mālik* (Cairo: Al-Bābī al-Ḥalabī, 1958).

Ibn Ḥajar al-ᶜAsqalānī, Aḥmad ibn ᶜAlī, *Fatḥ al-Bārī bi Sharḥ Ṣaḥīḥ al-Bukhārī*. Ed. Muhibb al-Din al-Khatib. 13 parts. (Beirut: Dār al-Maᶜrifah, no date).

Ibn Ḥanbal, Aḥmad, *Musnad al-Imām Aḥmad*. 6 parts. (Beirut: al-Maktab al-Islāmī, 1980).

Ibn Ḥazm al-Ẓāhirī, Abū Muḥammad ʿAlī ibn Aḥmad ibn Saʿīd, *Al-Muḥallā* (Beirut: Dār al-Āfāq al-Jadīdah).

Ibn Kathīr, *Al-Bidāyah wa al-Nihāyah fī al-Tārīkh* (Cairo: Maṭbaʿat al-Saʿādah).

Ibn Mājah, Abū ʿAbd Allāh Muḥammad ibn Yazīd al-Qazwīnī, *Sunan Ibn Mājah*. 3 parts. 2nd Edition (Riyadh: Sharikah al-Ṭibāʿah al-ʿArabiyyah al-Saʿūdiyyah, 1984).

Ibn al-Qayyim, *Iʿlām al-Muwaqqiʿīn* (Cairo: Maktabah al-Kulliyyāt al-Azhariyyah, 1968).

Ibn Taymiyyah, *Al-Ḥisbah* (Cairo: Maṭbūʿāh al-Shaʿb).

———, *Naqḍ al-Manṭiq* (Cairo: Maktabah al-Sunnah al-Muḥammadiyyah, 1951).

———, *Al-Fatāwā al-Kubrā* (Saudi Arabia, 1961–1966).

Ismail, Fatimah, *Al-Qur'ān wa al-Naẓar al-ʿAqlī* (London: The International Institute of Islamic Thought, 1993).

Al-Isnawī, *Nihāyah al-Sūl fī Sharḥ Minhāj al-Uṣūl*, with marginal commentary by Muhammad Najib al-Mutiʿi. 4 parts (ʿĀlam al-Kitāb).

———, *Zawā'id al-Uṣūl ʿalā Minhāj al-Wuṣūl* (Beirut: Mu'assasah al-Kutub al-Thaqāfiyyah).

Jumah, Ali, *Al-Madkhal* (London: The International Institute of Islamic Thought, 1996).

Al-Juwaynī, Imām al-Ḥaramayn, *Al-Burhān fī Uṣūl al-Fiqh* (Qatar, 1978).

Al-Khadimi, Nur al-Din ibn Mukhtar, *Al-Ijtihad al-Maqāṣidī*. (Qatar: Kitāb al-Ummah, 1998).

Al-Khamlishi, Ahmad, *Wujhah Naẓar* (Rabat: Dār Nashr al-Maʿrifah, 1998).

Al-Maysawi, Muhammad al-Tahir, *Al-Shaykh Muḥammad al-Ṭāhir ibn ʿĀshūr wa Kitābuhu Maqāṣid al-Sharīʿah al-Islāmiyyah* (*Taḥqīq wa Dirāsah*) (Al-Baṣā'ir, 1998).

Murad, Barakat Muhammad, *Manhaj al-Jadal wa al-Munāẓarah fī al-Fikr al-Islāmī* (Cairo: Al-Ṣadr li Khadamāt al-Ṭibāʿah, 1990).

Muslim, Abū al-Ḥusayn ibn al-Hajjāj, *Ṣaḥīḥ Muslim, Sharḥ al-Nawawī*. 6 parts (Cairo: Dār al-Rayyān li al-Turāth, 1986).

Al-Najjar, Abd al-Majid, *Fī Fiqh al-Tadayyun Fahman wa Tanzīlan* (Doha: Kitāb al-Ummah, 1999).

Al-Nasā'ī, Abū ʿAbd al-Raḥmān Aḥmad ibn Shuʿayb ibn ʿAlī ibn Yaḥyā, *Sunan al-Nasā'ī bi Sharḥ al-Ḥāfiẓ Jalāl al-Dīn al-Suyūṭī*. Edited and numbered by Abd al-Fattah Abu Ghuddah. 2nd Edition. 9 parts (Dār al-Bashā'ir al-Islāmiyyah, 1986).

Al-Nīsābūrī, Abū ʿAbd Allāh al-Ḥākim, *Al-Mustadrak ʿalā al-Ṣaḥīḥayn*. 4 parts (Beirut: Dār al-Kitāb al-ʿArabī, 1980).

Al-Qaradawi, Yusuf, *Madkhal li Dirāsah al-Sharīʿah al-Islāmiyyah* (Cairo: Maktabah Wahbah, 1990).

———, *Taysīr al-Fiqh* (*Fiqh al-ʿIlm*) (Cairo: Maktabah Wahbah, 1989).

———, *Kayfa Nataʿāmalu maʿa al-Qur'ān al-ʿAẓīm* (Doha: Qatar University, 1997).

Al-Qarrāfī, *Al-Furūq* (Beirut: ʿĀlam al-Kutub).

———, *Sharḥ Tanqīḥ al-Fuṣūl* (Cairo: Maktabah al-Kulliyyāt al-Azhariyyah), and (Beirut: Dār al-Fikr, 1997).

Al-Qummī, Ibn Bābawayh, *ᶜIlal al-Sharā'iᶜ* (Dār al-Balāghah, 1966).

Al-Raysuni, Ahmad, *Naẓariyyah al-Maqāṣid ᶜInd al-Imām al-Shāṭibī* (London: The International Institute of Islamic Thought, Al-Mu'assasah al-Jāmiᶜiyyah, 1992).

———, *Al-Fikr al-Maqāṣidī*, Pocketbook Series (Morocco: Manshūrāt al-Zaman, 1999).

Al-Rāzī, Fakhr al-Dīn, *Al-Maḥṣūl fī ᶜIlm Uṣūl al-Fiqh* (Riyadh: Al-Imam Muhammad ibn Saud University).

Al-Saᶜati, Abd al-Rahman, *Al-Fatḥ al-Rabbānī fī Tartīb Musnad al-Imām Aḥmad al-Shaybānī*.

Al-Sadr, Muhammad Baqir, *Iqtiṣādunā: Dirāsah Tatanāwalu bi al-Naqd wa al-Baḥth al-Madhāhib al-Iqtiṣādiyyah* (Beirut: Dār al-Fikr, 1974).

———, *Al-Sunan al-Tārīkhiyyah fī al-Qur'ān* (Damascus: Dār al-Taᶜāruf li al-Maṭbūᶜāt, 1989).

Al-Saghir, Abd al-Majid, *Al-Fikr al-Uṣūlī wa Ishkāliyah al-Sulṭah al-ᶜIlmiyyah fī al-Islām* (Beirut: Dār al-Muntakhab al-ᶜArabī, 1994).

Salih, Suad Ibrahim, *Mabādi' al-Niẓām al-Iqtiṣādī al-Islāmī wa Baᶜḍ Taṭbīqātihi*.

Al-Shāṭibī, Abū Isḥāq, Ibrāhīm ibn Mūsā al-Lakhmī al-Ghranāṭī al-Mālikī, *Al-Muwāfaqāt fī Uṣūl al-Sharīᶜah*. Ed. Abd Allah Darraz. 4 parts. 2nd Edition. (Beirut: Dār al-Maᶜrifah, 1975).

———, *Al-Iᶜtiṣām*, Al-Manār Edition, (1914).

Al-Subkī, Tāj al-Dīn, *Al-Ibhāj*.

———, *Ḥāshiyah al-Banānī ʿalā Sharḥ al-Muḥallā ʿalā Matn Jamʿ al-Jawāmiʿ* (Beirut: Dār al-Fikr).

Al-Suyūṭī, Jalāl al-Dīn, *Al-Ashbāh wa al-Naẓā'ir fī al-Furūʿ wa Sharḥayhi al-Mawāhib al-Saniyyah wa al-Farā'id al-Bahiyyah* (Dār al-Fikr).

———, *Al-Durr al-Manthūr fī al-Tafsīr al-Ma'thūr* (Beirut: Dār al-Maʿrifah, 1896).

Al-Tirmidhī, Abū ʿĪsā Muḥammad ibn ʿĪsā ibn Sūrah, *Al-Jāmiʿ al-Ṣaḥīḥ: Sunan al-Tirmidhī*. 5 parts. Ed. Ahmad Shakir (Beirut: Dār al-Kutub al-ʿIlmiyyah, no date).

Al-Ubaydi, Hammadi, *Al-Shāṭibī wa Maqāṣid al-Sharīʿah* (Beirut: Dār Qutaybah, 1992).

Yusuf, Yusuf Ibrahim, *Istrātījiyyah wa Taktīk al-Tanmiyah al-Iqtiṣādiyyah fī al-Islām* (Cairo: Al-Ittiḥād al-Dawlī li al-Bunūk al-Islāmiyyah, 1981).

———, *Al-Nafaqāt al-ʿĀmmah fī al-Islām: Dirāsah Muqāranah*, 2nd Edition (Doha: Dār al-Thaqāfah, 1988).

Al-Zarkashī, *Al-Baḥr al-Muḥīṭ* (Kuwait: Ministry of Religious Endowments and Islamic Affairs).

Al-Zarqa, Mustafa, *Al-Madkhal al-Fiqhī al-ʿĀmm*. (Beirut: Dār al-Fikr, 1967).

Al-Zuhayli, Wahbah, *Naẓariyyah al-Ḍarūrah al-Sharʿiyyah*. (Beirut: Dār al-Fikr, 1997).

ARTICLES AND PERIODICALS

Al Najaf, Abd al-Karim, "Review of *Naẓariyyah al-Maqāṣid 'ind al-Imām al-Shāṭibī* by Ahmad al-Raysuni," *Qaḍāyā Islāmiyyah Mu*ᶜ*āṣirah*, No. 4 (1997), 429-458.

Al-Alwani, Taha Jabir, "Al-Fiqh wa al-Mawrūth," *Qaḍāyā Islāmiyyah Mu*ᶜ*āṣirah*, No. 8, 96-126.

Attia, Gamal Eldin, "Maqāṣid ᶜIlm al-Iqtiṣād al-Islāmī," *Faculty of Islamic Law Annals*, (University of Qatar), No. 11 (1993) and *Qaḍāyā Islāmiyyah Mu*ᶜ*āṣirah*, No. 8, 175–194.

——, "Maqṣid Iᶜtibār al-ᶜAql," *al-Muslim al-Mu*ᶜ*āṣir*, No. 106, 17-31.

Barri, Baqir, "Fiqh al-Naẓariyyah ᶜind al-Shahīd al-Ṣadr," *Qaḍāyā Islāmiyyah Mu*ᶜ*āṣirah*, Nos. 11–12, 165–202.

Muhammad, Yahya, "Naẓariyyah al-Maqāṣid wa al-Wāqiᶜ," *Qaḍāyā Islāmiyyah Mu*ᶜ*āṣirah*, No. 8, 127-174.

Rahiman, Said, "Manhaj Iktishāf al-Milāk wa Atharuhu fī Taghayyur al-Aḥkām," *Qaḍāyā Islāmiyyah Mu*ᶜ*āṣirah*, Nos. 9-10, 174–198.

Al-Raysuni, Ahmad, "Al-Manḥā al-Maqāṣidī fī Fiqh ibn Rushd," *Qaḍāyā Islāmiyyah Mu*ᶜ*āṣirah*, No. 8, 207-224.

Shararah, Abd al-Jabbar, "A Review of *Naẓariyyah al-Maqāṣid* ᶜ*Ind al-Imām Muḥammad al-Ṭāhir ibn* ᶜ*Āshūr*, by Ismail al-Hasani," *Qaḍāyā Islāmiyyah Mu*ᶜ*āṣirah*, No. 4, 1997, 473–490.

Al-Ta'i, Sarmad, "Maqāṣid al-Sharīᶜah fī Āthār al-Shaykh Shams al-Dīn," *Qaḍāyā Islāmiyyah Mu*ᶜ*āṣirah*, Nos. 9-10, 225–242.

CONFERENCES AND SEMINARS

Abd al-Halim, Fatah al-Bab, "Maqāṣid al-Tarbiyah." Paper presented at a conference entitled, "Towards Building a Contemporary Islamic Theory of Education," (Amman, July 24–27, 1990).

Ali, Said Ismail, "Ahdāf al-Madāris al-Islāmiyyah," presented at a conference on educational and instructional methods, (Cairo, July 29-31, 1990).

Attia, Gamal Eldin, "Al-Awlawiyāt al-Shar^ciyyah," presented at a seminar sponsored by the International Institute of Islamic Thought, (Cairo Office, May 12, 1991).

———, "Sunan Allāh fī al-Āfāq wa al-Anfus," presented at a seminar sponsored by the International Institute of Islamic Thought, (Cairo Office, December 28, 1989, January 3, 1990 and January 10, 1990).

DISSERTATIONS AND UNPUBLISHED RESEARCH

Al-Ghazali, Ahmad, "Murāʿāh al-Maqāṣid fī Fiqh ʿUmar ibn al-Khaṭṭāb" (Rabat: Muhammad V University, 1999).

Hasan, Musaddiq, "Al-Handasah al-Wirāthiyyah wa Maqāṣid al-Sharīʿah" (Tunis: Zaytuna University, Faculty of *Uṣūl al-Dīn*, 1997).

Hirz Allah, Abd al-Qadir, "Al-Taʿlīl al-Maqāṣidī li Aḥkām al-Fasād wa al-Baṭlān" (Batinah, Algeria: Al-Maʿhad al-Waṭanī, 1997).

Al-Masri, Muhammad, Gamal Eldin Attia and Zaynab Attia, "Dalīl li Takshīf al-Qur'ān al-Karīm wa ʿAmal Makāniz li Aghrāḍ al-Takshīf" (London: The International Institute of International Thought, 1989).

Al-Rafayiah, Ahmad Muhammad, "Ahammiyyah Maqāṣid al-Sharīʿah fī al-Ijtihād" (Amman: University of Jordan, 1992).

Al-Turabi, Hasan, "Tajdīd al-Uṣūl al-Fiqhiyyah li al-Islām: Muḥāwalah li Tanẓīm Māddah Uṣūl al-Aḥkām al-Sharʿiyyah wa Daʿwah li Taṭwīr Fiqh Uṣūlī Muʿāṣir." [no date given]

GLOSSARY OF TERMS

Ahl al-Dhimmah: Non-Muslim subjects of an Islamic state.

Āḥād or solitary hadiths: A solitary hadith is a report narrated on the authority of the Prophet (pbuh) by one or more individuals, but whose chain of transmission does not fulfill the requirements of *tawātur.**

Appropriateness: See *Al-Munāsabah*

Batinites: A group of sects including the Ismaelites, the Alawis (or Nusayrites) and the Druze, who hold in common the belief that the hidden meanings of the Qur'an (*al-bāṭin*) negate its apparent meanings (*al-ẓāhir*).

Bay[c] al-Gharar: A term referring to a transaction involving buying and selling in which there is an element of uncertainty concerning the price, the merchandise being purchased, the deadline for payment and/or delivery, or the ability to deliver the merchandise.

Fatḥ al-Dharā'i[c]: The opposite of *sadd al-dharā'i[c]*, this term refers to the process of opening up paths which, despite some potential of harm, have at least as much potential of leading to benefit.

Fiqh: Islamic jurisprudence.

The definitions in this glossary of terms are drawn for the most part from the following sources: Koutoub Moustapha Sano, *Mu[c]jam Muṣṭalaḥāt Uṣūl al-Fiqh, [c]Arabī-Inkilīzī* (Concordance of Jurisprudence Fundamentals Terminology), (Damascus: Dār al-Fikr, 2000); Qalaji, Muhammad Rawwas, et. al., *Mu[c]jam Lughah al-Fuqahā'*, English-French-Arabic (Beirut: Dār al-Nafā'is, 1996); and Deeb al-Khudrawi, *A Dictionary of Islamic Terms, Arabic-English* (Damascus-Beirut: Dār al-Yamāmah, 1995).

ʿIllah: The underlying legal cause of *ḥukm*, its *ratio decidendi*, on the basis of which the accompanying *ḥukm* is extended to other cases.

Ijtihad, or independent reasoning: The effort exerted by a suitably qualified *fiqh* scholar to arrive at an accurate conceptualization of the divine will based on Muslim legal sources (the Qur'an, the Hadith, analogical deduction and consensus) and the means by which to apply this will in a given age and under given circumstances; as such, ijtihad is the effort exerted by such a scholar to derive a legal ruling from Muslim legal sources, and to reach certainty on questions of an ambiguous nature.

Inḍibāṭ: See *munḍabiṭ*.

Istidlāl: The literal meaning of the term *istidlāl* is to seek evidence (*dalīl*). In the context of Islamic law, it is the search for legal evidence, be it textual or otherwise, on the basis of which one may arrive at a sound ruling or judgment on this or that question or situation. In a broader sense, the term *istidlāl* refers simply to a process of reasoning, investigation, inference or argumentation.

Al-Istidlāl al-Mursal, or unrestricted reasoning: Reasoning or argumentation based on unrestricted interests.

Istiḥsān, or juristic preference: A decision, in the process of arriving at a legal decision, to refrain from applying to a given situation the same ruling which has been applied to analogous situations in favor of another ruling which is more in keeping with the intents of the Law. In other words, juristic preference involves giving human interests and the intents of the Law priority over the results of *qiyās*, or analogical deduction.

Istinbāṭ: Deduction, that is, the extraction of precise meanings from Islamic texts, including the process referred to as *istinbāṭ al-aḥkām*, or the derivation of Islamic legal rulings.

Istiṣḥāb: A judgment or ruling to the effect that a state of affairs which obtained at an earlier time continues to obtain now in the absence of evidence to the contrary.

Istiṣlāḥ, or reasoning based on unrestricted interests: The practice of issuing a legal ruling concerning a case which is not mentioned explicitly in any authoritative Islamic legal text and on which there is no consensus, based on consideration for unrestricted interests (see *al-maṣāliḥ al-mursalah*).

Iṭṭirād, or constancy, regularity: This term refers to the phenomenon whereby a legal ruling applies whenever its basis, or *ᶜillah*, is found, and does not apply whenever its basis is absent.

Jizyah, or poll tax: The tax imposed by a Muslim state on *ahl al-dhimmah*, that is, its non-Muslim subjects.

Kharāj, or land tax: Specifically, the tax levied by a Muslim state on lands which have been conquered by force, or with whose inhabitants it has entered into a peaceful agreement.

Maqāṣid: Literally, 'intents', 'aims' or 'purposes,' this term is frequently used alone to refer to the intents of Islamic law in general, that is, *maqāṣid al-sharīᶜah*.

Maqāṣid-based Ijtihad: A new understanding or reinterpretation of the Islamic edicts, based on an understanding of their purposes or final ends.

Al-Maṣāliḥ al-Mursalah, or unrestricted interests (sometimes referred to also as public interests): Interests which are not explicitly identified by any text in the Qur'an or the Sunnah but which are generally agreed upon based on circumstances which arise in human society. Examples of unrestricted interests include the paving of roads, the setting up of administrative offices to handle public needs, the use of traffic signals, the construction of sewers and waste disposal facilities, etc.

Mujtahid: Someone who engages in ijtihad,* or independent reasoning.

Al-Munāsabah, or 'appropriateness': The description of a situation in which a legal ruling and the situation upon which it is based are 'appropriate' to each other in such a way that the ruling leads to the preservation of an interest which is explicitly recognized in the source texts for Islamic law (i.e., the Qur'an and the Sunnah) and is supported by *ijmā*ᶜ, or the consensus of the Muslim community. An example of 'appropriateness' would be the prohibition of alcoholic beverages (legal ruling) based on the fact that such beverages cause inebriation (the situation upon which the ruling is based), where the interest being preserved through the prohibition is the preservation of the faculty of reason.

Sano (p. 446) defines that which is 'appropriate' (*munāsib*) in this sense as "a visible, measurable condition, sign or circumstance which, by serving as the basis or occasion for a given Islamic legal ruling [as, in the example above, when the power of alcoholic beverages to cause inebriation serves as the occasion for the legal prohibition against them], yields a result which is worthy of being considered an intent (*maqṣūd*) of the Lawgiver, such as the achievement or maximization of some human interest or the prevention or minimization of some type of harm, whether in this world or the next..." An alternative, more succinct, definition provided by Sano for the term *munāsib* is "that which one has good reason to identify as the wise purpose (*ḥikmah*) for the sake of which a given legal ruling was issued." An example of the practical application of the concept of *munāsib* in this sense is the proposal that the wise purpose behind the Islamic prohibition against a man's marrying two women who are sisters is to prevent a harmful sense of jealousy, envy, rivalry and resentment between two people whose relationship would otherwise be one of untainted harmony, cooperation and affection.

Munḍabiṭ, or consistent: This term is used to refer to a legal ruling which does not vary significantly from one person, place, time or circumstance to another.

Mutawātir: See *tawātur*.

Presumption of continuity: See *Istiṣḥāb*

Qadhf: Falsely accusing someone of sexual misconduct.

Qirāḍ, or 'sleeping partnership': An agreement between two people on the basis of which one of them will supply the funds while the other will undertake the work, after which whatever profits accrue will be shared by both; however, any loss is to borne by the person who supplied the funds.

Qiyās, or analogical deduction: The practice of basing a new legal ruling on a previous ruling concerning a similar case, given the similarity between the two cases with respect to their underlying basis or occasion (*ᶜillah*).

Sadd al-Dharā'iᶜ: The prohibition of evasive legal devices, or of anything which has the potential of leading to that which is forbidden.

Ṣalāh al-Ḥājah: The performance of two *rakᶜahs* for the fulfillment of a want.

Ṣalāh al-Istikhārah, or prayer for guidance: A prayer in which one asks God to guide him/her on the right path regarding a particular action, situation or decision with which one is confronted. After performing two *rakᶜahs* one prays to God, saying, "O God, I seek Your good help in Your great wisdom. I pray for the ability to act through your power. I ask for this out of Your goodness. You know, but I know not. You are Powerful, but I am not. You are the Knower of secrets. O God, if You know that the matter I am about to undertake is good for my religion, my life and my future, then make it easy and prosper me in it. But if it would be harmful to my religion, my life, or my future, then put it away from me, and show me what is good." The Arabic text of the prayer is: *Allāhumma, innī astakhīruka bi ᶜilmika wa 'astaqdiruka bi qudratika, wa'as'aluka min faḍlika al-ᶜaẓīm. Fa'innaka taqdir wa lā 'aqdiru, wa taᶜlamu wa lā aᶜlam, wa'anta ᶜallām al-ghuyūb. Allāhumma, in kunta taᶜlamu'anna hādha al-'amra khayrun lī fī dīnī wa maᶜāshī wa ᶜāqibati 'amrī, fa 'aqdirhu lī wa yassirhu lī, thumma bārik lī fīhi. wa'in kunta taᶜlam'anna hādha al-'amra sharrun lī fī dīnī wa maᶜāshī wa ᶜāqibati amrī, faṣrifhu ᶜannī waṣrifnī ᶜanhu, wa'aqdir lī al-khayra ḥaythu kāna, thumma arḍinī fīhi.*

Taᶜabbud/Taᶜabbudī, meaning literally, devotion or worship: Those commands or rulings in Islamic law for which one cannot arrive at an explanation through human reason, and for which there is no known basis or occasion. Examples of such rulings include the number of *rakᶜahs* of which the various ritual prayers consist, the prescribed punishments for violations such as sexual misconduct and slander, etc.

Taʿlīl: The process of identifying the basis (*ʿillah*) for a given legal ruling, and/or the situation out of which such a ruling arose.

Taḥqīq al-Manāṭ: The confirmation of the existence of the *ʿillah* in the new case (*farʿ*) to which a rule is to be extended through *qiyās*.

Tawaqquf, or failure to combine options: This terms refers to the inability to determine which of two apparently incompatible views should be favored over the other, and resignation to the existence of the incompatibility or contradiction until such time as there emerges evidence which resolves it. This approach is adopted by a group of *uṣūl* scholars known as *al-wāqifiyyah.**

Tawātur, or *Tawātur al-Khabar*: The report of an event by a group of individuals sufficiently large and disparate that it would be impossible for them to have colluded in an intent to falsify or deceive.

Thubūt: The manner in which an authoritative Islamic text, specifically, a text from the Qur'an or the Sunnah, has been narrated and passed down. It is said, for example, that the Qur'an is *qaṭʿī al-thubūt*; that is, it is of definitive reliability with respect to the manner in which it has been passed down to us. This is because the Qur'an was passed down in a manner which may be described as *mutawātirah** and which is, therefore, not subject to error or mere probability. As for the Sunnah, some of its texts are *qaṭʿī al-thubūt*, as in the case of reports described as *mutawātirah*, while others are described as *ẓannī al-thubūt*, that is, of presumptive reliability, as in the case of solitary hadiths, or *āḥād.**

Unrestricted interests: See *al-maṣāliḥ al-mursalah*.

ʿUshr: 1) Meaning literally 'one-tenth', or 'tithe', the *ʿushr* is a 10% tax which was once levied on the commerce of Jews and Christians whenever they crossed over the borders of a Muslim state. 2) The term *ʿushr* is also used to refer to the zakah collected on agricultural produce.

Uṣūl al-Fiqh: The principles or fundamentals of Islamic jurisprudence.

Al-Wāqifiyyah: See *al-tawaqquf*.

Zahirites (*al-Ẓāhiriyyah*): A literalist Islamic legal school, founded in 9th Century Iraq by Dāwūd Khalaf and later championed by Ibn Ḥazm, which insists on strict adherence to the literal or apparent meaning (*ẓāhir*) of the Qur'an and Hadith as the only source of Muslim law.

Ẓannī, or speculative: An adjective describing a term, phrase, or statement which is most likely to convey a particular meaning, with the possibility that it might be understood in some other way as well. In his definition of the term 'speculative evidence' (*al-dalīl al-ẓannī*), Mustafa Sano explains that evidence which is speculative is that which yields reasonable, but not conclusive, certainty, and that the speculative nature of a given piece of textual evidence will be attributable either to its chain of transmission (*sanad*), its content (*matn*), or both. Textual evidence which is deemed speculative based on its chain of transmission might include, for example, a hadith passed down on the authority of the Prophet (pbuh) by one, two or even more individuals but which does not meet the requirements of *tawātur*.* Any report or account which does not meet the standards for *tawātur* is deemed to be speculative rather than conclusive. As for the classification of textual evidence as speculative based on its content (*matn*), this is due to the fact that it is subject to more than one interpretation. Most Qur'anic verses are classified as speculative on this basis despite the fact that their chain of transmission is of unquestionable reliability. All hadiths are likewise speculative with respect to their *matn*, including those which meet the criteria for *tawātur*. As for texts which are classified as speculative in terms of both their *matn* and their *sanad*, they include all hadiths with the exception of those which are *mutawātirah* as well as all evidence based on independent reasoning or interpretation, including the processes of *qiyās, istiḥsān, sadd al-dharā'iʿ*, and the like.